Speaking and Listening to the English LANGUAGE!™

by Jane Fell Greene, Ed.D.

270 Oral Language Lessons for English Learners

Thanks to Jenny Hamilton and Martha Cooper for their assistance in the preparation of this book.

ISBN #1-57035-460-X

Edited by Annemarie Curran, Karen Butler, and Karen Altschuller
Cover and text layout design by Sue Campbell *and* Eileen Bechtold

06 05 04 03 02 01 6 5 4 3 2 1

Printed in the United States of America

Published and Distributed by:

SOPRIS
WEST

4093 Specialty Place • Longmont, Colorado 80504
(303) 651-2829 • www. sopriswest.com

For my ancestors, and yours, and the millions of new Americans
who, over the decades and centuries,
have mastered this language called English.

Jane Fell Greene, 2001

Table of Contents

Introduction vii

Daily Lessons 1

Glossary 273

Appendix A: Scope and Sequence 279

Appendix B: Basic English Sentence Patterns 287

Appendix C: Pronouns by Category 288

Appendix D: Positive, Comparative, and Superlative Adjective Forms 289

Appendix E: Irregular Verb Forms 290

Appendix F: Prepositions 291

Appendix G: Phrasal Verbs 292

Appendix H: Helping (Auxiliary) Verbs Used to Build Verb Phrases 293

Appendix I: Conjunctions 294

Appendix J: Picture Cards by Category 295

Appendix K: Manner and Place of Articulation of Phonemes 301

Appendix L: Research Institute Web Sites 306

Appendix M: Contrastive Analyses of English Learners' First Languages 307

Introduction

Rationale and Objectives

Growing numbers of English learners are being assigned to English and reading teachers in both general and special education classes. Many of these teachers are not specifically trained to teach English learners, yet they are responsible for their students' acquisition of English. This book provides teachers with a series of lessons designed to teach spoken Standard English to students who are English learners. Students may be of any age or background; the target language does not change.

Most adults who speak fluent Standard English would be unable to describe the linguistic phenomena required in this question/response task, yet even young children provide the correct response without difficulty.

This series of lessons does not address the acquisition of written English. Literacy, mastery of the written word, is taught in the master curriculum, ***LANGUAGE !***™, which integrates reading (decoding, fluency, and comprehension), spelling, vocabulary, grammar, and composition. The lessons in this book make it possible for teachers to introduce and develop spoken and written English simultaneously. When spoken and written English are taught simultaneously, students become able to access the regular curriculum much faster, so their active participation in education is not delayed. Teachers may elect to use this series of lessons independently; however, *Speaking and Listening to the English* ***LANGUAGE !*** is best used concurrently with ***LANGUAGE !***.

Curriculum: What Is the Content?

To begin to describe the complexities of spoken Standard English is a difficult undertaking. The language contains about a million words, most of which have been borrowed from other languages. But the vocabulary merely represents the surface of the language. The deep structure and function of the language are complex. Linguistic processes that native speakers take for granted are often difficult to explain, even for experts.

It would be helpful to analyze a segment of a single lesson, so that prospective teachers using this book might see just how difficult it is for someone to learn to speak English. What follows is a question/response task from the beginning of Lesson 152. The teacher provides the question and the "yes" stimulus; the student responds in a complete Standard English sentence.

Question: *Did I say I would (I'd) give you the book? (Yes.)*
Response: *"Yes, you said you would (you'd) give me the book."*

On the surface, this task seems simple enough. But what does a student need to know before providing the correct response? Here are some examples of the grammatic, semantic, syntactic, and pragmatic knowledge that students must master before providing the response above.

1. **Do** is an irregular verb. Its past tense is not formed by adding **-ed**.
2. **Did** is the past tense form of the verb **do**.
3. When a question begins with a form of **do** (in this case, **did**), the response form usually eliminates the verb **do** altogether. We don't usually say, "Yes, you did say you would give me the book"—unless we need to emphasize **did**.
4. Here, the speaker does not mean to emphasize **did**. Therefore, the response sentence requires deletion of the form of **do**.
5. The tense from the form of **do** (in this case, **did**, so the tense is past) is retained, even though the word itself is deleted.
6. The main predicate verb, **say**, seizes the past tense, changing it to **said**.
7. The personal pronoun **I** in the question requires a corresponding **you** in the response, in both positions.
8. **Would** is part of the verb phrase. It is a modal, a particular type of auxiliary (helping) verb, indicating the possibility of something happening.
9. In casual conversation, **I would** (in the question) would ordinarily be contracted to **I'd**; **you would** (in the response) would ordinarily be contracted to **you'd**. (Both language *use* and language *structure* are critical for English learners.)

Had enough? Certainly, these rules are not comprehensible to somebody who is *learning to speak English!* These rules are probably incomprehensible to most English speakers. Most adults who speak fluent Standard English would be unable to describe the linguistic phenomena required in this question/response task, yet even young children provide the correct response without difficulty. Most people communicate without difficulty, even though their knowledge about linguistic processes may be implicit rather than explicit. In other words, they don't speak the language because they are aware of myriad abstract grammatic rules. They have learned to speak the language by speaking it. They have listened to lots of modeling and have been provided ample opportunity to produce utterances.

Classroom Focus: Versions of English

We almost always shortchange English learners in the most critical area: abundant exposure and ample opportunity to produce spoken Standard English.

Spoken language is generally less formal than written language; few would argue that point. A controversy that has been debated for several decades revolves around the importance of teaching Standard English. Standard English is the term used to depict the dialects spoken and written by educated people; content-area textbooks are written in Standard English. The issue is student outcome: students who do not learn to comprehend Standard English rapidly and produce Standard English fluently do not possess the most essential skills necessary to access the content-area curriculum. *When we fail to insure that our students are fluent in*

Standard English, we rob them of the opportunity to participate fully in their own educations and, ultimately, in our society.

Does this philosophy of Standard English teaching mean that teachers should not accept nonstandard dialects? Does it mean that teachers should not permit students to speak informally? Absolutely not. Nearly every English speaker is able to code-switch; that is, in addition to speaking Standard English, the speaker is also able to converse in an informal, nonstandard, regional, or ethnic dialect. For many speakers, code-switching is language play. It is an important function of learning the differences between and among variations of a language.

... students who do not learn to comprehend Standard English rapidly and produce Standard English fluently do not possess the most essential skills necessary to access the content-area curriculum. When we fail to insure that our students are fluent in Standard English, we rob them of the opportunity to participate fully in their own educations and, ultimately, in our society.

Informal language is casual, but not necessarily grammatically incorrect. However, nonstandard English contains grammatically incorrect structures and functions. Acquisition of informal, nonstandard English does not need to be directly taught; it typically takes care of itself. Throughout each day, numerous verbal interactions with other speakers and various instances of communication provide English learners with ample exposures to informal and nonstandard English. English learners are continually exposed to informal and nonstandard language, both inside and outside their classrooms. In their interactions with various speakers at school and in their neighborhoods, through television and radio, in movies and videos, and in every form of communication, they experience hours and hours of exposure to informal language.

Even among well-educated speakers, few speak Standard English all day long. Why, then, do these lessons focus on Standard English? We almost always shortchange English learners in the most critical area: abundant exposure and ample opportunity to produce spoken Standard English. Accessing content-area textbooks and discussions requires that students: (1) Comprehend spoken Standard English; (2) Comprehend written Standard English; and (3) Independently generate both spoken and written Standard English.

In language and literacy classes, teachers should gently help their students reformulate statements or questions that students generate in informal or nonstandard English. Pragmatic language—learning the differences among the levels of usage, between formal and informal, nonstandard and Standard English—is critical to all English learners. The informal language to which English learners are exposed every day lacks the morphologic, semantic, grammatic, and syntactic exposure that students need if they are to be able to participate fully in their own education or in society.

Instruction: How Are These Lessons Taught?

The setting. These 270 sequential and cumulative lessons in spoken Standard English may be taught in a classroom, a small group, or one-to-one. The lessons are outlined briefly, simply, and clearly. They are easily adaptable, designed to be used in LED, ESL, bilingual, general, or special education classes.

... every student experiences abundant opportunity to produce many utterances during every lesson.

Time required. It is recommended that English learners receive an additional 45 minutes of intensive spoken language instruction each day—above and beyond the instruction they receive in written English. If we are to move these students into mainstream education as rapidly as possible, we will need to invest substantial time every day to do so.

Student involvement. A major aspect of instruction is student involvement. The teacher's most important instructional consideration is to optimize each student's output of spoken English. Teachers ensure that every student experiences abundant opportunity to produce many utterances during every lesson.

Utterances, not rules. Explanations of English structure are necessarily abstract; students have not yet mastered a level of English to comprehend such explanations. Teachers should not use linguistic terminology, nor should they directly teach grammar rules. (Grammar is taught in ***LANGUAGE !***, but only after students reach mastery levels that permit them to understand the abstract language of rules.)

Immediate feedback. As language learners begin to produce utterances in a new language, they are certain to make mistakes. Major questions for language learners have always involved whether and when to modify, adjust, correct, or alter their utterances. Teachers using these lessons are encouraged to model the correct version of an incorrect utterance and have students repeat it. For example, a teacher would: (1) Say, "Good, Mia! Now, let's say it again, in Standard English"; (2) Model a Standard English version of the student's response; and (3) Have the student repeat the Standard English version of the utterance. This last step's importance is rooted in what we know about how people learn.

Consequences of repetition. The relearning curve comprises a critical concept in educational psychology. Teachers know that as learners repeat something they have learned before (relearn), the behavioral objective (in this case, utterances in Standard English) gradually becomes permanently learned. Rapid learning requires frequent repetition. When English learners repeat utterances that contain *nonstandard* English, those utterances become more and more permanent. They become much harder to unlearn. Not only does the *nonstandard* production have to be unlearned; the *standard* production remains to be learned. As a result, achieving the behavioral objective becomes much more difficult and time-consuming.

Grouping. Grouping significantly reduces time on task. The teacher must balance these truths: If the teacher divides English learners from a single class into two groups, each group will necessarily receive less than half the time. If the students remain together in one group, everybody will make gains in spoken Standard English. While grouping is helpful in the acquisition of written English, students will likely make greater gains if they remain in one group during the spoken English segment of each day's lesson.

As quickly as they can, but as slowly as they must. To ensure that English learners move toward full participation in content-area subjects as rapidly and as efficiently as possible, classroom focus should be on Standard English. For each group of students, teachers should remain focused on mastery. Students should move as rapidly as they can, but as slowly as they must, through the series of lessons. Each of these lessons may need to be presented more than once, depending upon the English proficiency and development of the students whom you are teaching.

How Is the Content Organized?

The content is organized for ease of teacher use. *Speaking and Listening to the English* ***LANGUAGE!*** contains 270 daily lessons, which increase in difficulty. Five lessons constitute a week's worth of instruction. The scope and sequence charts, contained in Appendix A, provide detailed outlines of each week's lessons. Each thread of the language is woven sequentially and cumulatively, gradually creating a tightly woven tapestry that reflects mastery of all of the aspects of English. Because English is synergistic—much more complex than the sum of its threads—teachers are encouraged to return to previous lessons and repeat them as indicated.

The lesson series begins with the structures and functions most essential for English learners and are organized for continual spiraling back and integrating new language concepts, building on previously mastered elements of spoken Standard English. As new elements are integrated and mastered, fluency gradually develops. For example, in the earliest lessons, teachers focus on the verb **be**—the most commonly used verb in English. But **be** is also the most complex English verb, with its several forms: **am, are, is, was, were, be, been, being**. Several lessons later, after students master the simple use of **be**, they learn to use **be** in expanded verb phrases (**were** reading, **had been** going, might **be** walking, **are being** prepared). By the end of this book, English learners independently generate and produce oral presentations on diverse subjects.

If we really want to attain significant increase in literacy, we must be willing to make significant change in instruction.

If we really want to attain significant increase in literacy, we must be willing to make significant change in instruction. This series of lessons in the acquisition of spoken Standard English, used in conjunction with the ***LANGUAGE!*** curriculum, matches a body of scientific research that guides us toward significant gains in language acquisition and literacy.

Lesson 1

In this lesson, students will practice **is** (form of **be**: third person singular, present tense form of the English copula) and the possessive pronouns **my**, **your**, **his**, and **her**.

1. Pronounce a student's name and identify the student by gesturing toward him or her. Have everyone in the group repeat that student's name. Repeat for each student.

2. Approach individual students and say: Your name is (Ngoc). Model the student's response: My name is (Ngoc). The student should respond: "*My name is (Ngoc).*" You may have to model this several times for some students. Repeat with each student.

3. Have students repeat sentences using **my**. Point to yourself and say: My name is (Mr. Soto) to demonstrate. Then point to a student and model, using that student's name: My name is (Ngoc) The student should repeat your sentence. Repeat, selecting different students at random.

4. Have students repeat sentences that use **your**, **his**, and **her**. Point to a student and say: Your name is (Carlos). Have students repeat the sentence: "*Your name is (Carlos).*" If the student who is called on responds with the class, encourage that student to use the pronoun **my**. Select different students' names randomly and repeat the exercise. After modeling the pronoun **your** several times, repeat for **his** and **her**.

5. Solicit volunteers to attempt to produce sentences independently. If an error is made in production, model the corrected version and have the student repeat.

6. Encourage students to repeat these sentences throughout the school day.

Lesson 2

In this lesson, students will review and practice **is** (form of **be**: third person singular, present tense form of the English copula) and the possessive pronouns **my**, **your**, **his**, and **her**.

1. Review pronouns **your** and **my**. Prompt individual students by saying: Your name is (Jan). Model the student's response: My name is (Jan). The student should respond: *"My name is (Jan)."* Repeat with each student.

2. Approach individual students and say: Your name is (Pedro). Model the student's response: My name is (Pedro). The student should repeat: "*My name is (Pedro).*" Next, model: Your name is (Pedro). The student should repeat your sentence. Model and repeat several times.

3. Repeat, selecting students at random, and say: Your name is (Carlos). Have the selected student repeat the sentence using **my**. After a student says, "*My name is (Carlos),*" model and have the other students repeat several times: Your name is (Carlos).

4. Have students repeat sentences several times using **my**, **your**, **his**, and **her**. Point to yourself and say: My name is (Ms. Kam). Then point to various students and say: Your name is (Ramon); His name is (Vencott); Her name is (Kia). Have students repeat each sentence after you say it.

5. Solicit volunteers to attempt to produce sentences independently. If an error is made in production, model the corrected version and have the student repeat.

6. Encourage students to repeat the sentences throughout the school day.

Lesson 3

Materials: common classroom objects (e.g., book, chair, pencil, table)

In this lesson, students will review and practice **is** (form of **be**: third person singular, present tense form of the English copula) and familiar object words to make familiar object sentences.

1. Gesture to an object in the room and say: This is a table. Have students repeat the entire sentence. Repeat, indicating the following familiar objects: **chair**, **book**, **pencil**.
2. Stand next to or hold an object and say: This is a…. Don't complete the sentence; instead, have students fill in the object word. Student should respond as a class. Use **table**, **chair**, **book**, and **pencil**.
3. Stand next to or hold the same objects and prompt individual students to fill in the object word. Say: This is a…. Use **table**, **chair**, **book**, and **pencil**.
4. Model the adding of possessive pronouns. Stand next to the teacher's table and say: This is **my** table. Indicate a female student's chair and say: This is **her** chair. Point to a student's book and, looking directly at the student, say: This is **your** book. Indicate a male student's pencil and say: This is **his** pencil. Repeat, incorporating different students with the objects to demonstrate ownership and the possessive pronouns. Students should repeat each sentence after you say it.
5. Encourage individual students to produce sentences that contain **this** and a possessive pronoun. If an error is made in production, model the corrected version and have the student repeat.
6. Encourage students to repeat the sentences throughout the school day.

Lesson 4

Materials: common classroom objects (e.g., book, chair, pencil, table)

In this lesson, students will review and practice **is** (form of **be**: third person singular, present tense form of the English copula) with **this** at near point. Students will also use familiar object words to make familiar object sentences.

1. Gesture to an object in the room and say: This is a table. Have students repeat the entire sentence. Repeat using **chair**, **book**, and **pencil**.

2. Call on individual students to fill in the object word. Point to an object and say: This is a... After the selected student fills in the object word, have all the students repeat the sentence.

3. Have students fill in the sentence. Point to an object and say: This.... The students should respond: "*This is a (table, chair, book, pencil).*"

4. Model the addition of possessive pronouns. Move around the room, modeling: This is **my** table; This is **her** chair; This is **your** book; This is **his** pencil. Students should repeat each sentence after you say it. Then indicate various objects and provide the prompt This is.... Have students fill in the sentence using the correct possessive pronouns and object word. Repeat sentences if students use incorrect pronouns and have students repeat the correct sentence.

5. Call on students to produce sentences independently. If an error is made in production, model the corrected version and have the student repeat.

6. Encourage students to use these sentences throughout the school day.

Lesson 5

Materials: common classroom objects (e.g., book, chair, pencil, table)

In this lesson, students will review and practice **is** (form of **be**: third person singular, present tense form of the English copula) with **that,** using familiar objects at far point. Students will contrast far point and near point objects using **that** and **this**.

1. Point to a table at a far point and say: That is a table. Have students repeat the entire sentence. Repeat, pointing to a **chair**, **book**, and **pencil**.
2. Have students fill in the object word. Point to an object at far point and say: That is a/an.... Students should respond with the correct object word.
3. Have students complete each sentence. Point to an object at far point and say: That.... Students should respond with the correct object word.
4. Add other familiar nouns to further expand this exercise. Move away from an object and model: **That** is a chair. Then move near the object and model: **This** is a chair. Have students repeat each sentence after you model it. Stress that **this** is used for near point objects and **that** is used for far point objects. Repeat with other objects in the room, contrasting **this** and **that**.
5. Help each student to produce a sentence using **that** independently. If an error is made in production, model the corrected version and have the student repeat.
6. Encourage students to practice using **this** and **that** in sentences throughout the school day.

Lesson 6

Materials: picture cards (colors: black, blue, brown, gray, green, orange, pink, purple, red, white, yellow)

In this lesson, students will learn color words using color cards.

1. Hold up each color card, say the name, and have students repeat each name.
2. Call out a color name and have students touch other objects in the room (clothing, posters, furniture, small objects) that belong to the same color category. If students need help, hold up the color card.
3. Point to or touch solid color objects around the room. Say: This is.... Students should fill in the color word.
4. Continue this exercise, calling on individual students to complete the prompt This is... with the appropriate color word. Have all students repeat each sentence.
5. Solicit volunteers to touch objects around the room and to say *"This is ________,"* identifying the color. Have all students repeat each sentence. Make sure every student has a turn.
6. Practice color words with students each day. Encourage students to say English words for colors they see throughout the school day.

Lesson 7

Materials: picture cards (colors: blue, green, purple, red, white, yellow)

In this lesson, students will learn familiar action verbs (jump, skip, hop, sit, stand, squat); they will be combined with color words.

1. Say and demonstrate action verbs: **jump**, **skip**, **hop**, **sit**, **stand**, **squat**.

2. After demonstrating each verb, have students simultaneously say each word and demonstrate the action.

3. Assign each row or group of students a color card (**blue**, **white**, **yellow**, **green**, **purple**, **red**). Call out a color and an action command (**jump**, **skip**, **hop**, **sit**, **stand**, **squat**). The group assigned that color is to demonstrate the action. For example, if you say: Blue, jump!, the blue group should jump. Repeat using all commands and changing color assignments.

4. Distribute the color cards to individual students. Call out color word/action verb exercises for students to demonstrate (e.g., if you say: Red, skip!, the student with the red card should skip). Mix up the activities so students do not associate specific verbs with specific colors. Be sure that every student has a turn.

5. Distribute cards again and call on individual students to say and demonstrate color word/action verb activities. Students should identify their assigned color but may choose their action. Make sure each student has the opportunity to practice this activity.

6. Encourage students to practice saying action verbs and color names during the school day and at home.

Lesson 8

Materials: picture cards (animals: bird, cat, cow, dog, fish, frog, horse, mouse, pig, rabbit)

In this lesson, students will learn animal words. Also, students will review and practice **is** (form of **be**: third person singular, present tense form of the English copula).

1. Hold up pictures of animals and identify each animal name. Have students repeat each animal name as the picture is shown.

2. Once students recognize animal names, model a complete sentence: This is a dog. Have students repeat. Repeat for each animal name.

3. Prompt students to provide the missing word by saying: This is a/an.... Once they have mastered that, provide the prompt This... and have students complete the sentence.

4. Hold up a picture and call on individual students to complete sentences. Supply: This.... Have the class repeat each sentence.

5. Pass out animal pictures to individual students and have each student identify the picture using a complete sentence. If a mistake is made, correct the student and have the student repeat it correctly. Make sure each student has a turn.

6. Encourage students to look for animals in their neighborhood and practice their English names.

Lesson 9

Materials: picture cards (animals: bird, cat, cow, dog, fish, frog, horse, mouse, pig, rabbit)

In this lesson, students will combine animal words and action verbs.

1. Review animal names using pictures.
2. Model an action verb and pair it with an animal name: Dog jumps; Rabbit hops; Cat scratches; Mouse runs; Cow eats. Have students repeat each sentence.
3. Call on individual students to name an animal from the picture cards and pantomime an action. Have the class identify the action. Model the complete sentence and have students repeat.
4. Model English words for the following animal sounds: Dog barks; Cat meows; Cow moos.
5. Ask students if they can model any animal-sound words in their native languages. Then practice the English words, using complete sentences as above.
6. Encourage students to listen for animal sounds throughout the day and practice naming them.

Lesson 10

Materials: picture cards (animals: cat, dog, frog, mouse, rabbit; colors: brown, gray, green, white, yellow); classroom objects

In this lesson, students will combine animal words and color words. Also, students will practice **is** (third person present tense singular of **be**).

1. Review animal and color words, using pictures. Hold up each color card and have students supply the color name. Then identify the animals, modeling complete sentences: This is a (frog). Have students repeat each sentence.

2. Combine the color and animal concepts. Hold up the card and model for each animal: This is a (green frog). Have students repeat each sentence.

3. Move about the classroom. Point to an object and identify the color and the object. Say: This is a (yellow pencil). Repeat using familiar objects. Have students repeat each sentence.

4. Continue to point to objects. Have students finish the sentence given the following prompt: This.... Students should supply the object name and color.

5. Give each student a familiar object and have each create a sentence describing the object. If a mistake is made, model the correct sentence and have the student repeat it. Have the class repeat each student's sentence.

6. Encourage students to repeat the sentences throughout the school day, using different objects and color words.

Lesson 11

Materials: picture cards (animals: alligator, bear, elephant, giraffe, gorilla, kangaroo, lion, monkey, peacock, tiger, zebra)

In this lesson, students will expand their animal-name vocabulary and will reinforce usage of the sentence structure **This is**.

1. Show students the pictures of the zoo animals and name each animal. Say: This is (an alligator). Have students repeat. Repeat for each animal.

2. While holding up a picture of an animal, say: This is a/an.... Prompt students to fill in the object word.

3. Repeat, holding up the picture cards and supplying only the prompt This.... Call on individual students to complete each sentence.

4. Have students create complete sentences based on the pictures of zoo animals. Mix up the cards until every student has had a turn.

5. Some students may be able to name these animals in their first languages. If so, use this activity for contrastive analysis.

6. Encourage students to notice animals throughout the day and practice using their names in English.

Lesson 12

Materials: at least two each of common objects (e.g., books, chairs, pencils, pens)

In this lesson, students will expand their object word vocabulary, reinforce usage of **These are**, and delete **a/an** before plurals.

1. Display common classroom objects. Hold up one of each object and identify it in the singular. Model and have students repeat.
2. Indicate each group of objects, keeping them at near point. Model and have students repeat: These are (books). Name the plural while reinforcing **are** (third person present tense plural of **be**).
3. Have students complete sentences using object prompts. Supply the prompt: These.... Repeat for all objects.
4. Have students supply complete sentences for all object prompts.
5. Give each individual student the opportunity to create a complete sentence using objects. Have the class repeat each sentence. Some students may be able to name the objects in their first languages. If so, use this activity for contrastive analysis.
6. Encourage students to create sentences using **These are** throughout the day.

Lesson 13

Materials: at least two each of common objects (e.g., books, chairs, pencils, pens)

This is a cumulative practice lesson using **is/are** (third person singular and plural forms of **be**), singular and plural object words, and deletion of **a/an** from plurals.

1. Using common objects, model and have students produce sentences identifying first a single object and then the plural of that object. Say: This **is** a (book). Have students repeat. Then say: These **are** (books). Have students repeat. Repeat using classroom objects.
2. Indicate first a single object and then multiple objects. Say: This is a (chair). These .... Students should finish your sentence using **are** and the appropriate plural word.
3. Indicate an object or objects in random order. Provide the prompt This... or These... as appropriate. Have students complete the sentences using either **is** or **are**, depending on the number of objects indicated.
4. Indicate objects, again in random order. Have students produce complete sentences using **This is** or **These are** as appropriate. Do not provide prompts.
5. Have students indicate objects and say a sentence about the object or objects chosen, using **This is** or **These are**. Have the class repeat each sentence. If an error is made in production, model the corrected version and have the student repeat.
6. Encourage students to practice using these words and sentence formation throughout the day.

Lesson 14

Materials: three each of common objects (e.g., books, boxes, pencils), distinguishable by color

In this lesson, students will learn to distinguish between usage of **a** (pronounce */uh/*) and **the** (pronounce */thuh/*).

1. Gather objects that begin with consonants (e.g., pencils, papers, books, boxes) into groups of three. Hold up three pencils. Say to an individual student: Take **a** pencil. Permit the student to take any pencil.
2. To another student say: Take **the** pencil. Do not allow the student to take a pencil immediately. Illustrate the need to identify which of the two remaining pencils is **the** pencil (i.e., is it the red pencil or the yellow pencil?). Repeat the prompt with specific direction (e.g., Take **the** yellow pencil) and allow the student to take the appropriate pencil.
3. Hold up three books. Say: Take a book. Permit the selected student to take any book. Then say: Take the book. Do not allow the student to take a book until you have identified which of the two remaining books is **the** book. Then allow the student to take it.
4. Present pencils (or other objects) in clusters of three. Say: Take a.... Have students finish the sentence with the appropriate object word. Permit a student to take an object. With only two objects remaining, give the prompt Take the.... Have students complete the sentence with the appropriate description and object words (e.g., *"Take the red pencil"*). *(Note: Do not include objects that begin with vowels at this stage, since another difficult and confusing concept,* ***a/an****, would need to be included.)*
5. Ask each student to complete this sentence pattern. Have the class repeat each sentence. If an error is made by a student, model the correct response and have the student repeat it.
6. Encourage students to listen for the way **a** and **the** are used throughout the day. This is a very difficult concept for English learners and requires frequent repetition before students can master the concept.

Lesson 15

Materials: three each of common objects (e.g., books, boxes, markers, pencils), distinguishable by color

In this lesson, students will review the usage of **a** (pronounce */uh/*) and **the** (pronounce */thuh/*).

1. Gather three each of objects that begin with consonants (e.g., books, boxes, markers, pencils). Hold up three boxes. Say: Take a box. Permit a selected student to take any box. Then say: Take the box. Do not permit the student to take the box until the sentence has been repeated and the box has been identified (e.g., white box, brown box).

2. Repeat this activity several times with different objects and different students. *(Note: Do not include objects that begin with vowels at this stage, since another difficult and confusing concept,* ***a/an****, would need to be included.)*

3. Choose pairs of students to demonstrate this activity to the class. Have one student hold the three objects and direct the other student to take **a** thing and then to take **the** thing by providing the necessary color to identify the object. Then have students switch roles. Have the class repeat each direction given by the selected students.

4. Model the addition of a naming sentence to this activity: These are markers; Take a marker; Take the green marker. Have students repeat this set of sentences. Work with different students to model this additional sentence. Have students repeat each set of sentences.

5. Choose pairs of students to model this series of sentences using a cluster of three objects: *"These are (pencils). Take a (pencil). Take the (yellow pencil)."* As each pair demonstrates, have the class repeat each sentence.

6. Repeat steps above many times with different objects. This is a very difficult concept for English learners and requires frequent repetition before students can master the concept.

Lesson 16

Materials: picture cards (ambulance, apple, arm, bed, bird, cup, egg, elephant, envelope, football, pencil, penny)

In this lesson, students will learn to distinguish usage of **a** and **an**.

1. Gather pictures of objects that begin with vowels and objects that begin with consonants. Identify the object in each picture and have students repeat its name.

2. Model and have students repeat these sentences:

   This is **an** apple.
   This is **an** elephant.
   This is **an** envelope.

3. Contrast with these sentences:

   This is **a** pencil.
   This is **a** penny.
   This is **a** bed.

4. Show picture cards and have students complete sentences with either **a** or **an**, using pictures of objects that begin with vowels and consonants. Say: This is.... Students should finish the sentence using the correct form of **a** or **an** and the object word.

5. Give each student a picture. Ask each student to create a complete sentence that identifies the object in the picture using either **a** or **an**. Have the class repeat each sentence. If a mistake is made, model the correct production and have the student repeat it.

6. Encourage students to practice producing sentences independently using **a** and **an**. Frequent oral production is necessary for students to internalize the concept and use **a/an** correctly.

Lesson 17

Materials: picture cards (ambulance, apple, arm, bed, bird, cup, egg, elephant, envelope, football, pencil, penny)

In this lesson, students will review the usage of **a** and **an**.

1. Gather pictures of objects that begin with vowels and objects that begin with consonants. Hold up each picture and identify the object. Have students repeat names.

2. Model and have students repeat these sentences:

   This is **an** ambulance.
   This is **an** egg.
   This is **an** arm.

3. Contrast with these sentences:

   This is **a** bird.
   This is **a** cup.
   This is **a** football.

4. Hold up pictures in random order and have students complete sentences with either **a** or **an**, as appropriate.

5. Distribute one picture to each student. Have students hold up their pictures and create a complete sentence using **a** or **an**. Have the class repeat each sentence. If an error in production is made, model the correct sentence and have the student repeat it correctly.

6. Encourage students to practice producing sentences independently using **a** and **an**. Frequent oral production is necessary for students to internalize the concept and use **a/an** correctly.

Lesson 18

Materials: picture cards (alligator, ambulance, apple, arm, bed, bell, bird, cup, doll, egg, elephant, envelope, eye, football, pencil, penny, ship, umbrella)

In this lesson, students will review the usage of **a** and **an** using familiar words and action verbs.

1. Gather pictures of objects that begin with vowels and objects that begin with consonants. Have students repeat the name of each object as the picture is presented.

2. Model and have students repeat these sentences:

   This is **an** alligator. — **An** alligator swims.
   This is **an** eye. — **An** eye blinks.
   This is **an** umbrella. — **An** umbrella opens.

3. Contrast with these sentences. Model and have the students repeat.

   This is **a** bell. — **A** bell rings.
   This is **a** doll. — **A** doll sits.
   This is **a** ship. — **A** ship floats.

4. Give the prompt: This is…. Have students complete sentences with either **a** or **an**, using pictures of objects that begin with vowels and consonants. See if students can provide an action verb for each picture. Give the prompts: An (alligator)…. Repeat using different objects.

5. Give all students a picture. Have them create two sentences about the picture, using the sentence structure illustrated in steps 2 and 3 above. Have the class repeat each sentence pair. If a mistake in production is made, model correctly and have student repeat it correctly.

6. Encourage students to practice producing sentences independently using **a** and **an**. Frequent oral production is necessary for students to internalize the concept and use **a/an** correctly.

Lesson 19

Materials: picture cards (alligator, ambulance, apple, arm, arrow, bed, bell, bird, cup, desk, doll, egg, elephant, envelope, eraser, eye, flag, football, orange [food], pencil, penny, sandwich, ship, umbrella)

In this lesson, students will review the usage of **a** and **an**.

1. Gather pictures of objects that begin with vowels and objects that begin with consonants. Have students repeat the name of each object as the picture is presented.

2. Model and have students repeat these sentences:

   This is **an** apple.
   This is **an** arrow.
   This is **an** eraser.
   This is **an** orange.

3. Contrast with these sentences:

   This is **a** desk.
   This is **a** flag.
   This is **a** sandwich.
   This is **a** ship.

4. Select contrasting pairs of pictures or objects (one beginning with a vowel and one with a consonant). Hold up one picture or object. Say: This is a/an…. Have students name the object that would correctly finish the sentence. Have students repeat the entire sentence. Repeat with the contrasting picture object. Repeat activity holding up different pairs and altering the prompt between **a** and **an**.

5. Give each student two picture cards, one of an object that begins with a consonant and one of an object that begins with a vowel. Say: This is a/an…. Have students hold up the object card that correctly completes the sentence based on the given article. Choose some students to repeat the sentence, filling in the name of their pictured object. Repeat activity so that each student gets the opportunity to create a sentence for the class.

6. Encourage students to practice naming objects they see throughout the day and decide if **a** or **an** would be required. Continue to practice this concept throughout the week, as frequent oral production is necessary for students to internalize the concept and use **a/an** correctly.

Lesson 20

Materials: picture cards (alligator, ambulance, apple, arm, arrow, bed, bell, bird, cup, desk, doll, egg, elephant, envelope, eraser, eye, flag, flashlight, football, horse, island, onion, orange [food], owl, pencil, penny, sandwich, ship, umbrella, window)

In this lesson, students will review the usage of **a** and **an**.

1. Gather pictures of objects that begin with vowels and objects that begin with consonants. Have students repeat the name of each object as the picture is shown.

2. Model and have students repeat these sentences:

   This is **an** island.
   This is **an** onion.
   This is **an** owl.

3. Contrast with these sentences:

   This is **a** flashlight.
   This is **a** horse.
   This is **a** window.

4. Give each student a picture and say: This is **a** window. The student who has the picture of the window should hold it up and repeat the sentence. Repeat until every student has had a chance to match his or her picture with a sentence.

5. Redistribute pictures to each student, now giving each student two pictures, one of an object beginning with a consonant and one of an object beginning with a vowel. Give each student the opportunity to come up to the front of the room and create a sentence for each picture. All students should demonstrate using **a** and **an** in their sentences. If a mistake is made, model the correct sentence and have the student repeat it correctly.

6. Encourage students to practice naming objects throughout the day and deciding if the objects would use **a** or **an**. Frequent oral production is necessary for students to internalize the concept and use **a/an** correctly.

Lesson 21

Materials: picture cards (ant, arrow, ax, chair, circle, clock, egg, globe, hat, jacket, oval, oven); common objects (multiples of each, distinguishable by color)

In this lesson, students will learn to distinguish the usage of **a**, **an**, and **the**.

1. Gather objects that begin with vowels and objects that begin with consonants. Name each object and have students repeat each name.

2. Model and have students repeat these sentences:

   This is **an** ant.
   This is **an** egg.
   This is **an** oven.

   Contrast with these sentences:

   This is **a** clock.
   This is **a** hat.
   This is **a** jacket.

3. Display the picture cards. Call on individual students. Say: Show me a hat. Have the selected student point to the hat and say: "*This is **a** hat.*" Provide ample opportunity for students to practice using **This is a** sentence construction.

4. Gather common objects in different colors. Name each object and have students repeat each object name.

5. Say: Show me the (jacket). Explain to students that **the** indicates you are looking for a specific object among several similar objects. They cannot know which object you mean until an indicator is given. Then say: Show me the (red jacket). Have a student approach and point to the appropriate object and say: "*This is the (red jacket).*" Provide ample opportunity for students to practice using **This is the** sentence construction.

6. Emphasize the difference between the general (**a/an**) and the specific (**the**).

Lesson 22

Materials: picture cards (ant, ax, chair, circle, globe, oval); common classroom objects

In this lesson, students will learn more about distinguishing the usage of **a**, **an**, and **the**.

1. Gather pictures of objects that begin with vowels and objects that begin with consonants. Name each object and have students repeat each name.

2. Model these sentences requiring **an** and have students repeat them:

   This is **an** ant.
   This is **an** ax.
   This is **an** oval.

3. Contrast with these sentences requiring **a** and have students repeat them:

   This is **a** chair.
   This is **a** circle.
   This is **a** globe.

4. Ask students to find general objects in the classroom. Say: Show me a chair. The student should point to a chair and say: "*This is **a** chair.*" Repeat using familiar classroom objects.

5. Ask students to find specific classroom objects. Say: Show me the teacher's chair. The student should say: "*This is the teacher's chair.*" Help students realize that **the** requires an indicator. Repeat exercises using different objects, distinguishing the usage of **a**, **an**, and **the**.

6. Emphasize the difference between the general (**a/an**) and the specific (**the**).

Lesson 23

Materials: objects beginning with consonants and vowels (multiples of each, distinguishable by color)

In this lesson, students will review distinguishing the usage of **a**, **an**, and **the**.

1. Gather objects that begin with vowels and objects that begin with consonants.
2. Identify each object beginning with a vowel. Say: This is **an** (eraser). Have students repeat the sentences.
3. Identify each object beginning with a consonant. Say: This is **a** (pen). Have students repeat the sentences.
4. Ask individual students to "show and tell" by coming up to "show" the object and "tell" by using **This is** construction with the proper indicator. Say: Show me an eraser. The students should respond: "*This is an eraser.*" Repeat for all objects, giving indicators as needed.
5. Help students to realize that **the** requires an indicator. Repeat exercises using different objects, distinguishing the usage of **a**, **an**, and **the**.
6. Emphasize the difference between the general (**a/an**) and the specific (**the**).

Lesson 24

Materials: picture cards (airplane, angel, ant, arrow, ax, chair, circle, clock, egg, fork, globe, hat, ice cream cone, jacket, knife, oval, oven, plate, spoon); common objects (multiples of some)

In this lesson, students will review distinguishing the usage of **a**, **an**, and **the**.

1. Hold up pictures of objects that begin with vowels and objects that begin with consonants. Say the objects' names and have students repeat.

2. Choose pictures at random. Give the prompt: This is.... Have students complete the sentence. Be sure students are correctly distinguishing between **a** and **an**.

3. Hold up pictures again and have students create complete sentences using **a** or **an**.

4. Hold up several picture cards and say: Show me the (airplane). Select students to come up and indicate the specific object and say: "*This is the (airplane).*" Notice that when there is only one of the specified objects in a group, an indicator is not required. Repeat, using different configurations of cards.

5. Display common objects. Pair up students to come to the front of the group. Have one student ask to be shown a general or specific object. The second student should point to the object and identify it verbally, using **This is** sentence construction and the correct article.

6. Emphasize the difference between the general (**a/an**) and the specific (**the**).

Lesson 25

Materials: common objects beginning with consonants and vowels (multiples of each, distinguishable by color)

In this lesson, students will review distinguishing the usage of **a**, **an**, and **the**.

1. Gather objects that begin with vowels and objects that begin with consonants.
2. Identify each object beginning with a vowel. Say: This is an (envelope). Have students repeat the sentences.
3. Identify each object beginning with a consonant. Say: This is a (cup). Have students repeat the sentences.
4. Ask individual students to show an object and tell what it is, using **This is** and the proper indicator. Say: Show me **a** cup. The students should respond: *"This is a cup."* Repeat for all the objects, giving indicators as needed.
5. Repeat exercises using different objects, distinguishing the usage of **a**, **an**, and **the**. Emphasize that **the** requires an indicator.
6. Emphasize the difference between the general (**a/an**) and the specific (**the**).

Lesson 26

Materials: common objects (12 different object categories, multiples of each)

In this lesson, students will learn familiar object words, number words, and **are** (present tense plural form of **be**).

1. Using objects, reinforce student vocabulary. Introduce at least 12 objects, indicate each object, and say its name. Have students repeat.
2. Model and have students repeat number words (1–10). Display at least two each of several common objects. Model using the number word with the pluralized object word (e.g., Three pencils; Six books). Explain that the addition of number words (except one) requires pluralizing the object word.
3. Keeping objects or pictures at near point, have students repeat complete sentences using the sentence construction **Here are**. Remember that **here** is for near point and **there** is for far point. Model: Here are (five pens). Repeat using common objects.
4. Indicate common objects to be used in sentences. Give the prompt Here… and have students complete the sentences.
5. Select students to create complete sentences using object prompts. Reinforce **here** and **are** in each sentence. Have the class repeat each student's sentence. If an error is made in production, model the corrected version and have the student repeat.
6. Encourage students to continue naming and counting objects throughout the day.

Lesson 27

Materials: common objects (12 different object categories, multiples of each)

In this lesson, students will learn familiar object words, number words, and **are** (present tense plural form of **be**).

1. Place objects or pictures at far point. Stress that **here** is used for near point objects and **there** is used for far point objects. Say the pluralized name and number of each object and have students repeat.
2. With the objects at far point, model complete sentences and have students repeat:

   There **are** four chairs.
   There **are** two windows.
   There **are** three books.
3. Indicate an object around the classroom and give the prompt: There are.... Have students complete the sentences.
4. Giving the class a number word and object name, call on students to complete the sentence correctly. Have the class repeat the sentence. For example, say: Four pencils. The students will say: "*There are four pencils.*" If an error is made in production, model the corrected version and have the students repeat.
5. Place objects on each student's desk. Have the student walk away from his or her desk and say: "*There are (four pencils).*" If an error is made in production, model the corrected version and have the student repeat.
6. Encourage students to repeat the sentences throughout the day.

Lesson 28

Materials: common objects (12 different object categories, multiples of each)

In this lesson, students will learn familiar object words, number words, and **are** (present tense plural form of **be**).

1. Place objects for counting at far point. Say each object's name and number and have students repeat.
2. Model complete sentences and have students repeat. Say: There are (three balls). Remember to keep objects at far point. Repeat for all objects.
3. Point to various objects and give the prompt: There are.... Have students complete the sentences.
4. Give the students a name and number prompt to create a complete sentence. Select a student to say the sentence and have the class repeat each sentence. If an error is made in production, model the corrected version and have the student repeat.
5. Assign a group of objects to each student. Have each student create a complete sentence using **There are**. If an error is made in production, model the corrected version and have the student repeat.
6. Encourage students to repeat the sentences throughout the day.

Lesson 29

Materials: common objects (12 different object categories, multiples of each)

In this lesson, students will learn familiar object words, number words, and **are** (present tense plural form of **be**).

1. Place objects for counting at near point and far point. Say the name and number of each object and have students repeat.
2. Indicating far point objects first, model complete sentences. Say: There are (four windows). Have students repeat. Repeat for all objects.
3. Contrast sentences with near point objects. Say: Here are (six books). Have students repeat. Repeat for all objects.
4. Give the prompts **Here are...** and **There are...** and have students complete sentences. Be sure they are recognizing **here** is for near point and **there** is for far point:
5. Give students the prompts **Here...** or **There...** and have them create complete sentences. Call on students to say the sentence and have the class repeat the sentence. If an error is made in production, model the corrected version and have the student repeat.
6. Remind students to practice repeating the sentences throughout the day.

Lesson 30

Materials: common objects (12 different object categories, multiples of each)

In this lesson, students will learn familiar object words, number words, and **are** (present tense plural form of **be**).

1. Place objects for counting at near point and far point. Emphasize to students that some objects are at near point and some are at far point. Say the name and number of each object and have students repeat.
2. Indicating far point objects first, model complete sentences. Say: There are (two bookcases). Have students repeat. Repeat for all objects.
3. Move to near point objects. Model complete sentences. Say: Here are (three folders). Have students repeat. Repeat for all objects.
4. Provide prompts for both far point and near point objects and have students complete the sentences with the number and object words. Use the prompts **There are...** and **Here are....**
5. Give students the name of an object and have them create complete sentences using **Here/There** and number words. Have the class repeat each sentence. If an error is made in production, model the corrected version and have the student repeat.
6. Encourage students to repeat the sentences throughout the day.

Lesson 31

In this lesson, students will learn abstract words (adjectives) that represent feelings. They will also practice the first and third person present tense forms of **be** (**am, is**).

1. Pantomime various emotions to introduce "feeling" words: **sad**, **happy**, **worried**, **excited**, **angry**, **scared**. Say: I am scared. I am happy. Emphasize first person present tense: **am**.
2. Have all students imitate your facial expressions. Have students say: "*I am (happy).*" Repeat for all six emotions.
3. Call on individual students to pantomime each emotion. Say: (Mikoto) is happy. The class should repeat: "*(Mikoto) is happy.*" The selected student should say "*I am happy.*" Repeat for all emotions.
4. Pair up students. Have students say to each other: "*(He/She) is happy. I am happy,*" while pantomiming the emotion. Have each pair of students practice for the class using **am** and **is**.
5. Review the practice of **is** (third person present tense singular of **be**). Call on individual students to create simple sentences using **am** and **is**.
6. Repeat sentences using **sad**, **happy**, **worried**, **excited**, **angry**, and **scared** to describe traits of students. Remain focused on students' oral output.

Lesson 32

In this lesson, students will review abstract words (adjectives) that represent feelings and practice of first and third person present tense forms of **be** (**am, is**).

1. Have individual students role-play the previous day's abstract words for feelings: **sad**, **happy**, **worried**, **excited**, **angry**, **scared**. Have the other students guess what emotion is being portrayed. Model using complete sentences: (Giancarlo) is (happy). Have the student role-playing then say: "*I am (happy).*"

2. Introduce new emotion words by role playing **hurt**, **tired**, **content**, **exhausted**, **jealous**, **confident**. Have students repeat the name of each feeling. These words are difficult to grasp. Be sure to explain what the words mean as simply as possible.

3. Have groups of students demonstrate each of these abstract words, while saying these sentences: "*I am hurt*"; "*I am tired*"; "*I am content*"; "*I am exhausted*"; "*I am jealous*"; "*I am confident.*"

4. Have individual students demonstrate these emotion words and have the class guess the emotion. The class should say: "*(Tomas) is (tired).*" Then have the student say: "*I am (tired).*"

5. Select individual students to create simple sentences using **am** and **is** and emotion words. Encourage them to remember yesterday's words as well as today's.

6. Repeat sentences using emotion words to describe traits of students or other people they know. Continue to remain focused on students' oral output.

Lesson 33

In this lesson, students will learn abstract words (adjectives) that represent individually identifiable characteristics. They will also practice first and third person present tense forms of **be (am, is)**.

1. Ask students to describe their classmates. The list might include these abstract descriptors: **short**, **tall**, **blonde**, **brunette**, **strong**, **injured**. Have students share the descriptive traits in complete sentences.

2. Ask individual students to role-play or identify abstract words that represent individual characteristics. (No student should be identified by a potentially hurtful characteristic such as overweight.)

3. Model sentences based on students' characteristics (e.g., Nguyen is tall). Have students repeat the sentences.

4. Have individual students select the appropriate adjectives that describe their own identifiable characteristics.

5. Solicit individual students to independently create simple sentences using **am** and **is**.

6. Repeat sentences using adjectives that describe traits of students or other people they know. Continue to remain focused on students' oral output.

Lesson 34

In this lesson, students will review abstract words (adjectives) that represent individually identifiable characteristics. They will also practice first and third person present tense forms of **be** (**am, is**).

1. Have individual students pantomime or indicate the previous day's adjectives for individual characteristics—**short**, **tall**, **strong**, **injured**, **blonde**, **brunette**—and have the class guess the word. Once the class has guessed the word, have the class say: "*(Stephanie) is (strong).*" Remember, no student should be identified by a potentially hurtful characteristic such as overweight.

2. Encourage the students to describe their classmates using new words: **little**, **big**, **old**, **young**, **dark-skinned**, **light-skinned**. Have students create complete sentences describing their classmates.

3. Ask the students to think about their neighbors and family. Elicit additional sentences describing characteristics of those people, focusing on physical descriptors.

4. Have individual students select the appropriate adjectives that describe their own identifiable characteristics using the sentence construction: "*I am (tall).*" Have the class repeat each sentence using the construction "*(Vincente) is (tall).*"

5. Select individual students to create simple sentences using **am** and **is** and additional vocabulary of their choosing.

6. Encourage students to practice creating sentences using adjectives that describe the people around them throughout the day. As sentences are repeated to review these descriptors, continue to remain focused on students' oral output.

Lesson 35

In this lesson, students will review abstract words (adjectives) that represent individually identifiable characteristics. They will also practice first and third person present tense forms of **be** (**am, is**).

1. Have individual students role-play or indicate all of the adjectives that have been taught during the previous four lessons: **sad**, **happy**, **worried**, **excited**, **angry**, **scared**, **hurt**, **tired**, **content**, **exhausted**, **jealous**, **confident**, **short**, **tall**, **strong**, **injured**, **blonde**, **brunette**, **little**, **big**, **old**, **young**, **dark-skinned**, **light-skinned**.
2. Have different students role-play abstract words. Once students have guessed the abstract word, have the student doing the role-play say: "*I am (scared).*" The class should say: "*(Joseph) is (scared).*"
3. Elicit additional sentences describing characteristics of neighbors or family members.
4. Have individual students select the appropriate adjectives that describe their own identifiable characteristics and complete these sentences using the construction **I am**.
5. Select individual students to create simple sentences using **am** and **is** with additional vocabulary of their choosing.
6. Model sentences using all of the abstract words representing individually identifiable characteristics to describe traits of students and others and have students repeat. Continue to remain focused on students' oral output.

Lesson 36

In this lesson, students will learn abstract words (verbs).

1. Demonstrate groups of verbs that are similar in meaning, such as words related to touch: **touch**, **tap**, **knock**, **pat**, **rap**, **bang**. Model, then have students repeat.

2. Model each action and put it into a complete sentence. Have the students copy your movements and then repeat the sentence.

   Touch your desk.
   Tap on your desk.
   Knock on your desk.
   Pat your desk.
   Rap on your desk.
   Bang on your desk.

3. Select several students to model each action. Have the class create a complete sentence that matches the action. Have students select a verb concept, then suggest related words.

4. Ask students for ideas about other concepts and related verbs, such as **see**: **watch**, **stare**, **look**, **peek**. If students are having a hard time generating related verbs, model and then label them for the students. Have the students repeat the new verbs.

5. Model each action along with a complete sentence. Have students repeat the sentence. Select different students to create complete sentences for the class to repeat. Listen carefully for correct language production and make sure all students are engaged.

6. Encourage students to practice complete sentences using these verbs during the school day.

Lesson 37

In this lesson, students will practice using abstract words (verbs), applying present and past tense.

1. Demonstrate verbs related to movement, modeling sentences in the present tense: **walk**, **skip**, **jump**, **hop**, **run**. Model sentences and have students repeat: He walks; She skips; He jumps; He hops; She runs.

2. Model the following words related to movement, first in third person present tense and then third person past tense: Walks, walked; Skips, skipped; Jumps, jumped; Hops, hopped; Runs, ran. Supply the present tense forms and then have students supply the past tense forms. Note the one irregular past tense: **ran**.

3. Next, model sentences in the present tense, then have students respond, changing the tense to past.

   stimulus: She walks. response: *"She walked."*
   stimulus: She skips. response: *"She skipped."*
   stimulus: She jumps. response: *"She jumped."*
   stimulus: He hops. response: *"He hopped."*
   stimulus: He runs. response: *"He ran."*

4. Select students to pantomime movements and have the class produce sentences describing the motion in present tense and then past tense, using the selected students' names (e.g., *"Juan walks; Juan walked"*).

5. Have individual students create complete sentences, using words related to movement in present tense form. Have students respond, changing the tense to past. Encourage them to think about the animal names they learned in previous weeks and how those animals move.

6. Encourage students to practice forming complete sentences using verbs in present and past tense.

Lesson 38

In this lesson, students will practice using abstract words (verbs).

1. Model and demonstrate groups of verbs that are related. For example, model words that are related to speech volume at the appropriate volume: **whisper**, **speak**, **call**, **shout**, **scream**. Have students repeat the words.

2. Say a word related to speech volume at the usual volume and have students repeat the word at the volume indicated: **whisper**, **speak**, **call**, **shout**, **scream**.

3. Repeat the exercises above, this time using words related to walking speed: **trudge**, **stroll**, **walk**, **scurry**, **run**. Demonstrate, then have students enact and say these related words.

4. Select students to enact a related word. Have students say the word and then create a complete sentence. For example, if a student says something quietly, the class should respond: "*Whisper; Luis whispers.*"

5. Call on individual students to create a complete sentence using one of the related words. Have the class repeat the sentence. Remain focused on students' oral language.

6. Encourage students to practice complete sentences using verbs during the school day.

Lesson 39

In this lesson, students will practice using abstract words (verbs) applying present and past tense.

1. Model a group of verbs related to movement: **walk**, **skip**, **jump**, **hop**, **run**. Have students repeat abstract words.

2. Model words related to movement and have students respond by creating their own sentences, first using present tense and then using past tense. Students should use **I**. Use the words **today** and **yesterday** to help prompt correct tense.

   stimulus: Walk. response: *"Today, I walk; yesterday, I walked."*
   stimulus: Skip. response: *"Today, I skip; yesterday, I skipped."*
   stimulus: Jump. response: *"Today, I jump; yesterday, I jumped."*
   stimulus: Hop. response: *"Today, I hop; yesterday, I hopped."*
   stimulus: Run. response: *"Today, I run; yesterday, I ran."*

3. Encourage students to generate other words that are related to movement. Help them think of animals or objects that move.

4. Select students to pantomime movement and have the class guess the movement word. The student who is doing the pantomime should create a sentence for the action, first in present tense and then in past tense. The class should repeat the sentence, changing first person to third person.

5. Call on different students to create complete sentences using words related to movement in present tense, then past tense.

6. Encourage students to practice forming complete sentences using verbs, present and past tense.

Lesson 40

In this lesson, students will build awareness of opposite concepts.

1. Model and have students repeat the following word pairs: Push/pull; Come in/go out; Sit/stand; Stop/start; Come/go; Speak/listen. Focus on students' oral language production.

2. Discuss the concept of opposites with students.

3. Call on students to demonstrate the word pairs modeled in step 1. As the word pairs are acted out, have the class repeat the words.

4. Model complete sentences with these terms. Contrast first person present tense with third person present tense (e.g., I can push; He can pull). Have students repeat sentences.

5. Call on individual students to create their own sentences using these opposite word pairs.

6. Encourage students to practice forming complete sentences using verbs, mastering awareness of opposite concepts.

Lesson 41

In this lesson, students will learn to change statements to questions.

1. Model and have students repeat stimulus sentences.

   You go to school.
   You like recess.
   You eat lunch.
   You take a nap.

2. Give a stimulus and model the question formation.

   stimulus: You go to school. response: Do I go to school?
   stimulus: You like recess. response: Do I like recess?
   stimulus: You eat lunch. response: Do I eat lunch?
   stimulus: You take a nap. response: Do I take a nap?

3. Provide the stimulus, then have students respond with the question format. Say: You go to school. Students should respond: "*Do I go to school?*" Repeat with the stimulus sentences given in step 1.

4. Ask individual students to respond to stimuli with a question formation.

5. Continue to model stimulus sentences, then have students respond with the appropriate question formation. If an error is made in formation, model the correct question and have the student repeat.

6. Encourage students to practice daily the transformation of statements to questions.

Lesson 42

In this lesson, students will learn to answer questions with positive statements.

1. Model and have students repeat stimulus questions.

   Do you go to school?
   Do you like recess?
   Do you eat lunch?
   Do you take a nap?

2. Model these question/answer pairs and have students repeat.

stimulus: Do you go to school?	response: Yes, I go to school.
stimulus: Do you like recess?	response: Yes, I like recess.
stimulus: Do you eat lunch?	response: Yes, I eat lunch.
stimulus: Do you take a nap?	response: Yes, I take a nap.

3. Next, give a question and ask students to provide the appropriate response. Use the question stimulus sentences given in step 1.

4. Ask a question and have individual students provide the appropriate response. Use the question stimulus sentences given in step 1.

5. Call on students to create their own questions and ask classmates to answer them. If an error is made in formation, model the correct statement and have the student repeat.

6. Encourage students to practice the transformation of questions to positive statements.

Lesson 43

In this lesson, students will learn to answer questions with positive statements, third person singular.

1. Model and have students repeat the stimulus questions.

   Does he go to school?
   Does she like recess?
   Does he eat lunch?
   Does she take a nap?

2. Model question/answer pairs and have students repeat.

   stimulus: Does he go to school? response: Yes, he goes to school.
   stimulus: Does she like recess? response: Yes, she likes recess.
   stimulus: Does he eat lunch? response: Yes, he eats lunch.
   stimulus: Does she take a nap? response: Yes, she takes a nap.

3. Ask a stimulus question and have students provide the appropriate response. Use the stimulus questions given in step 1.

4. Provide stimulus questions and ask individual students to provide the appropriate response. Use the stimulus questions in step 1.

5. Select individual students to create their own questions and have another student answer with the appropriate statement. If an error is made in formation, model the correct statement and have the student repeat.

6. Encourage students to practice the transformation of questions to positive statements.

Lesson 44

In this lesson, students will learn to answer questions with negative statements (with contractions) using first and second persons singular.

1. Model and have students repeat stimulus questions.

   Do you drive to school?
   Do you sleep at recess?
   Do you sit on your lunch?
   Do you sing during class?
   Do you color on the wall?

2. Model question/sentence pairs and have students repeat.

   stimulus: Do you drive to school? response: No, I don't drive to school.
   stimulus: Do you sleep at recess? response: No, I don't sleep at recess.
   stimulus: Do you sit on your lunch? response: No, I don't sit on my lunch.
   stimulus: Do you sing during class? response: No, I don't sing during class.
   stimulus: Do you color on the wall? response: No, I don't color on the wall.

3. Ask a question and have students respond with the appropriate negative statement. Use the questions given in step 1.

4. Ask individual students to respond with the appropriate negative statement. Use the questions given in step 1.

5. Select individual students to ask a question and have another student answer it with the appropriate statement. If an error is made in formation, model the correct statement and have the student repeat.

6. Encourage students to practice the transformation of questions to negative statements.

Lesson 45

In this lesson, review exercises for the previous four days: changing statements to questions; answering questions with positive statements; answering questions with a positive statement, third person singular; and answering questions with negative statements, first and second persons singular.

1. Model stimulus statements and have students change the statements to questions.

   stimulus: You go to school. response: *"Do I go to school?"*
   stimulus: You like recess. response: *"Do I like recess?"*
   stimulus: You eat lunch. response: *"Do I eat lunch?"*
   stimulus: You take a nap. response: *"Do I take a nap?"*

2. Ask a question and have students respond with the appropriate positive statement:

   stimulus: Do you go to school? response: *"Yes, I go to school."*
   stimulus: Do you like recess? response: *"Yes, I like recess."*
   stimulus: Do you eat lunch? response: *"Yes, I eat lunch."*
   stimulus: Do you color pictures? response: *"Yes, I color pictures."*

3. Ask a question and have students respond with the appropriate positive statement, third person singular.

   stimulus: Does he go to school? response: *"Yes, he goes to school."*
   stimulus: Does she like recess? response: *"Yes, she likes recess."*
   stimulus: Does he eat lunch? response: *"Yes, he eats lunch."*
   stimulus: Does she take a nap? response: *"Yes, she takes a nap."*

4. Ask a question and have students respond with the appropriate negative statement:

   stimulus: Do you drive to school? response: *"No, I don't drive to school."*
   stimulus: Do you sleep at recess? response: *"No, I don't sleep at recess."*
   stimulus: Do you sit on your lunch? response: *"No, I don't sit on my lunch."*
   stimulus: Do you color on the wall? response: *"No, I don't color on the wall."*

5. Select students to ask questions of their own, following one of the above configurations. Choose another student to answer the question using the appropriate statement. Statements can be positive or negative. Remain focused on students' oral language output.

6. Encourage students to practice the transformation of questions to statements, both positive and negative.

Lesson 46

In this lesson, students will learn to change statements to questions.

1. Model and have students repeat stimulus sentences.

   Ivan rides the bus to school.
   Ngoc draws good pictures.
   Sana helps other students.
   Anita likes to sing.
   Tran puts the books away.

2. Give a stimulus and model the question formation. Have students repeat each stimulus and response.

   stimulus: Ivan rides the bus to school. response: Does Ivan ride the bus to school?
   stimulus: Ngoc draws good pictures. response: Does Ngoc draw good pictures?
   stimulus: Sana helps other students. response: Does Sana help other students?
   stimulus: Anita likes to sing. response: Does Anita like to sing?
   stimulus: Tran puts the books away. response: Does Tran put the books away?

3. Provide the stimulus, then have students respond with the question format. Use the stimulus sentences given in step 1.

4. Ask individual students to respond to stimuli with a question formation. Use the stimulus sentences given in step 1.

5. Call on individual students to create a statement and transform it into a question. Draw from previous lessons for question samples if needed.

6. Encourage students to practice the transformation of statements to questions.

Lesson 47

In this lesson, students will learn to change statements to questions using pronoun referents.

1. Model and have students repeat the stimulus sentences.

   Ivan rides the bus to school.
   Ngoc draws good pictures.
   Sana helps other students.
   Anita likes to sing.
   Tran puts the books away.

2. Give a stimulus and model the question formation using pronoun referents.

   stimulus: Ivan rides the bus to school. response: Does he ride the bus to school?
   stimulus: Ngoc draws good pictures. response: Does he draw good pictures?
   stimulus: Sana helps other students. response: Does she help other students?
   stimulus: Anita likes to sing. response: Does she like to sing?
   stimulus: Tran puts the books away. response: Does he put the books away?

3. Provide the stimulus, then have students respond with the question format. Use the stimulus sentences given in step 1.

4. Ask individual students to respond to stimuli with a question formation, using pronoun referents. Use the stimulus sentences given in step 1.

5. Call on individual students to create a statement and transform it into a question. Encourage students to use pronoun referents. Draw from previous lessons for question samples if needed.

6. Encourage students to practice the transformation of statements to questions.

Lesson 48

In this lesson, students will learn to change statements to negative questions.

1. Model and have students repeat stimulus sentences.

   LaTanya dances.
   Susan draws.
   Kim plays ball.
   Tommy reads books.
   Mrs. Nakamura tells stories.

2. Give a stimulus and model the negative question formation. Have students repeat the stimulus and question response.

   stimulus: LaTanya dances. response: Doesn't LaTanya dance?
   stimulus: Susan draws. response: Doesn't Susan draw?
   stimulus: Kim plays ball. response: Doesn't Kim play ball?
   stimulus: Tommy reads books. response: Doesn't Tommy read books?
   stimulus: Mrs. Nakamura tells stories. response: Doesn't Mrs. Nakamura tell stories?

3. Provide the stimulus, then have students respond with the question format. Use the sentence stimuli given in step 1.

4. Ask individual students to respond to stimuli with a question formation. Use the sentence stimuli given in step 1.

5. Select individual students to create a statement and transform it into a question. Prompt students to use negative questions. Remain focused on students' oral output.

6. Encourage students to practice the transformation of statements to questions.

Lesson 49

In this lesson, students will learn to change statements to negative questions using pronoun referents.

1. Model and have students repeat the stimulus sentences.

   LaTanya dances.
   Susan draws.
   Kim plays ball.
   Tommy reads books.
   Mrs. Nakamura tells stories.

2. Give a stimulus and model the negative question formation using pronoun referents.

stimulus: LaTanya dances.	response: Doesn't she dance?
stimulus: Susan draws.	response: Doesn't she draw?
stimulus: Kim plays ball.	response: Doesn't he play ball?
stimulus: Tommy reads books.	response: Doesn't he read books?
stimulus: Mrs. Nakamura tells stories.	response: Doesn't she tell stories?

3. Provide the stimulus, then have students respond with the appropriate question format. Use the stimuli given in step 1.

4. Ask individual students to respond to stimuli with a question formation, using pronoun referents. Use the stimuli given in step 1.

5. Select individual students to create a statement and transform it into a question. Encourage students to use pronoun referents. Remain focused on students' oral output.

6. Encourage students to practice the transformation of statements to questions.

Lesson 50

In this lesson, students will review the statement/question transformations of the previous four lessons, producing complete statements and questions.

1. Model several statements and have students change the stimulus statements to questions:

   stimulus: Ivan rides the bus to school. response: *"Does Ivan ride the bus to school?"*
   stimulus: Ngoc draws good pictures. response: *"Does Ngoc draw good pictures?"*
   stimulus: Sana helps other students. response: *"Does Sana help other students?"*
   stimulus: Anita likes to sing. response: *"Does Anita like to sing?"*
   stimulus: Tran puts the books away. response: *"Does Tran put the books away?"*

2. Model several statements and have students change the stimulus statements to questions, using appropriate pronoun referents:

   stimulus: Ivan rides the bus to school. response: *"Does he ride the bus to school?"*
   stimulus: Ngoc draws good pictures. response: *"Does he draw good pictures?"*
   stimulus: Sana helps other students. response: *"Does she help other students?"*
   stimulus: Anita likes to sing. response: *"Does she like to sing?"*
   stimulus: Tran puts the books away. response: *"Does he put the books away?"*

3. Model several statements and have students change the stimulus statements to negative questions:

   stimulus: LaTanya dances. response: *"Doesn't LaTanya dance?"*
   stimulus: Susan draws. response: *"Doesn't Susan draw?"*
   stimulus: Kim plays ball. response: *"Doesn't Kim play ball?"*
   stimulus: Tommy reads books. response: *"Doesn't Tommy read books?"*
   stimulus: Mrs. Nakamura tells stories. response: *"Doesn't Mrs. Nakamura tell stories?"*

4. Model several statements and have students change the stimulus statements to negative questions, using appropriate pronoun referents:

   stimulus: LaTanya dances. response: *"Doesn't she dance?"*
   stimulus: Susan draws. response: *"Doesn't she draw?"*
   stimulus: Kim plays ball. response: *"Doesn't he play ball?"*
   stimulus: Tommy reads books. response: *"Doesn't he read books?"*
   stimulus: Mrs. Nakamura tells stories. response: *"Doesn't she tell stories?"*

5. Review the statement/question transformations of the previous four lessons, eliciting complete statements and questions. Emphasize use of the appropriate pronoun referent structures. Remain focused on students' oral output.

6. Encourage students to practice the transformation of statements to questions. Make sure that each student produces several sentences each day.

Lesson 51

Materials: picture cards (action verbs: dancing, driving, hopping, jumping, looking, reading, sitting, standing, walking, writing)

In this lesson, students will practice present progressive forms of **be** as auxiliary verbs while using first, second, and third person personal pronouns.

1. Model and have students repeat pattern sets several times. Using the verbs **reading**, **sitting**, **standing**, **walking**, and **writing**, conjugate each verb with all pronouns (first, second, and third person, singular and plural). Display the appropriate picture card while conjugating each verb.

   I am reading.
   You are reading.
   He is reading.
   She is reading.
   We are reading.
   They are reading.

   Emphasize the pronoun and how the verb changes to agree with the pronoun. Repeat sequences, changing the order of the pronouns with all the verbs.

2. Provide students with a sentence and pronoun stimulus and have them generate a new sentence. Say: I am reading. They.... Students should respond: "*They are reading.*" Repeat, scrambling the pronoun stimuli and verbs.

3. Model and have students repeat sentences as in step 1, using new verbs: **dancing**, **driving**, **hopping**, **jumping**, **looking**. Emphasize the pronoun and how the verb changes to agree with the pronoun.

4. As in step 2, provide students with the sentence and pronoun stimulus and have them generate a new sentence. Say: They are jumping. It.... Students should respond: "*It is jumping.*" Repeat, scrambling the pronoun stimuli and verbs.

5. Providing a pronoun stimulus and an action verb picture card, select an individual student to create a sentence. Have another student change the sentence using a new pronoun stimulus. Call on students until all pronouns have been used. Begin the process again with a new verb and pronoun prompt. Use all verbs, giving each student ample opportunity to practice.

6. Review various pattern sentences daily.

Lesson 52

Materials: picture cards (action verbs: biking, climbing, coloring, eating, fishing, helping, marching, running, skipping, sleeping, talking)

In this lesson, students will practice present progressive forms of **be** as auxiliary verbs while using first, second, and third person personal pronouns.

1. Using the verbs **biking**, **climbing**, **coloring**, **eating**, and **fishing**, conjugate each verb with all pronouns (first, second, and third person, singular and plural). Display the appropriate picture card while conjugating each verb.

   I am biking.
   You are biking.
   He is biking.
   She is biking.
   We are biking.
   They are biking.

   Model sentences for students and have them repeat each sentence. Emphasize the pronoun and how the verb changes to agree with the pronoun. Repeat sequences, changing the order of the pronouns with all the verbs.

2. Provide students with a sentence and pronoun stimulus and ask them for the correct response. Say: I am biking. They…. Students should respond: "*They are biking.*" Repeat, selecting pronouns and verbs randomly.

3. Model and have students repeat sentences as in step 1, using the following verbs: **marching**, **running**, **skipping**, **sleeping**, **talking**.

4. As in step 2, provide students with the sentence and pronoun stimulus and solicit a revised sentence using the new verbs. Repeat using all pronouns and verbs.

5. Provide a pronoun stimulus and a picture card to a student and have that student create a sentence. Have another student change the sentence using a new pronoun stimulus. Continue to make sentences using the pictured verb until all pronouns have been used. Prompt the next student using a new verb until all students have had a turn. If an error is made, model the correct response and have students repeat it.

6. Review various pattern sentences daily.

Lesson 53

Materials: picture cards (action verbs: biking, climbing, coloring, dancing, driving, eating, fishing, helping, hopping, jumping, looking, marching, reading, running, sitting, skipping, sleeping, standing, talking, walking, writing)

In this lesson, students will practice using the present progressive forms of **be** as auxiliary verbs while using first, second, and third person personal pronouns. Students will begin to generate appropriate sentences independently based on the pronoun stimuli provided.

1. Model and have students repeat pattern sets several times. Use the following verbs: **practicing, resting, washing, working**.

   I am practicing.
   You are practicing.
   He is practicing.
   She is practicing.
   We are practicing.
   They are practicing.

   Repeat for all verbs.

2. Scramble the pronouns and action verbs and have students repeat.

3. Model sentences and provide pronoun stimuli. Have students respond, using complete sentences. Say: She is practicing. You.... Students should respond: "*You are practicing.*"

4. Scramble and repeat. Provide stimulus sentences and pronouns and prompt students to respond using complete sentences. Practice with all verbs introduced in Lessons 51 and 52, using picture cards as appropriate.

5. Select individual students to create sentences. Provide a pronoun stimulus and a picture card. Have another student change the sentence using a new pronoun stimulus. Repeat, changing verbs and pronoun stimuli, until every student has had a turn. If an error is made, model the correct response and have the student repeat it.

6. Review various pattern sentences daily.

Lesson 54

Materials: picture cards (action verbs: biking, climbing, coloring, dancing, driving, eating, fishing, hopping, jumping, looking, marching, reading, running, sitting, skipping, sleeping, standing, talking, walking, writing)

In this lesson, students will practice forms of **be** (past tense) while using first, second, and third person personal pronouns. Students need to internalize the past tense forms of **be**, associating them with the appropriate personal pronouns, until they are automatic.

1. Model and have students repeat pattern sets several times.

   I was leaving.
   You were coming.
   He was thinking.
   She was stopping.
   It was there.
   We were going.
   They were happy.

2. Scramble verbs, adverbs, and pronoun stimuli and repeat.

3. Model and have students repeat new pattern sets several times. Use the verbs taught in Lessons 51–53. Be sure to use the past tense form of **be**.

4. Select individual students to create sentences. Provide a pronoun stimulus and a picture card. Have another student change the sentence using a new pronoun stimulus. Repeat, changing picture cards and pronoun stimuli, until every student has had a turn. Be sure students are using the past tense of **be**.

5. Provide students with pronoun stimuli and familiar adjectives and encourage them to create sentences with past tense forms of **be**. Repeat until every student has had a turn.

6. Review various pattern sentences daily.

Lesson 55

In this lesson, review sentences of the previous four days, reviewing sentence patterns and emphasizing pronouns associated with various forms of **be**. Remain focused on students' oral language.

1. Model and have students repeat present progressive pattern sets several times using common verbs.

   I am standing.
   You are sitting.
   She is walking.
   We are writing.
   I am kneeling.

   Scramble the pronouns and verbs and repeat.

2. Model a sentence and have students independently generate more sentences based on the pronoun stimuli provided. Say: She is practicing. You…. Students should respond: "*You are practicing.*" Scramble the pronoun and verb stimuli and repeat.

3. Practice sentence patterns using personal pronouns and the past tense forms of **be**. Say: I was leaving. You…. Students should respond: "*You were leaving.*" Scramble the pronoun and verb stimuli and repeat.

4. Model a sentence and have students independently generate more sentences based on the pronoun stimuli provided. Emphasize past tense forms of **be** in each sentence.

5. Select individual students to create complete sentences using pronouns and present progressive forms of **be**. Contrast present tense with past tense forms of **be** in student sentences.

6. Review various pattern sentences daily.

Lesson 56

In this lesson, students will practice past tense forms of **be** while using first, second, and third person personal pronouns.

1. Model and have students repeat pattern sets several times. Use the following verbs: **coming, going, leaving, stopping, walking**.

   I was coming.
   You were coming.
   She was coming.
   It was coming.
   We were coming.
   They were coming.

   Repeat with all verbs.

2. Scramble the pronoun stimuli and repeat.

3. Model and have students repeat new sets of pattern sentences several times. Use the following adjectives: **confident, content, happy, hurt, jealous, sad**.

   I was confident.
   You were confident.
   He was confident.
   She was confident.
   We were confident.
   They were confident.

   Scramble the pronouns and adjectives and repeat several times.

4. Model sentences as above and provide new pronoun stimuli. Have students complete the pattern sentences. Use the verbs and adjectives from steps 1 and 3.

5. Provide a pronoun prompt and ask students to create complete sentences. Make sure sentences contain past tense forms of **be**.

6. Review various pattern sentences daily, focusing on students' oral language.

Lesson 57

Materials: picture cards (action verbs: bathing, dressing, helping, painting, reading, sharing, singing, sweeping, talking, writing)

In this lesson, students will practice past tense forms of **be**, while using first, second, and third person personal pronouns. Students need to internalize the past tense forms of **be**, associating them with the appropriate personal pronouns, until they are automatic.

1. Model and have students repeat pattern sets several times. Use the following verbs: **painting**, **reading**, **sharing**, **talking**, **writing**.

   I was painting.
   You were painting.
   She was painting.
   We were painting.
   They were painting.

   Repeat with all verbs.

2. Scramble the pronouns and verbs and repeat.

3. Model and have students repeat new sets of pattern sentences several times. Use the following verbs: **bathing**, **dressing**, **helping**, **singing**, **sweeping**.

   I was bathing.
   You were bathing.
   He was bathing.
   We were bathing.
   They were bathing.

   Repeat with all verbs. Scramble the pronouns and verbs and repeat several times.

4. Model new sentences and provide pronoun stimuli. Have students complete new pattern sentences. Say: We were working. It …. Students should respond: "*It was working.*"

5. Provide students with a pronoun stimulus and a picture card and ask them to create sentences of their own. Emphasize the past tense form of **be** that belongs with each pronoun.

6. Review various pattern sentences daily, focusing on students' oral language.

Lesson 58

In this lesson, students will practice past tense forms of **be** while using first, second, and third person personal pronouns.

1. Model and have students repeat pattern sets several times. Use the following verbs: **going**, **helping**, **listening**, **playing**, **talking**.

   I was going.
   You were going.
   She was going.
   We were going.
   They were going.

2. Next, scramble the pronouns and verbs and repeat.

3. Model and have students repeat new sets of pattern sentences several times. Use the following verbs: **cutting**, **planting**, **pushing**, **resting**, **washing**.

   I was cutting.
   You were cutting.
   He was cutting.
   We were cutting.
   They were cutting.

4. Model a pattern sentence and a pronoun stimuli: They were playing. He…. Have student finish the pattern set: "*He was playing.*" Scramble the pronouns and verbs and repeat.

5. Select students to create their own sentences utilizing pronouns and past tense forms of **be**. If an error is made, model the correct sentence and have student repeat.

6. Review various pattern sentences daily, focusing on students' oral language.

Lesson 59

In this lesson, students will practice present and past tense forms of **be** while using first, second, and third person personal pronouns and time stimuli.

1. Model a sentence, then use **today** and **yesterday** to elicit new sentences. Say: I **am** talking. Yesterday, I **was** talking. Have students repeat.

   She **is** helping. Yesterday, she **was** helping.
   You **are** sitting. Yesterday, you **were** sitting.
   You **were** here. Today, you **are** here.
   We **were** reading. Today, we **are** reading.
   I **was** writing. Today, I **am** writing.

2. Scramble the cues **yesterday** and **today**. Repeat several times.

3. Model a sentence, then use **today** and **yesterday** to elicit independently generated sentences. Say: She is helping. Yesterday…. Students should respond: *"She was helping."* Scramble the pronoun, verb, and time stimuli, and repeat several times. Students need to internalize the present and past tense forms of **be**, associating them with the appropriate personal pronouns, until they are automatic.

4. Provide students with a time prompt and have them create their own sentences. If an error is made, model the sentence correctly and have the student repeat it.

5. Have students work in pairs to create sentences that incorporate forms of **be** as well as previous concept words like opposites and related verb groups (e.g., *"She was pushing; he was pulling"*). Refer to Lessons 36–40 if students need more practice with these concepts.

6. Review various pattern sentences daily, focusing on students' oral output.

Lesson 60

Materials: picture cards (action verbs: dancing, helping, painting, reading, running, sitting, talking, walking, writing)

In this lesson, review sets of personal pronouns plus present and past tense forms of **be** from the previous four lessons. Remain focused on students' oral language. Each student should produce several sentences.

1. Model and have students repeat pattern sets several times. Scramble and repeat.

   I was leaving.
   You were coming.
   She was stopping.
   We were going.
   You were there.
   They were happy.

2. Model and have students repeat different pattern sets several times. Scramble and repeat.

   I was listening.
   You were talking.
   She was helping.
   We were reading.
   You were sitting.
   They were writing.

3. Model another set of sentences and have students complete the pattern sets using the pronoun stimulus. Say: I was talking. You…. Students should respond: "*You were talking.*" Repeat several times, scrambling the pronoun stimuli and verbs. After several repetitions, call on individual students to respond.

4. Model a sentence, then use **today** and **yesterday** to elicit independently generated sentences. Say: I am talking. Yesterday…. Students should respond: "*I was talking.*" After several repetitions, call on individual students to respond.

5. Use picture cards of familiar action words to elicit sentences from individual students. Make sure sentences contain pronouns and forms of **be**. Have the class repeat the sentences.

6. Review various pattern sentences daily, focusing on students' oral language.

Lesson 61

Materials: picture cards (food: apple, apples, burrito, cake, carrots, cherries, cookies, corn, egg, eggs, juice, lettuce, milk, orange, oranges, soup; school things: board, book, chalk, crayons, eraser, glue, paints, paper, pencil, pencils, scissors, tape dispenser)

In this lesson, students will learn deletion of **a/an** before plurals and before some English nouns. In many first languages, this linguistic phenomenon does not exist. Model and stay focused on students' oral production rather than teacher explanation. (Much of English defies explanation!)

1. Select picture cards of food items. Using singular and plural cards when possible and appropriate, review the name of each food with students. Have students identify the relationship of the pictured objects.

2. Place cards at far point. Using a pointer to indicate each card, model deletion of **a/an**, using complete sentences.

   That is an orange.
   Those are Ø oranges.
   That is Ø lettuce.

   Use all the cards in sentences, emphasizing **a/an** or its deletion.

3. Repeat sentences in random order and have students repeat them.

4. Select picture cards of school things. Review the names of the objects. Set the cards at far point and, using a pointer to indicate each card, model complete sentences, emphasizing **a/an** or its deletion.

   That is a pencil.
   Those are Ø pencils.
   That is Ø chalk.

   Use all the cards in sentences. Have students repeat each sentence. Have students identify the relationship of the pictured objects.

5. Select individual students to create their own sentences using noun cards. Make sure each sentence uses **that** or **those** and listen for correct sentence construction. If an error is made, model the correct sentence and have the student repeat.

6. Encourage students to practice using **that** with singular nouns and **those** with plural nouns outside of class, focusing on proper usage or deletion of **a/an**.

Lesson 62

Materials: picture cards (clothing: boots, dress, gloves, hat, hats, jacket, jeans, overalls, pajamas, pants, shirt, shoes, shorts, sneakers, sweater; tools: broom, bucket, fire extinguisher, glasses, hammer, hammers, ladder, rake, rakes, saw, shovel, shovels)

In this lesson, students will practice deletion of **a/an** before plurals and before some English nouns. Continue to stay focused on students' oral production rather than teacher explanation.

1. Select clothing picture cards. Using singular and plural cards when possible and appropriate, review the name of each article of clothing with students. Have students identify the relationship of the pictured objects.

2. Place cards at far point. Using a yardstick or pointer to indicate each card, model the use or deletion of **a/an**, using complete sentences.

   That is a sweater.
   Those are Ø pants.
   Those are Ø jeans.

   Use all the cards in sentences, emphasizing **a/an** or its deletion.

3. Repeat sentences in random order and have students repeat them.

4. Select picture cards of tools. Review the names of the objects. Have students identify the relationship of the pictured objects. Set the cards at far point and, using a yardstick or pointer to indicate each card, model complete sentences, emphasizing **a/an** or its deletion.

   That is a shovel.
   Those are Ø hammers.
   That is a rake.

   Use all the cards in sentences. Have students repeat each sentence.

5. Select individual students to create their own sentences using noun cards from both groups. Make sure each sentence uses **that** or **those** and listen for correct sentence construction. If an error is made, model the correct sentence and have student repeat.

6. Encourage students to practice using **that** with singular nouns and **those** with plural nouns outside of class.

Lesson 63

Materials: picture cards (vehicles: ambulance, boat, boats, bus, car, cars, train, truck, trucks; toys: blocks, doll, jacks, jump rope, marbles, puppets, puzzle, yo-yo)

In this lesson, students will practice deletion of **a/an** before plurals and before some English nouns. Continue to stay focused on students' oral production rather than teacher explanation.

1. Select vehicle picture cards. Using singular and plural cards when possible and appropriate, review the name of each item with students. Have students identify the relationship of the pictured objects.

2. Place cards at far point. Model deletion of **a/an**, using complete sentences.

   That is a car.
   Those are Ø boats.
   That is a train.

   Use all the cards in sentences, emphasizing **a/an** or its deletion.

3. Repeat sentences and have students repeat them.

4. Select toy picture cards. Review the names of the objects. Set the cards at far point and model complete sentences, emphasizing **a/an** or its deletion.

   That is a puzzle.
   Those are Ø blocks.
   That is a jump rope.

   Use all the cards in sentences. Have students repeat each sentence.

5. Select individual students to create their own sentences using noun cards. Make sure each sentence uses **that** or **those** and listen for correct sentence construction. If an error is made, model the correct sentence and have the student repeat.

6. Encourage students to practice using **that** with singular nouns and **those** with plural nouns outside of class, focusing on proper use or deletion of **a/an**.

Lesson 64

Materials: picture cards from Lessons 61–63 (clothing; food; school things; tools; toys; vehicles)

In this lesson, students will practice deletion of **a/an** before plurals and before some English nouns. Continue to stay focused on students' oral production rather than teacher explanation.

1. Create groups of three to five students of approximately the same level of spoken English development. Give each group a stack of noun cards that belong to the same category. *(Note: The side of the card **without** the word should face up.)* Use the categories (clothing, food, school things, tools, toys, vehicles) that have been reviewed in the last three days.

2. Have students take turns identifying the item pictured on the top card using a complete sentence (e.g., *"Those are Ø oranges"*). If the student is successful, that student keeps the card. If the student incorrectly names the item or is unable to create a complete sentence, the card is kept on top of the pile. Play passes to the student to the left (clockwise). If no student in the group is able to produce a sentence from a picture card, the card is set aside for reteaching to the whole class.

3. Model sentences using any cards with which groups had difficulty. Rotate cards so that each group has a new set of cards and repeat activity.

4. Collect all the cards and place them at far point. Call on students and allow them to select a card and produce a sentence using **That** or **Those**. If an error is made, model the correct sentence and have student repeat.

5. With cards at far point, begin a sentence: That is… or Those are…. Call on students to complete the sentence. Challenge students to find all the cards that would fit the prompt.

6. Encourage students to practice using **that** with singular nouns and **those** with plural nouns outside of class, focusing on proper use or deletion of **a/an**.

Lesson 65

Materials: picture cards from Lessons 61–63 (clothing; food; school things; tools; toys; vehicles)

Review all noun categories taught during Lessons 61–63.

1. Using the picture cards for all the noun categories that were practiced in the previous three lessons, hold up one card at a time. Call on individual students to properly identify the object, using **a/an** where appropriate and deleting where appropriate.

2. Continue to use the picture cards as prompts and have individual students identify the object correctly using or deleting **a/an.**

3. Pass out all the cards. Students may have several cards. Have each student hold up a card and properly identify the object using or deleting **a/an**. Continue until all the cards have been properly identified.

4. Collect the cards. Set them up at far point in categories. Call on individual students to name all the objects in a category. Say: All of these are…. Prompt students into giving the name of the category (e.g., clothing, vehicles). Go through the categories in random order until the students can automatically name the objects and the category.

5. Set some cards at near point and leave some at far point. Say: This is (a pictured object that is at near point). Indicate a far point object and say: That is (a pictured object that is at far point). Call on students to produce pairs of sentences contrasting **this/that** or **these/those**. If an error is made, model the sentences correctly and have the student repeat.

6. Encourage students to identify common objects throughout the school day and review proper usage or deletion of **a/an**.

Lesson 66

Materials: picture cards (action verbs: helping, opening, walking)

In this lesson, students will learn verb tense inflections. *(Note: It is important to incorporate very high-frequency irregular verbs such as* **be** *and* **go** *early in the lesson; these words are critical to communication.)*

1. Model sentences using **be** and **go,** showing various verb tense inflections. Have the students repeat.

   I go.
   You are going.
   She goes.
   He will go.

2. Select action verb picture cards. Hold up each card and say the action. Model sentences, showing various verb tense inflections.

   I walk.
   You are walking.
   She walks.
   He will walk.

   Scramble the pronouns, verbs, and tenses. Have the students repeat each sentence.

3. Choose a few verbs and call on several students to help demonstrate. Change the tense and the pronoun in sentences. Walk, and say: I am walking. Have a student walk, and say: You are walking. Have a male student walk and then stop, and say: He walked. Have the rest of the class repeat the sentences as they are being demonstrated.

4. Provide a stimulus and have students complete the sentence. Say: I open the door.

stimulus: Now you…	response: *"are opening the door."*
stimulus: Yesterday, she...	response: *"opened the door."*
stimulus: Tomorrow, he…	response: *"will open the door."*

   Continue to change the starting sentence and have the students complete the sentence based on the stimulus.

5. Provide another starting sentence. Say: I go to school. Use time indicators and pronouns as a stimulus again, and call on individual students to complete the sentence. Give all students an opportunity to complete a sentence. If an error is made, model the correct sentence and have the student repeat.

6. Encourage students to practice verb tenses and sentence construction throughout the school day.

Lesson 67

Materials: picture cards (action verbs: eating, emptying, riding, sweeping)

In this lesson, students will learn verb tense inflections. *(Note: It is important to incorporate very high-frequency irregular verbs such as* **be** *and* **go** *early in the lesson; these words are critical to communication.)*

1. Model sentences using **be** and **go,** showing various verb tense inflections. Have the students repeat.

2. Select action verb picture cards. Hold up each card and say the action. Model sentences, showing various verb tense inflections.

   I ride.
   You are riding.
   She rode.
   He will ride.

   Scramble the pronouns, verbs, and tenses. Have the students repeat each sentence.

3. Choose a few verbs and call on several students to help demonstrate. Change the tense and the pronoun in sentences. Pantomime sweeping, and say: I am sweeping. Have a student pantomime sweeping, and say: You are sweeping. Have a female student pantomime sweeping and then stop, and say: She swept. Have the rest of the class repeat the sentences as they are being demonstrated.

4. Provide a stimulus and have students complete the sentence. Say: I empty the trash.

stimulus: Now you…	response: *"are emptying the trash."*
stimulus: Yesterday, she...	response: *"emptied the trash."*
stimulus: Tomorrow, he…	response: *"will empty the trash."*

   Continue to change the starting sentence and have the students complete the sentence based on the stimulus.

5. Provide another starting sentence. Say: I help other students. Use time indicators and pronouns as stimuli, and call on individual students to complete the sentence. Give all students an opportunity to complete a sentence. If an error is made, model the correct sentence and have the student repeat.

6. Encourage students to practice verb tenses and sentence construction throughout the school day.

Lesson 68

Materials: picture cards (action verbs: eating, emptying, helping, opening, riding, sweeping, walking, writing)

In this lesson, students will learn verb tense inflections. *(Note: It is important to incorporate very high-frequency irregular verbs such as* **be** *and* **go** *early in the lesson; these words are critical to communication.)*

1. Choose several picture card verbs that can be easily pantomimed (e.g., **sweeping, walking, writing**). Pantomime each verb and say the action. Have students repeat. Use each verb several times and incorporate **be** and **go**.

2. Pantomime a verb from step 1. Model sentences showing various verb tense inflections.

   I walk.
   You are walking.
   She walks.
   He will walk.

   Scramble the pronouns, verbs, and tenses. Have the students repeat each sentence.

3. Choose a few verbs and call on several students to help demonstrate. Change the tense and the pronoun in sentences. Pantomime writing, and say: I am writing. Have a student pantomime writing, and say: You are writing. Have a female student pantomime writing and then stop, and say: She wrote. Have the rest of the class repeat the sentences as they are being demonstrated.

4. Provide a stimulus and have students complete the sentence. Say: I play ball.

stimulus: Now you…	response: *"are playing ball."*
stimulus: Yesterday, she...	response: *"played ball."*
stimulus: Tomorrow, he…	response: *"will play ball."*

   Continue to change the starting sentence and time stimulus and have the students complete the sentence based on the stimulus.

5. Provide another starting sentence. Say: I watch television. Use time indicators and pronouns as stimuli and call on individual students to complete the sentence. Give all students an opportunity to complete a sentence. If an error is made, model the correct sentence and have the student repeat.

6. Encourage students to practice verb tenses and sentence construction throughout the school day.

Lesson 69

Materials: picture cards (action verbs: driving, eating, emptying, helping, opening, reading, riding, sweeping, swimming, walking, writing)

In this lesson, students will learn verb tense inflections. *(Note: It is important to incorporate very high-frequency irregular verbs such as* **be** *and* **go** *early in the lesson; these words are critical to communication.)*

1. Choose several picture card verbs that can be easily pantomimed (e.g., **driving, eating, opening**). Pantomime each verb and say the action. Have the students repeat. Use each verb several times and incorporate **be** and **go**.

2. Hold up a picture card from step 1. Model sentences showing various verb tense inflections.

   I drive.
   You are driving.
   She drove.
   He will drive.

   Scramble the pronouns, verbs, and tenses. Have the students repeat each sentence.

3. Choose a few verbs and call on several students to help demonstrate. Change the tense and the pronoun in sentences. Pantomime eating, and say: I am eating. Have a student pantomime eating, and say: You are eating. Have a female student pantomime eating and then stop, and say: She ate. Have the rest of the class repeat the sentences as they are being demonstrated.

4. Provide a stimulus and have students complete the sentence. Say: I read.

stimulus: Now you…	response: *"are reading."*
stimulus: Yesterday, she...	response: *"read."*
stimulus: Tomorrow, he…	response: *"will read."*

   Continue to change the starting sentence and have the students complete the sentence based on the stimulus.

5. Provide another starting sentence. Say: I go to the store. Use time indicators and pronouns as a stimulus again, and call on individual students to complete the sentence. Give all students an opportunity to complete a sentence. If an error is made, model the correct sentence and have the student repeat.

6. Encourage students to practice verb tenses and sentence construction throughout the school day.

Lesson 70

Materials: picture cards (action verbs: driving, eating, emptying, helping, opening, reading, riding, sweeping, swimming, walking, writing)

Review sentences modeling verb tense inflections from the previous four lessons. Make sure that every student produces at least five or six sentences independently. Focus on spoken language of individual students.

1. Pantomime several verbs and say the action. Have the students repeat. Use all verbs from Lessons 66–69 several times and incorporate **be** and **go**.

2. Hold up a picture card from step 1. Model sentences, showing various verb tense inflections.

   I ride.
   You are riding.
   She rode.
   He will ride.

   Scramble the pronouns, verbs, and tenses. Have the students repeat each sentence.

3. Provide a stimulus and have students complete the sentence. Say: I am here.

   stimulus: Now you… — response: *"are here."*
   stimulus: Yesterday, she... — response: *"was here."*
   stimulus: Tomorrow, he… — response: *"will be here."*

4. Choose a group of four students. Give them a verb card. Help them create four sentences that follow the stimulus model from step 2. Have each student take a turn creating a sentence with different pronouns and verb tense. Have the rest of the class repeat each sentence.

5. Provide another starting sentence like the one in step 3. Say: I swim in the pool. Use time indicators and pronouns as a stimulus again, and call on individual students to complete the sentence. Give all students an opportunity to complete a sentence. If an error is made, model the correct sentence and have the student repeat.

6. Encourage students to practice verb tenses and sentence construction throughout the school day.

Lesson 71

In this lesson, students will learn active/passive voice sentences using personal and objective pronouns.

1. Model passive voice sentences using personal pronouns (**I, you, he, she, it, we, they**) as subjects. Have students repeat sentences.

   You were seen by Mika.
   She was driven by Mario.
   They were shown by Kendra.
   I was found by Ana.
   He was told by Nguyen.
   We were helped by Ilsa.

2. Model passive voice sentences and active voice responses that contain objective pronouns as direct objects (**me, you, him, her, it us, them**). Have students repeat each sentence and then the response.

You were seen by Mika.	Mika saw **you**.
She was driven by Mario.	Mario drove **her**.
They were shown by Kendra.	Kendra showed **them**.
I was found by Ana.	Ana found **me**.
He was told by Nguyen.	Nguyen told **him**.
We were helped by Ilsa.	Ilsa helped **us**.

   Scramble the pronouns and verbs and repeat.

3. Model passive voice sentences and active voice responses. Elicit the objective pronoun that is the direct object. Say: I was found by Ana. Ana found.... Students should supply the missing pronoun: *"me."* Repeat using the sentences in step 2.

4. Model passive voice sentences and elicit active voice responses that contain objective pronouns as direct objects. Say: She was driven by Mario. Students should respond: *"Mario drove her."* Repeat, using the sentences in step 2.

   Scramble the pronouns and verbs and repeat.

5. Model passive voice sentences and call on individual students to produce active voice responses that contain objective pronouns as direct objects. If an error is made, model the correct response and have the student repeat.

6. Encourage students to use both types of sentence construction and review concepts throughout the unit.

Lesson 72

In this lesson, students will learn about objective case pronouns.

1. Model sentences in which verbs are followed by indirect objects of the main predicate verb, using objective pronouns (**me, you, him, her, it, us, them**). Have students repeat the sentences.

   Ana found **me** a sweater.
   Lani showed **you** a dress.
   Nguyen told **him** a story.
   Mario gave **her** a book.
   Ilsa made **us** a cake.
   Norma showed **them** the paper.

2. Model sentences with objective pronouns as indirect objects, followed by related sentences using the objective case pronouns. Have students repeat each sentence.

Ana found **me** a sweater.	Ana found a sweater for **me**.
Lani showed **you** a dress.	Lani showed a dress to **you**.
Nguyen told **him** a story.	Nguyen told a story to **him**.
Mario gave **her** a book.	Mario gave a book to **her**.
Ilsa made **us** a cake.	Ilsa made a cake for **us**.
Norma showed **them** the paper.	Norma showed the paper to **them**.

3. Model related sentence pairs and elicit the missing objective case pronouns. Say: Kendra sold **us** the tickets. Kendra sold the tickets to.... Students should supply the missing pronoun: *"us."* Repeat, using the sentences above.

4. Model sentences with objective pronouns as indirect objects and elicit the related sentence, using the objective case pronouns. Say: Mario gave **her** the book. Students should respond: *"Mario gave the book to her."* Repeat, using the sentences provided in step 2.

5. Model sentences with objective pronouns as indirect objects and call on individual students to produce the pattern sentence, using the objective case pronouns. If an error is made in production, model the correct response and have the student repeat.

6. Encourage students to practice these sentence constructions and review these concepts throughout the unit.

Lesson 73

In this lesson, students will learn prepositional phrases and will fill in objective pronouns as objects of the preposition.

1. Model sentences in which verbs are followed by prepositional phrases (**at, for, to, with, from, about, around, beside**) Have students repeat sentences.

   I went to the cafeteria **with** Karl.
   He came in the morning **with** Linh.
   She stood on the sidewalk **beside** Sani.
   They lived in a house **near** Mona.

2. Provide sentences with prepositional phrases followed by a related sentence, using the objective case pronouns as objects of the preposition. Have students repeat each sentence.

I went to the cafeteria with Karl.	Karl went to the cafeteria with **me**.
He came in the morning with Linh.	Linh came in the morning with **him**.
She stood on the sidewalk beside Sani.	Sani stood on the sidewalk beside **her**.
They lived in a house near Mona.	Mona lived in a house near **them**.

3. Model related sentence pairs and have students complete them, using the objective case pronouns. Say: I went to the cafeteria with Karl. Karl went to the cafeteria with…. Students should supply the pronoun: *"me."* Repeat, using the sentences in step 2.

4. Model related sentence pairs and call on individual students to complete them, using the objective case pronouns.

5. Provide sentences with prepositional phrases and call on individual students to provide the related sentence. Say: I went to the cafeteria with Karl. The student should respond: *"Karl went to the cafeteria with me."* Repeat, using the sentences or variations of the sentences provided in step 2.

   Provide ample opportunity for students to practice this sentence construction. If an error is made, model the correct response and have the student repeat.

6. Encourage students to practice these sentence constructions and review throughout the unit.

Lesson 74

In this lesson, students will review sentence patterns from Lessons 71–73. They will practice primary uses of objective case pronouns (direct objects, indirect objects, objects of prepositions) in English sentences.

1. Provide passive voice stimulus sentences with personal pronouns as subjects. Elicit active voice sentences in which verbs are followed by direct objects that are objective pronouns. Prompt students to produce complete sentences.

   stimulus: I was found by Ana. — response: *"Ana found me."*
   stimulus: You were seen by Mika. — response: *"Mika saw you."*
   stimulus: He was told by Nguyen. — response: *"Nguyen told him."*
   stimulus: She was driven by Mario. — response: *"Mario drove her."*
   stimulus: They were shown by Kendra. — response: *"Kendra showed them."*

2. Provide stimulus sentences in which verbs are followed by indirect objects of the main predicate verb, using objective pronouns. Elicit complete sentences in which the indirect object becomes the object of the preposition.

   stimulus: Ana found me a sweater. — response: *"Ana found a sweater for me."*
   stimulus: Mario gave her the book. — response: *"Mario gave the book to her."*
   stimulus: Kendra sold us the tickets. — response: *"Kendra sold the tickets to us."*
   stimulus: Ilsa made them a cake. — response: *"Ilsa made a cake for them."*

3. Provide stimulus sentences that use subject pronouns and verbs followed by prepositional phrases. Elicit complete sentences in which the subject pronouns and objects of the prepositions are changed.

   stimulus: He came in the morning with Nguyen. — response: *"Nguyen came in the morning with him."*
   stimulus: They lived in a house near Mona. — response: *"Mona lived in a house near them."*
   stimulus: Sara stayed at school with Ms. Soto. — response: *"Ms. Soto stayed at school with her."*

4. Move between sentence patterns and provide students ample opportunity to recognize and generate related sentences. Use students' names in sentence prompts.

5. Provide stimulus sentences for each pattern and call on individual students to complete the pattern, using complete sentences. Make sure each student has the opportunity to respond to all three patterns. If an error is made, model the correct sentence construction and have the student repeat.

6. Encourage students to practice the different sentence constructions and review throughout the unit.

Lesson 75

In this lesson, students will review sentence patterns from Lessons 71–73. They will practice primary uses of objective case pronouns (direct objects, indirect objects, objects of prepositions) in English sentences.

1. Provide passive voice stimulus sentences with personal pronouns as subjects. Elicit active voice sentences in which verbs are followed by direct objects that are objective pronouns. Prompt students to produce complete sentences.

   stimulus: They were told by Kendra. response: *"Kendra told them."*
   stimulus: We were helped by Ilsa. response: *"Ilsa helped us."*
   stimulus: He was driven by Nguyen. response: *"Nguyen drove him."*

   Scramble pronouns and verbs and repeat several times.

2. Provide stimulus sentences in which verbs are followed by indirect objects of the main predicate verb using objective pronouns. Elicit complete sentences in which the indirect object becomes the object of the preposition.

   stimulus: Nguyen told him the story. response: *"Nguyen told the story to him."*
   stimulus: Ilsa made us a cake. response: *"Ilsa made a cake for us."*
   stimulus: Kendra showed him the picture. response: *"Kendra showed the picture to him."*

   Scramble pronouns and verbs and repeat several times.

3. Provide stimulus sentences that use subject pronouns and verbs followed by prepositional phrases. Elicit complete sentences in which the subject pronouns and objects of the prepositions are changed.

   stimulus: He walked to the store with Nguyen. response: *"Nguyen walked to the store with him."*
   stimulus: I went to the cafeteria with Karl. response: *"Karl went to the cafeteria with me."*
   stimulus: We sang to the teacher with Kendra. response: *"Kendra sang to the teacher with us."*

   Scramble pronouns and verbs and repeat several times.

4. Move between sentence patterns and provide students ample opportunity to recognize and generate related sentences. Use students' names in sentence prompts.

5. Provide stimulus sentences for each pattern and call on individual students to complete the pattern, using complete sentences. Make sure each student has the opportunity to respond to all three patterns. If an error is made, model the correct sentence construction and have the student repeat.

6. Encourage students to practice the different sentence constructions and review throughout the unit.

Lesson 76

In this lesson, students will expand their vocabulary and mastery of action verb tenses. Students will learn to conjugate action verbs (e.g., **bending*, bouncing, collapsing, drooping, flopping, leaning, rising*, sagging, slouching, wiggling**). *(Note: Verbs denoted with an asterisk are irregular; it is important to emphasize these throughout the lesson.)*

1. Select five action verbs from above. Pantomime the verb while conjugating it. Emphasize the irregular verbs. Scramble the pronouns, verbs, and tenses. Have students repeat each sentence.

   I bend.
   Now, I am bending.
   Yesterday, I bent.
   Tomorrow, I will bend.

   Scramble pronouns and verbs and repeat several times.

2. Using the same five verbs, pantomime the action. Start each sentence and prompt students to complete the sentence with the proper tense of the verb.

   stimulus: I... response: *"flop."*
   stimulus: Now, I am... response: *"flopping."*
   stimulus: Yesterday, I... response: *"flopped."*
   stimulus: Tomorrow, I... response: *"will flop."*

   Scramble the pronouns, verbs, and tenses. Repeat exercise until responses become automatic.

3. Select five new action verbs and repeat step 1.

4. Using the new verbs, pantomime the action. Repeat step 2.

5. At random, pantomime verbs previously introduced. Call on individual students to produce sentences using the verb. Have students change the tenses.

6. Encourage students to practice sentence construction using various verb tenses and review throughout the unit.

Lesson 77

Materials: picture cards (action verbs: closing, dancing, driving*, hugging, jumping, looking, opening, planting, pushing, reading*)

In this lesson, students will continue to expand their vocabulary and mastery of action verb tenses. *(Note: Verbs denoted with an asterisk are irregular. It is important to emphasize these during the lesson.)*

1. Select five action verb picture cards. Hold up each card, say the action in all tenses (e.g., *look, looking, looked, will look*), and have students repeat until they know them readily. Emphasize the irregular verbs and their conjugation.

2. Select a card and pantomime the action. Start each sentence and prompt students to complete the sentence with the proper tense of the verb.

stimulus: I…	response: *"drive."*
stimulus: Now, I am…	response: *"driving."*
stimulus: Yesterday, I…	response: *"drove."*
stimulus: Tomorrow, I…	response: *"will drive."*

   Repeat this process with all the verbs.

3. Select five new action verb picture cards and repeat step 1.

4. Using the new cards, pantomime the action. Repeat step 2.

5. At random, hold up picture cards or act out verbs previously introduced. Call on individual students to produce sentences using the verb. Have students change the tenses.

6. Encourage students to practice sentence construction using various verb tenses and review throughout the unit.

Lesson 78

Materials: picture cards (action verbs: climbing, closing, dancing, driving*, eating*, hugging, jumping, looking, opening, planting, pushing, raking, reading*, riding*, sitting*)

In this lesson, students will expand their vocabulary and mastery of action verb tenses. *(Note: Verbs denoted with an asterisk are irregular. It is important to emphasize these during the lesson.)*

1. Pantomime the following action verbs: **shaking*, spinning*, stretching, swaying**. Say each verb in all tenses (e.g., *shake, shaking, shook, will shake*) and have students repeat until they know them readily. Emphasize the irregular verbs and their conjugation.

2. Pantomime **swaying** and have students identify the verb. Give the following stimulus prompts and have students complete the sentence with the proper tense of the verb.

stimulus: I…	response: *"sway."*
stimulus: Now, I am…	response: *"swaying."*
stimulus: Yesterday, I…	response: *"swayed."*
stimulus: Tomorrow, I…	response: *"will sway."*

   Repeat this process with **shaking, spinning,** and **stretching**.

3. Display the picture cards of the action verbs. Have students identify each verb and conjugate in all tenses.

4. Using the same verb picture cards, pantomime each action. Prompt students to produce sentences with the verb in all learned tenses (e.g., *"I eat; Now, I am eating; Yesterday, I ate; Tomorrow, I will eat"*).

5. At random, hold up picture cards or act out verbs previously introduced. Call on individual students to produce sentences using the verbs. Have students change the tenses.

6. Encourage students to practice sentence construction using various verb tenses.

Lesson 79

Materials: picture cards (action verbs: climbing, closing, cooking, dancing, driving*, eating*, exercising, fishing, hugging, jumping, looking, mixing, opening, planting, pushing, raking, reading*, riding*, sitting*, writing*)

In this lesson, students will continue to expand their vocabulary and mastery of action verb tenses. *(Note: Verbs denoted with an asterisk are irregular. It is important to emphasize these verbs during the lesson.)*

1. Select five action verb picture cards. Hold up each card, say the action in all tenses (e.g., *cook, cooking, cooked, will cook*) and have students repeat until they know them readily. Emphasize the irregular verbs and their conjugation.

2. Using the same five verbs, pantomime the action. Start each sentence and prompt students to complete the sentence with the proper tense of the verb.

   stimulus: I … response: *"sit."*
   stimulus: Now, I am … response: *"sitting."*
   stimulus: Yesterday, I … response: *"sat."*
   stimulus: Tomorrow, I … response: *"will sit."*

   Repeat this process with all the verbs, emphasizing the irregular verbs.

3. Review the remaining action verbs using the picture cards. With each card, have students identify and conjugate the verb in all tenses.

4. Review action verbs introduced in Lessons 76 and 78 (**bending*, bouncing, collapsing, drooping, flopping, leaning, rising*, sagging, shaking*, slouching, spinning*, stretching, swaying, wiggling**) by pantomiming each verb. Prompt students to produce sentences with the verb in all tenses.

5. At random, hold up picture cards or act out verbs previously introduced. Call on individual students to produce sentences using the verb. Have students change the tenses.

6. Encourage students to continue practicing sentence construction using various verb tenses.

Lesson 80

Materials: picture cards (action verbs: climbing, closing, cooking, dancing, driving*, eating*, exercising, fishing, hugging, jumping, looking, mixing, opening, planting, pushing, raking, reading*, riding*, sitting*, writing*)

In this lesson, students will continue to expand their vocabulary and mastery of action verb tenses.

1. Select ten action verbs used in Lessons 76–79 and review. As you display each card or pantomime each action, have students identify and conjugate the verb in all tenses. Emphasize the irregular verbs and their conjugation.

2. Select a picture card and pantomime the action. Start each sentence and prompt students to complete it with the proper tense of the verb.

stimulus: I ...	response: "*write.*"
stimulus: Now, I am ...	response: "*writing.*"
stimulus: Yesterday, I ...	response: "*wrote.*"
stimulus: Tomorrow, I ...	response: "*will write.*"

   Repeat this process with all picture card verbs, emphasizing the irregulars.

3. Select another ten action verbs from Lessons 76–79 and review. Have students produce sentences with the verb conjugated in all learned tenses.

4. Using the same action verbs, call on individual students to produce one sentence with the verb. Call on different students until the verb has been completely conjugated. Work through verbs at random, making sure that each student is called on several times. Pantomime when appropriate.

5. Pass cards out to students. Call on individual students to hold up their picture cards, say the verb, and then produce four sentences conjugating the verb using the pronoun **I**. If an error is made, model the correct sentence construction and have the student repeat. Continue until all students have produced sentences.

6. Encourage students to practice sentence construction using various verb tenses.

Lesson 81

Materials: picture cards (climbing, cooking, dancing, driving, fishing, juggling, jumping, looking, marching, sharing, sipping, sitting, sliding, swimming)

In this lesson, students will review and practice pronoun usage.

1. Choose five verbs from the previous week's lessons (**climbing, dancing, driving, fishing, sitting**). Using picture cards, have students identify each verb. Pantomime if possible.

2. Hold up a picture card. Encourage students to pantomime the pictured action verb while completing the following sentence patterns:

   stimulus: **I** can slide. — response: *"You slide with **me**."*
   stimulus: **He** can slide. — response: *"You slide with **him**."*
   stimulus: **She** can slide. — response: *"You slide with **her**."*
   stimulus: **We** can slide. — response: *"You slide with **us**."*
   stimulus: **They** can slide. — response: *"You slide with **them**."*

   Repeat this sentence pattern with all picture card verbs, emphasizing how the pronouns change.

3. Choose five more action verbs from the previous week's lessons (**bending, bouncing, drooping, rising, wiggling**). Have students identify each verb. Pantomime if possible.

4. Encourage students to pantomime each action verb while completing the sentence patterns as in step 2. Provide a pronoun prompt and hold up a picture card to elicit the correct verb.

5. Provide a pronoun stimulus and hold up a picture card. Call on individual students to produce one of the patterned sentences. Say: I can (march). The student should respond: *"You (march) with me."* Continue to call on individual students until all the pronouns have been used. Randomly work through all verbs, making sure that each student has several opportunities to model correct sentence construction.

6. Encourage students to practice sentence construction using various verb tenses and pronouns.

Lesson 82

Materials: picture cards (action verbs: combing, gluing, jogging, skipping, walking)

In this lesson, students will review and practice pronoun usage.

1. Display the picture cards. Pantomime each action and identify the verb. Have students repeat.

2. Hold up a picture card. Encourage students to pantomime an action verb while completing the following sentence patterns.

stimulus:	**I** can jog.	response:	"*You jog with* ***me.***"
stimulus:	**He** can jogs.	response:	"*You jog with* ***him.***"
stimulus:	**She** can jogs	response:	"*You jog with* ***her.***"
stimulus:	**We** can jog.	response:	"*You jog with* ***us.***"
stimulus:	**They** can jog.	response:	"*You jog with* ***them.***"

   Repeat this sentence pattern with all picture card verbs, emphasizing how the pronouns change.

3. Pantomime the following verbs: **creeping**, **dodging**, **galloping**, **limping**, **running.** Identify each verb. Have students repeat.

4. Encourage students to pantomime these verbs while completing the sentence patterns as in step 2. Repeat, using all five verbs.

5. Provide a pronoun stimulus while pantomiming an action or holding a picture card. Call on individual students to produce one of the patterned sentences. Say: I can (skip). The student should respond: *"You (skip) with me."* Continue to call on individual students until all the pronouns have been used. Randomly work through all ten verbs, making sure each student has several opportunities to model the correct sentence construction.

6. Encourage students to practice sentence construction using various verb tenses and pronouns.

Lesson 83

Materials: picture cards (action verbs: climbing, combing, cooking, dancing, driving, fishing, gluing, jogging, juggling, jumping, looking, marching, sharing, sipping, sitting, skipping, sliding, swimming, walking)

In this lesson, students will review and practice pronoun usage.

1. Review verbs from Lessons 81 and 82, using picture cards or pantomiming. Repeat until verbs are automatic for students.

2. Hold up a picture card or pantomime an action and elicit the correct verb. Have students complete these sentence patterns.

   stimulus: **I** can fish. — response: *"You fish with **me**."*
   stimulus: **He** can fish. — response: *"You fish with **him**."*
   stimulus: **She** can fish. — response: *"You fish with **her**."*
   stimulus: **We** can fish. — response: *"You fish with **us**."*
   stimulus: **They** can fish. — response: *"You fish with **them**."*

   Repeat this sentence pattern with all verbs, emphasizing how the pronouns change.

3. Choose five more verbs from the previous week's lessons (**dancing, jumping, leaning, riding, slouching**). Hold up picture cards or pantomime the action and have students identify each verb.

4. Using these five verbs, have students complete the sentence patterns outlined in step 2. Pantomime action, or hold up the picture card, to prompt the student.

5. Provide a pronoun stimulus while pantomiming or holding a picture card. Call on individual students to produce one of the patterned sentences. Say: I can (juggle). The student should respond: *"You (juggle) with me."* Continue to call on individual students until all the pronouns have been used. Randomly work through all verbs, making sure each student has several opportunities to model the correct sentence construction.

6. Encourage students to continue practicing sentence construction using various verb tenses and pronouns.

Lesson 84

Materials: picture cards (action verbs: climbing, combing, cooking, dancing, driving, fishing, gluing, jogging, juggling, jumping, looking, marching, sharing, sipping, sitting, skipping, sliding, swimming, walking)

In this lesson, students will review and practice pronoun usage.

1. Review verbs from Lessons 81–83. Use picture cards when possible to prompt verb. Pantomime when verb is not depicted on a card. Review until verbs are automatic for students.

2. Hold up a picture card or pantomime an action to elicit the correct verb. Have students complete these sentence patterns.

   stimulus: **I** can climb. response: *"You climb with **me**."*
   stimulus: **He** can climb. response: *"You climb with **him**."*
   stimulus: **She** can climb. response: *"You climb with **her**."*
   stimulus: **We** can climb. response: *"You climb with **us**."*
   stimulus: **They** can climb. response: *"You climb with **them**."*

   Repeat this sentence pattern with all verbs, emphasizing how the pronouns change.

3. Identify and pantomime the following verbs: **leaping, sprinting, staggering, strolling, tripping**. Pantomime again and have students identify each verb.

4. Encourage students to pantomime an action verb while completing the sentence patterns as in step 2. Repeat using all five verbs.

5. Provide a pronoun stimulus while pantomiming or holding a picture card. Call on individual students to produce one of the patterned sentences. Say: I can (sprint). The student should respond: *"You (sprint) with me."* Continue to call on individual students until all the pronouns have been used. Randomly work through all verbs, making sure each student has several opportunities to model the correct sentence construction.

6. Encourage students to continue practicing sentence construction using various verb tenses and pronouns.

Lesson 85

Materials: picture cards (action verbs: climbing, combing, cooking, dancing, driving, fishing, gluing, jogging, juggling, jumping, looking, marching, sharing, sipping, sitting, skipping, sliding, swimming, walking)

In this lesson, students will review and practice pronoun usage.

1. Review verbs from Lessons 81–84, using picture cards or pantomiming. Review until verbs are automatic for students.

2. Hold up a picture card or pantomime an action to prompt the correct verb. Have students complete these sentence patterns.

   stimulus: **I** can stroll. response: *"You stroll with **me**."*
   stimulus: **He** can stroll. response: *"You stroll with **him**."*
   stimulus: **She** can stroll. response: *"You stroll with **her**."*
   stimulus: **We** can stroll. response: *"You stroll with **us**."*
   stimulus: **They** can stroll. response: *"You stroll with **them**."*

   Repeat this sentence pattern with all verbs, emphasizing how the pronouns change.

3. Provide a pronoun stimulus while holding up a picture card or pantomiming. Call on individual students to produce one of the patterned sentences. Say: I can (gallop). The student should respond: *"You (gallop) with me."* Continue to call on individual students until all the pronouns have been used. Randomly work through all verbs, making sure each student has several opportunities to model the correct sentence construction.

4. Group students into pairs and distribute picture cards. Each pair should produce all five sentence sets demonstrating pronoun usage based on the given verb. After a few minutes, each pair should share the sentences with the class. If an error is made, model the correct sentence construction and have both students repeat.

5. Gather the cards and bring the class back together. Holding up an action picture card, call on individual students to create all five sentence sets demonstrating pronoun usage. Make sure each student has the opportunity to demonstrate mastery.

6. Encourage students to practice sentence construction using various verb tenses and pronouns.

Lesson 86

In this lesson, students will review and practice first person personal pronouns with present, present progressive, past, and future tense verbs.

1. Select five verbs, regular and irregular, to use as prompts (e.g., **driving, riding, smiling, talking, writing**). Model sentences with subject pronouns and varying verb tenses.

   I smile.
   I am smiling.
   Yesterday, **I** smiled.
   Tomorrow, **I** will smile.

   Model sentences with all verbs. Have students repeat each sentence.

2. Provide a stimulus sentence and have students respond with complete sentences, using the three remaining tenses. Say: I talk. Students should respond: *"I am talking. Yesterday, I talked. Tomorrow, I will talk."* Repeat with all verbs.

3. Select five more verbs, regular and irregular, to use in a stimulus sentence (e.g., **eating**, **playing**, **reading**, **sliding**, **standing**). Have students respond with complete sentences, using the three remaining tenses as outlined in step 2.

4. Provide a stimulus sentence using the ten verbs in this lesson. Call on individual students to produce complete sentences using **I** and the verb in one of the three remaining tenses. If an error is made, model the correct sentence construction and have the student repeat.

5. Repeat the stimulus sentences. Call on individual students to produce complete sentences using **I** and the verb in all three remaining tenses.

6. Encourage students to practice changing verb tenses.

Lesson 87

In this lesson, students will review and practice first and third person personal pronouns with present, present progressive, past, and future tense verbs. Emphasize subject/verb agreement.

1. Model sentence pairs using subject pronouns and objective case pronouns in present tense using action verbs from Lesson 86 (**driving**, **eating**, **playing**, **reading**, **riding**, **sliding**, **smiling**, **standing**, **talking**, **writing**). Have students repeat each sentence.

I smile.	Smile at **me**.
They play.	Play with **them**.
He reads.	Read with **him**.

   Repeat patterns with all verbs and pronouns.

2. Provide a stimulus sentence and have students respond with the correct pronoun.

stimulus: **She** speaks. Speak to…	response: *"**her**."*
stimulus: **We** drive. Drive with…	response: *"**us**."*
stimulus: **They** ride. Ride with…	response: *"**them**."*

   Repeat stimulus with all verbs and pronouns. Practice until responses become automatic.

3. Provide a stimulus sentence and have students respond with the complete sentence.

stimulus: **We** stand.	response: *"Stand with **us**."*
stimulus: **I** drive.	response: *"Drive with **me**."*
stimulus: **He** sits.	response: *"Sit with **him**."*

   Repeat, using all verbs and pronouns, using both subject and objective case. Practice until responses become automatic.

4. Call on individual students and provide them with a verb. Have a student produce a stimulus sentence. Call on a second student to produce the response sentence. Use the verbs in step 1. If an error is made in production, model the correct sentence construction and have the student repeat.

5. Call on individual students and provide them with a verb. Have students produce both a stimulus sentence and a response sentence. Make sure all students have an opportunity to participate and can demonstrate mastery of the concept.

6. Encourage students to practice changing subject pronouns to objective case pronouns.

Lesson 88

Materials: picture cards (book, car, cat, computer, dog, flashlight, hat, gloves, jacket, magazine, map, paper, truck)

In this lesson, students will review and practice possessive pronouns with present tense forms of **be**. Focus on subject/verb agreement, using **this** or **these** as subjects.

1. Display picture cards. Model sentence patterns to review and practice usage of possessive pronouns with present tense form of **be**. Have students repeat each sentence.

   These are **my** gloves. These gloves are **mine**.
   This is **your** jacket. This jacket is **yours**.
   This is **his** magazine. This magazine is **his**.
   This is **her** book. This book is **hers**.
   This is **our** map. This map is **ours**.
   This is **their** truck. This truck is **theirs**.

   Continue to model sentences, interchanging all possessive pronouns and picture cards.

2. Supply stimulus sentences and have students fill in the appropriate possessive pronoun. Say: This is **their** computer. This computer is.... Students should supply the possessive pronoun: *"theirs."* Repeat, interchanging all possessive pronouns and picture cards.

3. Provide stimulus sentences and have students respond with complete sentences that manipulate the possessive pronouns. Say: This is **my** cat. Students should respond: *"This cat is mine."* Continue to model sentences until all nouns and possessive pronouns have been prompted repeatedly. Practice until student responses become automatic.

4. Using picture cards, prompt a stimulus sentence. Because **this** and **these** indicate near point, hand the card to the student chosen to produce a sentence (e.g., *"This is her dog"*). After the correct sentence is produced, hand the card to a second student who is to produce the response using the correct possessive pronoun (e.g., *"This dog is hers"*). Repeat these steps until all students have had an opportunity to produce sentences and vocabulary has been reinforced.

5. Using the picture cards, prompt a stimulus and response from individual students. Continue to hand cards to students, encouraging them to use the same noun with a different pronoun, keeping the prompt at near point. Use all cards and make sure all students have an opportunity to produce sentences.

6. Encourage students to practice creating sentences that use possessive pronouns.

Lesson 89

Materials: picture cards (book, car, cat, computer, dog, flashlight, hat, gloves, jacket, magazine, map, paper, truck)

In this lesson, students will review and practice possessive pronouns with past tense forms of **be**. Focus on subject/verb agreement, using **that** and **those** as subjects.

1. Model sentence patterns to review and practice usage of possessive pronouns with past tense forms of **be**. Have students repeat each sentence.

   That was **your** jacket. That jacket was **yours.**
   That was **his** map. That map was **his.**
   That was **her** book. That book was **hers.**
   That was **our** magazine. That magazine was **ours.**
   Those were **my** gloves. Those gloves were **mine.**
   That was **their** truck. That truck was **theirs.**

   Model sentences using all picture cards and interchanging all possessive pronouns.

2. Supply stimulus sentences and have students fill in the appropriate possessive pronoun. Say: That was their computer. That computer was.... Students should supply the possessive pronoun: *"theirs."* Repeat, interchanging all possessive pronouns and picture cards.

3. Provide stimulus sentences and have students respond with complete sentences that manipulate the possessive pronouns. Say: That was my cat. Students should respond: *"That cat was mine."* Continue to model sentences until all nouns and possessive pronouns have been prompted repeatedly. Practice until student responses become automatic.

4. Using picture cards, prompt a stimulus sentence (e.g., *"That was her dog"*). Because **that** and **those** indicate far point, keep the card at a distance from the student chosen to produce the sentence. After the correct sentence is produced, keep the card at far point and select a second student to produce the response using the correct possessive pronoun (e.g., *"That dog was hers"*). Repeat these steps until all students have had an opportunity to produce sentences and vocabulary has been reinforced.

5. Using the picture cards, prompt a stimulus and response from individual students (e.g., *"That was our computer. That computer was ours"*). Continue to keep cards at far point and encourage students to use the same noun with a different pronoun. Use all cards and make sure all students have an opportunity to produce sentences.

6. Encourage students to practice creating sentences that use possessive pronouns.

Lesson 90

Materials: picture cards (book, car, cat, computer, dog, flashlight, hat, gloves, jacket, magazine, map, paper, truck)

In this lesson, students will review verb tense, pronoun case, subject/verb agreement, and present and past tense forms of **be**.

1. Model sentences that review first person personal pronouns. Use present, present progressive, past, and future tense verbs. Select verbs from earlier lessons that the students have mastered.

   I smile. **I** am smiling.
   Yesterday, **I** smiled. Tomorrow, **I** will smile.

   Scramble the pronouns, verbs, and tenses. Have students repeat each sentence.

2. Continue to use verbs that the students have mastered. Model sentences using first and third person objective case pronouns in present tense.

   I run. Run with **me**.
   She speaks. Speak to **her**.
   They walk. Walk with **them**.

   Scramble the pronouns and verbs. Have students repeat each sentence.

3. Display picture cards and model sentences using possessive pronouns with present tense forms of **be**.

   This is **their** truck. This truck is **theirs**.
   These are **my** gloves. These gloves are **mine**.
   That is **his** paper. That paper is **his**.

   Scramble the pronouns and nouns. Have students repeat each sentence.

4. Display picture cards and model sentences that review possessive pronouns and the past tense of **be**.

   That was **your** paper. That paper was **yours**.
   Those were **his** gloves. Those gloves were **his**.
   That was **our** book. That book was **ours**.

   Repeat sentences, using all cards and possessive pronouns.

5. Review steps 1–4 by prompting students to complete each pattern. Model each pattern before asking students to complete it. Review each step extensively, allowing students opportunities to respond in a group and then individually.

6. Encourage students to look for ways to practice these concepts throughout the day.

Lesson 91

In this lesson, students will learn and conjugate 12 new action verbs.

1. Pronounce each of the following action verbs: **cackling, calling, chuckling, coughing, crying, daydreaming, gasping, giggling, groaning, growling, grunting, hiccupping**. Have students repeat each verb.

2. Pronounce each verb, demonstrate the appropriate action, and say the verb again. Have students repeat each verb.

3. Say a verb, pantomime the action, and conjugate the verb.

   I daydream.
   You daydream.
   He daydreams.
   We daydream.
   They daydream.

   Scramble the pronouns and conjugate each verb again. Have students repeat each sentence.

4. Call on individual students and give them an action verb to demonstrate. Have the rest of the class generate a sentence that tells what the student is doing. For example, say: Marta, cough. (Marta should cough.) Students should respond: *"Marta coughs."* Repeat, scrambling verbs from step 1, until all students have demonstrated an action.

5. Call on individual students and assign each an action verb from step 1. Have the student produce a complete sentence using the verb and demonstrate the appropriate action. Have all students repeat each sentence. Give each student an opportunity to produce a sentence. If an error is made, model the correct sentence and have the student repeat.

6. Encourage students to practice making complete sentences using these and other action verbs throughout the day.

Lesson 92

In this lesson, students will review the 12 action verbs from Lesson 91, while learning 12 new action verbs.

1. Pronounce each of the following action verbs: **cackling, calling, chuckling, coughing, crying, daydreaming, gasping, giggling, groaning, growling, grunting, hiccupping, hissing, humming, laughing, mumbling, muttering, panting, screaming, singing, sneezing, snickering, sniffing, sobbing**. Have students repeat each verb.

2. Pronounce each verb, demonstrate the appropriate action, and say the verb again. Have students repeat each verb.

3. Say a verb, pantomime the action, and conjugate the verb.

   I laugh.
   You laugh.
   He laughs.
   We laugh.
   They laugh.

   Scramble the pronouns and conjugate each verb again. Have students repeat each sentence.

4. Call on individual students and give them an action verb to demonstrate. Have the rest of the class generate a sentence that tells what the student is doing. For example, say: Nguyen, hum. (Nguyen should hum.) Students should respond: *"Nguyen hums."* Repeat, scrambling verbs from step 1, until all students have demonstrated an action.

5. Call on individual students and assign each an action verb from step 1. Have the student demonstrate the action and use it in a complete sentence. Have the class repeat each sentence. Give each student an opportunity to produce a sentence. If an error is made, model the correct sentence and have the student repeat.

6. Encourage students to practice making complete sentences using these and other action verbs throughout the day.

Lesson 93

In this lesson, students will review the 24 action verbs from Lessons 91 and 92 and learn six new action verbs.

1. Pronounce each of the following action verbs: **cackling, calling, chuckling, coughing, crying, daydreaming, gasping, giggling, groaning, growling, grunting, hiccupping, hissing, humming, laughing, mumbling, muttering, panting, screaming, sobbing, singing, sneezing, snickering, sniffing, snoring, sobbing, wailing, wheezing, whimpering, whining, whistling**. Have students repeat each verb.

2. Pronounce each verb, demonstrate the appropriate action, and say the verb again. Have students repeat each verb.

3. Say a verb, pantomime the action, and conjugate the verb.

   I wheeze.
   You wheeze.
   He wheezes.
   We wheeze.
   They wheeze.

   Scramble the pronouns and conjugate each verb again. Have students repeat each sentence.

4. Call on individual students and give them an action verb to demonstrate. Have the rest of the class generate a sentence that tells what the student is doing. For example, say: Keisha, whistle. (Keisha should whistle.) Students should respond: *"Keisha whistles."* Repeat, scrambling verbs from step 1, until all students have demonstrated an action.

5. Call on individual students and assign each an action verb from step 1. Have the student demonstrate the action and use it in a complete sentence. Have the class repeat each sentence. Give each student an opportunity to produce a sentence. If an error is made, model the correct sentence and have the student repeat.

6. Encourage students to practice making complete sentences using these and other action verbs throughout the day.

Lesson 94

Materials: picture cards (balloon, bee, bell, bird, car, cat, clock, dog, mouse, pig, steak, telephone)

In this lesson, students will expand their vocabulary of action verbs by learning, demonstrating, and making sentences with verbs associated with objects and animals.

1. The following action verbs are associated with objects or animals, rather than people: **barking, buzzing, chirping, clanging, clicking, honking, popping, purring, ringing, sizzling, squeaking, squealing**. Pronounce each verb and have students repeat.
2. Pronounce each verb again while holding up the correlating picture card or object. Have students repeat each verb.
3. Hold up a picture card or object and ask individual students to name the verb associated with it. Have all students repeat the correct response. Repeat until all the students have had an opportunity to identify a verb.
4. Hold up a picture card and model a complete sentence using the action verb associated with it. Have the students repeat each sentence. For example, while holding the picture card of the telephone, say: The telephone rings. Repeat with all verbs.
5. Hold up a picture card and have individual students produce a complete sentence using the action verb associated with it. Have students repeat each sentence. Give each student an opportunity to produce a sentence. If an error is made, model the correct response and have the student repeat.
6. Encourage students to practice making complete sentences using these and other action verbs throughout the day.

Lesson 95

Materials: picture cards (balloon, bee, bell, bird, car, cat, clock, dog, mouse, pig, steak, telephone)

This lesson is a cumulative review of the action verbs learned in Lessons 91–94.

1. Provide a clear pronunciation of each of the following action verbs: **barking, buzzing, cackling, calling, chirping, chuckling, clanging, clicking, coughing, crying, daydreaming, gasping, giggling, groaning, growling, grunting, hiccupping, hissing, honking, humming, laughing, mumbling, muttering, panting, popping, purring, ringing, screaming, singing, sizzling, sneezing, snickering, sniffing, snoring, sobbing, squeaking, squealing, wailing, wheezing, whimpering, whining, whistling**. Have students repeat each verb.

2. Pronounce each verb again and demonstrate the action (if it is a verb associated with people) or show the correlating picture card (if it is a verb associated with animals or objects). Pronounce the verb again and have students repeat.

3. Prompt students with one of the action verbs associated with people. Have individual students demonstrate the action. Repeat, using all possible verbs from step 1. Make sure each student has an opportunity to demonstrate an action.

4. Pantomime a verb associated with people and have individual students produce a complete sentence using that verb. Ask each student to demonstrate the action and form a sentence. Have the class repeat each sentence. Use all appropriate verbs from step 1. Give each student an opportunity to produce a complete sentence.

5. Hold up a picture card and call on individual students to generate the verb associated with it. Ask the student to produce a complete sentence using the verb and have the class repeat it. Use all appropriate verbs from step 1. Make sure each student produces at least one complete sentence using the action verb. If an error is made, model the correct response and have the student repeat.

6. Encourage students to practice making complete sentences using these and their own action verbs throughout the day.

Lesson 96

In this lesson, students will review action verbs associated with people.

1. Pronounce and demonstrate each of the following action verbs: **cackling, calling, chuckling, coughing, crying, daydreaming, gasping, giggling, groaning, growling, grunting, hiccupping**. Have students repeat each verb.

2. Pantomime verbs and have students identify. Assign individual students verbs to pantomime and have the class guess the verb. Have the class answer in a complete sentence (e.g., *"Noriko coughs"*).

3. Model sentences in the present, present progressive (**-ing**), and past (**-ed**) tense of each verb.

   Linh hiccups.
   Today, Linh is hiccupping.
   Yesterday, Linh hiccupped.

   Use all the verbs from step 1 and have students repeat each sentence.

4. Provide students with a stimulus sentence that contains the present tense of the action verb. Have students respond with complete sentences, using the **-ing** and **-ed** verb endings along with the words **today** and **yesterday**. Say: Dogs growl. Students should respond: *"Today, dogs are growling. Yesterday, dogs growled."* Repeat, using different nouns and scrambling the verbs from step 1.

5. Call on individual students and provide one of the action verbs from this lesson. Ask the student to create a simple sentence (present tense). Have two different students each provide a response. Ask one to respond with the present progressive tense (**-ing**) and ask the other to respond with the past tense (**-ed**).

   stimulus: I chuckle.　　response: *"I am chuckling."*
   response: *"I chuckled."*

   Repeat the sequence, ensuring each student has ample opportunity to practice. If a mistake is made, model the correct response and have the student repeat.

6. Encourage students to practice using action verbs and adding inflectional endings throughout the day.

Lesson 97

In this lesson, students will review action verbs.

1. Pronounce and demonstrate each of the following action verbs: **cackling, calling, chuckling, coughing, crying, daydreaming, gasping, giggling, groaning, growling, grunting, hiccupping, hissing, humming, laughing, mumbling, muttering, panting, screaming, sneezing, snickering, sniffing, sobbing**. Have students repeat each verb.

2. Pantomime verbs and have students identify. Give individual students verbs to pantomime and have the class identify the verb. Have the class answer in a complete sentence (e.g., *"Zoe sneezes"*).

3. Model sentences in the present, present progressive (**-ing**), and past (**-ed**) tense of each verb.

   Keisha sobs.
   Right now, Keisha is sobbing.
   Yesterday, Keisha sobbed.

   Use all the verbs from step 1 and have students repeat each sentence.

4. Provide students with a stimulus sentence that contains the present tense of the action verb. Have students respond with complete sentences using the **-ing** and **-ed** verb endings along with the words **today** and **yesterday**. Say: Jim groans. Students should respond: *"Today, Jim is groaning. Yesterday, Jim groaned."* Repeat, using different nouns and scrambling the verbs from step 1.

5. Call on individual students and provide one of the action verbs from this lesson. Ask the student to create a simple sentence (present tense). Have two different students each provide a response. Ask one to respond with the present progressive tense (**-ing**) and ask the other to respond with the past tense (**-ed**).

   stimulus: They snicker. response: *"They are snickering."*
   response: *"They snickered."*

   Repeat the sequence, ensuring each student has ample opportunity to practice. If a mistake is made, model the correct response and have the student repeat.

6. Encourage students to practice using action verbs and adding inflectional endings throughout the day.

Lesson 98

Materials: picture cards (balloon, bell, car, clock, dog, telephone)

In this lesson, students will review action verbs while adding inflectional endings to mark tense. Some of the verbs listed in step 1 relate to objects or animals, rather than people.

1. Pronounce and demonstrate each of the following action verbs (hold up the corresponding picture card where appropriate): **barking, cackling, calling, chuckling, clanging, clicking, coughing, crying, daydreaming, gasping, giggling, groaning, growling, grunting, hiccupping, hissing, honking, humming, laughing, mumbling, muttering, panting, popping, ringing, screaming, sneezing, snickering, sniffing, snoring, sobbing, wailing, wheezing, whimpering, whining, whistling**. Have students repeat each verb.

2. Pantomime or hold up a picture card to prompt verbs. Have students identify. Give individual students a verb to pantomime. Have the class answer in a complete sentence (e.g., *"Kate daydreams"*). For verbs that cannot be pantomimed, say the verb and ask individual students to produce a sentence with it (e.g., *"The balloon pops"*). Give each student an opportunity to produce a sentence.

3. Model sentences in the present, present progressive (**-ing**), and past (**-ed**) tense of each verb.

   Lavona cries.
   Right now, Lavona is crying.
   Yesterday, Lavona cried.
   Tomorrow, Lavona will cry.

   Use all the verbs from step 1 and have students repeat each sentence.

4. Provide students with a stimulus sentence that contains the present tense of the action verb. Have students respond with complete sentences using the **-ing** and **-ed** verb endings, along with the words **today** and **yesterday**. Say: Maria sobs. Students should respond: *"Today, Maria is sobbing. Yesterday, Maria sobbed."* Repeat, using different nouns and scrambling the verbs from step 1.

5. Call on individual students and provide one of the action verbs from this lesson. Ask the student to create a simple sentence (present tense). Have two different students each provide a response. Have them both choose a new pronoun and have one respond with the present progressive tense (**-ing**) and the other respond with the past tense (**-ed**).

   stimulus: They cough. response: *"She is coughing."*
   response: *"He coughed."*

6. Encourage students to practice using action verbs and adding inflectional endings throughout the day.

Lesson 99

Materials: picture cards (balloon, bee, bell, bird, car, cat, clock, dog, mouse, pig, steak, telephone)

In this lesson, students will review action verbs while adding inflectional endings to mark tense. Some of the verbs listed in step 1 relate to objects or animals, rather than people.

1. Pronounce each of the following action verbs (hold up the corresponding picture card where appropriate): **barking, buzzing, cackling, calling, chirping, chuckling, clanging, clicking, coughing, crying, daydreaming, gasping, giggling, groaning, growling, grunting, hiccupping, hissing, honking, humming, laughing, mumbling, muttering, panting, popping, purring, ringing, screaming, sizzling, sneezing, snickering, sniffing, snoring, sobbing, squeaking, squealing, wailing, wheezing, whimpering, whining, whistling**. Have students repeat each verb.
2. Pantomime or hold up a picture card to prompt verbs. Have students identify. Give individual students a verb to pantomime. Have individual students identify by producing a complete sentence (e.g., *"Kade snores"*). For verbs that cannot be pantomimed, say the verb and ask individual students to produce a sentence with it (e.g., *"The bell clangs"*). Use all the verbs listed in step 1. Give each student an opportunity to produce a sentence.
3. Model sentences in the present, present progressive (**-ing**), and past (**-ed**) tense of each verb. Use all the verbs from step 1 and have students repeat each sentence.
4. Provide students with a stimulus sentence that contains the present tense of an action verb. Have students respond with complete sentences using the **-ing** and **-ed** verb endings, along with the words **today** and **yesterday**. Say: Tran chuckles. Students should respond: *"Today, Tran is chuckling. Yesterday, Tran chuckled."* Repeat, using different nouns and scrambling the verbs from step 1.
5. Hold up a picture card or demonstrate an action. Have individual students provide a complete sentence with the correct action verb. Have two different students each provide a complete sentence using the same verb. Ask one to use the present progressive tense (**-ing**) and the other to use the past tense (**-ed**).

   stimulus: The bee buzzes. response: *"It is buzzing."*
   response: *"It buzzed."*
6. Encourage students to practice using action verbs and adding inflectional endings throughout the day.

Lesson 100

Materials: picture cards (balloon, bee, bell, bird, car, cat, clock, dog, mouse, pig, steak, telephone)

This lesson is a comprehensive review of the present progressive and past tenses. Some of the verbs listed in step 1 relate to objects or animals, rather than people.

1. Pronounce and demonstrate each of the following action verbs (hold up the corresponding picture card or object where appropriate): **barking, buzzing, cackling, calling, chirping, chuckling, clanging, clicking, coughing, crying, daydreaming, gasping, giggling, groaning, growling, grunting, hiccupping, hissing, honking, humming, laughing, mumbling, muttering, panting, popping, purring, ringing, screaming, sizzling, sneezing, snickering, sniffing, snoring, sobbing, squeaking, squealing, wailing, wheezing, whimpering, whining, whistling**. Have students repeat each verb.

2. Model sentences in the present, present progressive (**-ing**) and past tense (**-ed**) of each verb. Use all the verbs from step 1 and have students repeat each sentence.

3. Provide students with a stimulus sentence that contains the present tense of the action verb. Have students respond with complete sentences using the **-ing** and **-ed** verb endings, along with the words **today** and **yesterday**. Say: Alfredo calls. Students should respond: *"Today, Alfredo is calling. Yesterday, Alfredo called."* Repeat, using different nouns and scrambling the verbs from step 1.

4. Demonstrate an action and have individual students provide a complete sentence with the correct action verb. Have two different students each provide a complete sentence using the same verb with a different pronoun and verb tense. Ask one to use the present progressive tense (**-ing**) and the other to use the past tense (**-ed**).

   stimulus: Mr. Kam hums. response: *"Mr. Kam is humming."*
   response: *"Mr. Kam hummed."*

5. Hold up a picture card and have individual students provide a complete sentence using the corresponding action verb. Have two different students each provide a complete sentence using the same verb with a different pronoun and verb tense. Ask one to use the present progressive tense (**-ing**) and the other to use the past tense (**-ed**) as in step 4. Make sure each student has several opportunities to produce a sentence.

6. Encourage students to practice using action verbs and adding inflectional endings throughout the day.

Lesson 101

Materials: picture cards (action verbs: biking, climbing, cutting, helping, reading, singing, sitting, walking)

In this lesson, students will review forms of **be**, using action verbs to expand the lesson.

1. Review forms of **be (am, are, is, was, were, be, been, being).** Model sentences using be as the main predicate verb. Next, hold up each picture card and model sentences using the pictured action verbs as the main verb and be as the helping verb. Have students repeat each sentence. Say: I was going. He is reading. I am being helped. Use all verbs.

2. Display the picture cards and model sentences with the action verbs without **be**. Next, use the same pronoun and action verb in a complete sentence with a conjugate of **be** as the helping verb.

I cut.	I **am** cutting.
He sits.	He **is** sitting.
She works.	Yesterday, she **was** working.
We sing.	Yesterday, we **were** singing.
You read.	Yesterday, you **were** reading.

   Scramble pronouns, verbs, and verb tenses. Have students repeat each sentence.

3. Hold up an action verb picture card and provide a simple sentence stimulus. Have individual students add a helping verb in any tense.

stimulus: I walk.	response: *"I (**was** walking; am walking)."*
stimulus: We climb.	response: *"We (**are** climbing; were climbing)."*
stimulus: They sing.	response: *"They (**are** singing; were singing)."*

   Repeat with all verbs.

4. Hold up an action verb picture card. Have individual students use the verb along with a form of **be** as the helping verb. Give each an opportunity to produce a sentence, making sure all forms of the verb have been used.

*"I **am** cutting."*	*"She **is** cutting."*	*"They **are** cutting."*
*"Yesterday, he **was** cutting."*	*"Last week, they **were** cutting."*	*"Tomorrow, they **will be** cutting."*

   Repeat with all verbs and pronouns. Have all students repeat the sentence.

5. Hold up a picture card. Have individual students create a set of five complete sentences containing the pictured verb and five forms of **be**. Make sure each student has an opportunity to produce five sentences.

6. Encourage students to name their actions during the day and practice sentence construction using **be** as the helping verb.

Lesson 102

Materials: picture cards (action verbs: biking, climbing, cooking, cutting, dancing, driving, eating, exercising, fishing, helping, juggling, jumping, singing, sitting, reading, singing, walking, writing)

In this lesson, students will review forms of **be**, using action verbs to expand the lesson.

1. Review forms of **be (am, are, is, was, were, be, been, being)**. Model sentences using **be** as the main predicate verb. Next, display the picture cards and model sentences using the pictured action verbs as the main verb with **be** as the helping verb. Have students repeat each sentence.

2. Model sentences using the pictured verbs without **be**. Next, use the same pronoun and verb in a complete sentence with **be** as the helping verb.

I drive.	I **am** driving.
She fishes.	She **is** fishing.
He eats.	Yesterday, he **was** eating.
We juggle.	Yesterday, we **were** juggling.
You cook.	You **were** cooking.

   Scramble the pronouns, verbs, and verb tenses. Use all verbs. Have students repeat each sentence.

3. Provide a simple sentence. Have individual students respond by adding be as the helping verb in any tense.

stimulus: I write.	response: *"I (**am** writing; **was** writing)."*
stimulus: You dance.	response: *"You (**are** dancing; **were** dancing)."*
stimulus: He reads.	response: *"He (**is** reading; **was** reading)."*

   Scramble the pronouns and repeat with all verbs. Have students repeat each response sentence.

4. Hold up an action verb picture card. Have individual students use the verb along with a form of be as the helping verb. Give each student an opportunity to produce a sentence, making sure all forms of the verb have been used.

*"I **am** cutting."*	*"She **is** cutting."*	*"We **are** cutting."*
*"Yesterday, he **was** cutting."*	*"Last week, you **were** cutting."*	*"Tomorrow, they **will be** cutting."*

   Repeat with all verbs and pronouns. Have students repeat each sentence.

5. Hold up a picture card. Have individual students create a set of five complete sentences containing the action verb and five forms of **be**. Make sure each student has an opportunity to produce five sentences.

6. Encourage students to name their actions during the day and practice sentence construction using **be** as the helping verb.

Lesson 103

Materials: picture cards (action verbs: bathing, closing, kicking, sipping, skating)

In this lesson, students will review forms of **have** using action verbs.

1. Review forms of **have** (**have, has, had**). Model sentences using **have** as the main predicate verb. Next, model sentences using action verbs as the main verb with **have** as the helping verb. Hold up the appropriate picture card and have students repeat each sentence.

2. Model sentences with the verbs above without **have**. Next, use the same pronoun and verb in a complete sentence with a form of **have** as the helping verb.

I skate.	I **have** skated.
He sips.	He **has** sipped.
You close.	You **have** closed.
We bathe.	We **have** bathed.
They kick.	They **have** kicked.

   Scramble the pronouns and repeat with all verbs. Have students repeat each response sentence.

3. Provide a simple sentence. Have individual students respond by adding **have** as the helping verb.

stimulus: I skate.	response: *"I (**have** skated; **had** skated)."*
stimulus: We bathe.	response: *"We (**have** bathed; **had** bathed)."*
stimulus: They kick.	response: *"They (**have** kicked; **had** kicked)."*

   Scramble the pronouns and repeat with all verbs. Have students repeat the response sentence.

4. Hold up an action verb picture card to prompt students. Have individual students use the verb along with a form of **have** as the helping verb. Give each student an opportunity to produce a sentence, making sure all forms of the verb have been used. Repeat with all verbs and pronouns and have all students repeat each sentence.

5. Hold up a picture card. Have individual students create a set of three complete sentences containing the action verb and three forms of **have**. Make sure each student has an opportunity to produce three sentences.

6. Encourage students to name their actions during the day and practice sentence construction using a form of **have** as the helping verb.

Lesson 104

In this lesson, students will review forms of **have,** using action verbs to expand the lesson.

1. Review forms of **have** (**have, has, had**). Model sentences using **have** as the main predicate verb. Next, model sentences using the following action verbs as the main verb with **have** as the helping verb: **cackling, calling, coming, coughing, daydreaming, gasping, giggling, going, groaning, grunting, laughing, mumbling, panting, serving, stopping, working**. Have students repeat each sentence. Review action verbs from Lessons 101–103, using **have** as the helping verb.

2. Model sentences using the verbs above without **have**. Next, use the same pronoun and verb in a complete sentence with a form of **have** as the helping verb.

We cough.	We **have** coughed.
You pant.	You **have** panted.
She daydreams.	She **has** daydreamed.

   Scramble all pronouns and verbs. Have students repeat each sentence.

3. Provide a simple sentence. Have individual students respond by adding **have** as the helping verb.

stimulus: Phillipe cackles.	response: *"Phillipe (**has** cackled; **had** cackled)."*
stimulus: Libby works.	response: *"Libby (**has** worked; **had** worked)."*
stimulus: Rowi laughs.	response: *"Rowi (**has** laughed; **had** laughed)."*

   Repeat with all verbs. Have students repeat each response sentence.

4. Assign individual students an action verb. Have each student create a sentence using that verb with a form of **have** as the helping verb. Give each student an opportunity to produce a sentence, making sure all forms of the verb have been used with each pronoun. Have all students repeat each sentence.

5. Give individual students an action verb and have each person create a set of three complete sentences containing that verb and three forms of **have**. Make sure each student has an opportunity to produce three sentences. Use the action verbs above and from Lessons 101–103.

6. Encourage students to name their actions during the day and practice sentence construction using a form of **have** as the helping verb.

Lesson 105

Materials: picture cards (action verbs: bathing, biking, climbing, closing, cooking, cutting, dancing, driving, eating, exercising, fishing, helping, juggling, jumping, kicking, reading, singing, sipping, sitting, skating, walking, writing)

This lesson is a comprehensive review of **have**.

1. Model a question using one of the following action verbs and **have** as the helping verb: **bathing, biking, cackling, calling, climbing, closing, coming, cooking, coughing, cutting, dancing, daydreaming, driving, eating, exercising, fishing, gasping, giggling, going, groaning, grunting, helping, juggling, jumping, kicking, laughing, mumbling, panting, reading, serving, singing, sipping, sitting, skating, stopping, walking, working, writing**. Respond to each question.

Have you worked?	You **have** worked.	**Have** we served?	We **have** served.
Had they bathed?	They **had** bathed.	**Have** I helped?	I **have** helped.
Has he called?	He **has** called.	**Has** she gone?	She **has** gone.

   Use all pronouns and verbs. Have students repeat each question and statement.

2. Using the model from step 1, make each question the stimulus and have the students provide the appropriate response.

   stimulus: **Have** you worked? — response: *"You **have** worked."*
   stimulus: **Have** I helped? — response: *"I **have** helped."*
   stimulus: **Has** she cut? — response: *"She **has** cut."*

   Use all pronouns and verbs from step 1. Have the class repeat each response.

3. Act out an action or hold up a picture card. Ask students to form questions using that verb and **have** as the helping verb. Have others respond. Give each student several opportunities to ask and respond.

4. Using the verbs from step 1, provide a stimulus statement and have individual students respond using the same verb and a new pronoun.

   stimulus: We **have** eaten. — response: *"You **have** eaten."*
   stimulus: They **have** driven. — response: *"She **has** driven."*
   stimulus: I **have** read. — response: *"He **has** read."*

   Scramble the verbs and pronouns until each student has had several opportunities to respond.

5. Act out an action or hold up a picture card. Have individual students create a question and response containing a pronoun, the action verb, and **have** as the helping verb, as in step 1. Have other students generate different questions and responses using the same action verb until all forms have been used. Use all verbs listed above. Have each student create several distinct questions and responses.

6. Encourage students to name their actions during the day and practice sentences with a form of have as the helping verb.

Lesson 106

Materials: picture cards (action verbs: climbing, eating, exercising, helping, reading, singing, skating, sleeping)

In this lesson, students will review three forms of **do** (**do, does, did**), using action verbs to further expand the lesson.

1. Display the picture cards. Model complete sentences using the pictured verb and **do** as the helping verb. Emphasize that the verb remains the same; only the form of **do** changes.

I **do** sleep.	I **did** sleep.	We **do** sing.	We **did** sing.
You **do** help.	You **did** help.	You **do** skate.	You **did** skate.
He **does** read.	He **did** read.	They **do** climb.	They **did** climb.

   Have students repeat each sentence.

2. Provide individual students with a simple sentence using the action verbs from step 1. Have each student produce a complete sentence using forms of **do** as the helping verb.

stimulus: I sleep.	response: *"I (**do** sleep, **did** sleep)."*
stimulus: He skates.	response: *"He (**does** skate, **did** skate)."*
stimulus: She climbs.	response: *"She (**does** climb, **did** climb)."*

   Scramble pronouns and verbs, giving each student an opportunity to respond.

3. Model a sentence using **do** as the helping verb. Provide a pronoun prompt and have individual students create a complete sentence using the new pronoun (e.g., say: He **does** read. We.... The student should respond: *"We **do** read"*). Have the class repeat the response.

4. Hold up a picture card and have individual students identify the appropriate verb. Next, ask the student to create a complete sentence using any pronoun, the action verb, and a form of **do** as the helping verb.

   *"I **do** read."* *"She **does** read."* *"They **do** read."* *"We **did** read."* *"You **did** read."*

   Repeat until all the pronouns, action verbs, and forms of **do** have been used and each student has had an opportunity to respond.

5. Hold up a picture card. Have individual students create a set of three complete sentences containing the action verb and three forms of **do** (**do, does, did**) as the helping verb. Make sure each student has an opportunity to produce at least three different sentences. If a mistake is made, model the correct response and have the student repeat.

6. Encourage students to name their actions during the day and produce sentences with a form of **do** as the helping verb.

Lesson 107

Materials: picture cards (action verbs: climbing, cutting, driving, eating, exercising, fishing, helping, juggling, jumping, reading, singing, skating, skipping, sleeping)

In this lesson, students will review three forms of **do** (**do, does, did**), using action verbs to further expand the lesson.

1. Model sentences that contain the following action verbs with **do** as the helping verb: **climbing, crying, cutting, driving, eating, exercising, fishing, hearing, helping, juggling, jumping, listening, reading, seeing, singing, skating, skipping, sleeping, stopping, trying, working.** Repeat, pantomiming the action verb or holding up the appropriate picture card when possible. Emphasize that the verb remains the same, only the form of **do** changes. Have the students repeat each sentence.

2. Provide individual students with a simple sentence using the action verbs from step 1. Have each student produce a complete sentence using forms of **do** as the helping verb.

   stimulus: I cry. — response: *"I (**do** cry, **did** cry)."*
   stimulus: You stop. — response: *"You (**do** stop, **did** stop)."*
   stimulus: They see. — response: *"They (**do** see, **did** see)."*

   Scramble pronouns and verbs, giving each student an opportunity to respond.

3. Model a sentence using **do** as the helping verb. Provide a pronoun prompt and have individual students create a complete sentence using the new pronoun. For example, say: They fish. We.... The student should respond: *"We **did** fish."* Have the class repeat the response.

4. Pantomime an action, hold up a picture card, or say a verb to prompt students. Ask each student to create a complete sentence using any pronoun, the action verb provided, and **do** as the helping verb. For example, if you provide the verb **listening**, a student should respond: *"We **do** listen."* or *"We **did** listen."* Repeat until all the pronouns, action verbs, and forms of **do** have been used.

5. Pantomime an action, hold up a picture card, or say a verb to prompt students. Have individual students create a set of three complete sentences containing that action verb and three forms of **do** (**do, does, did**) as the helping verb. Make sure each student has an opportunity to produce at least three different sentences. If a mistake is made, model the correct response and have the student repeat.

6. Encourage students to name their actions during the day and produce sentences with a form of **do** as the helping verb.

Lesson 108

Materials: picture cards (action verbs: bathing, climbing, cutting, dressing, driving, eating, exercising, fishing, helping, juggling, jumping, looking, marching, mixing, painting, reading, singing, sitting, skating, skipping, sleeping)

In this lesson, students will review forms of **be** (**am, are, is, was, were, be, been, being**), using action verbs to further expand the lesson.

1. Model simple sentences using **be**. Have students repeat. Next, model sentences containing the following action verbs with the present or past forms of **be** as the helping verb: **bathing, climbing, coming, crying, cutting, dressing, driving, eating, exercising, fishing, going, hearing, helping, juggling, jumping, listening, looking, marching, mixing, painting, reading, seeing, serving, singing, sitting, skating, skipping, sleeping, starting, stopping, talking, trying, working.**

   I **am**.
   He **is** sitting.
   She **was** bathing.
   They **have been** painting.
   You **were**.
   The dog **is** eating.
   We **were** marching.
   Lunch **is being** served.
   They **are**.
   I **was** going.
   You **may be** starting.
   He **was** painting.

   Have the students repeat each sentence.

2. Model a sentence using the action verbs from step 1 without a helping verb. Follow with a sentence using the same pronoun and action verb and the present or past forms of **be** as the helping verb.

   I dress. I **am** dressing.
   We came. We **were** coming.
   She helps. She **is** helping.

   Scramble pronouns, verbs, and verb tenses. Have students repeat each sentence.

3. Provide a simple sentence. Have individual students respond by adding **be** as the helping verb.

   stimulus: I talk. response: *"I (**am** talking; **was** talking; **have been** talking)."*
   stimulus: She goes. response: *"She (**is** going; **was** going; **will be** going)."*
   stimulus: He started. response: *"He (**is** starting; **was** starting; **has been** starting)."*

   Scramble the pronouns and verbs. Have students repeat each response sentence.

4. Pantomime an action, hold up a picture card, or say a verb. Have individual students use the verb along with a form of **be** in a complete sentence. Repeat until all the forms of **be** are used as helping verbs with all action verbs listed in step 1.

5. Have individual students create a set of five complete sentences containing an action verb and **be** as the helping verb. Make sure each student has an opportunity to produce at least five different sentences. If a mistake is made, model the correct response and have the student repeat.

6. Encourage students to produce sentences using the present or past forms of **be** as the helping verb.

Lesson 109

Materials: picture cards (action verbs: bathing, climbing, cutting, dressing, driving, eating, exercising, fishing, helping, juggling, jumping, looking, marching, mixing, painting, reading, singing, sitting, skating, skipping, sleeping)

In this lesson, students will review forms of **have** (**have, has, had**) using action verbs.

1. Model sentences containing the following action verbs with **have** as the helping verb: **bathing, chuckling, climbing, coming, coughing, crying, cutting, daydreaming, dressing, driving, eating, exercising, fishing, gasping, giggling, going, groaning, hearing, helping, juggling, jumping, laughing, listening, looking, marching, mixing, mumbling, painting, reading, screaming, seeing, serving, singing, sitting, skating, skipping, sleeping, sneezing, snoring, sobbing, squealing, starting, stopping, talking, trying, working.**

   I **have** mumbled. You **have** laughed. He **has** daydreamed. She **has** chuckled.
   It **has** squealed. We **have** screamed. You **have** sneezed. They **had** groaned.

   Scramble the pronouns and verbs and have students repeat each sentence.

2. Model a sentence using the action verbs from step 1 without a helping verb. Follow with a sentence using the same pronoun and action verb, and a form of **have** as the helping verb. For example:

I giggled.	I **have** giggled.
She daydreamed.	She **has** daydreamed.
We gasp.	We **have** gasped.

   Scramble the pronouns and verbs and have students repeat each sentence.

3. Provide a simple sentence. Have individual students respond by adding **have** as the helping verb.

stimulus: I sneeze.	response: *"I (**have** sneezed, **had** sneezed)."*
stimulus: You cough.	response: *"You (**have** coughed, **had** coughed)."*
stimulus: She sobs.	response: *"She (**has** sobbed, **had** sobbed)."*

   Scramble the pronouns and verbs and have students repeat each sentence.

4. Pantomime an action, hold up a picture card, or say a verb. Have individual students use the verb along with a form of **have** in a complete sentence. Repeat until all the forms of **have** are used as helping verbs with all the verbs in step 1.

5. Pantomime an action or hold up a picture card. Have individual students create a set of three complete sentences containing the action verb and a form of **have** as the helping verb. Make sure each student has an opportunity to produce at least three different sentences. If a mistake is made, model the correct response and have the student repeat.

6. Encourage students to produce sentences using **have** as a helping verb throughout the day.

Lesson 110

Materials: picture cards (action verbs: bathing, climbing, cutting, dressing, driving, eating, exercising, fishing, helping, juggling, jumping, looking, marching, mixing, painting, reading, singing, sitting, skating, skipping, sleeping)

This lesson is a comprehensive review of **be**, **have**, and **do**.

1. Model a question using one of the following action verbs and **be**, **have**, or **do** as the helping verb: **bathing, chuckling, climbing, coming, coughing, crying, cutting, daydreaming, dressing, driving, eating, exercising, fishing, gasping, giggling, going, groaning, hearing, helping, juggling, jumping, laughing, listening, looking, marching, mixing, mumbling, painting, reading, screaming, seeing, serving, singing, sitting, skating, skipping, sleeping, sneezing, snoring, sobbing, squealing, starting, stopping, talking, trying, working**. Respond to each.

Is he sleeping?	He **is** sleeping.	**Has** it stopped?	It **has** stopped.
Are we singing?	We **are** singing.	**Did** we hear?	We **did** hear.

   Use all pronouns and verbs. Have students repeat each question and statement.

2. Using the model from step 1, make each question the stimulus, and have the students answer with the appropriate response.

   stimulus: **Have** you heard? — response: *"You **have** heard."*
   stimulus: **Are** they trying? — response: *"They **are** trying."*
   stimulus: **Did** he listen? — response: *"He **did** listen."*

   Use all pronouns and verbs. Have students repeat each response.

3. Pantomime an action, hold up a card, or say a verb. Have individual students form a question using that verb and **be**, **have,** or **do** as the helping verb. Have other students respond. Use all verbs from step 1. Give each student several opportunities to ask a question and respond.

4. Using the verbs from step 1, provide a statement and have individual students respond using the same verb and a new pronoun.

   stimulus: She has screamed. — response: *"You have screamed."*
   stimulus: We have laughed. — response: *"She has laughed."*

   Scramble the verbs and pronouns until each student has had several opportunities to respond.

5. Act out an action, hold up a card, or say a verb to prompt students. Have individual students create a question and response containing pronouns, an action verb, and the proper form of **be**, **have**, or **do**, as in step 1. Have other students generate different questions and responses using the same action verb until all forms have been used. Use all the verbs from Lessons 106–109. Have each student create several distinct questions and responses.

6. Encourage students to practice identifying their actions using **be**, **have**, or **do** as the helping verb.

Lesson 111

In this lesson, students will create sentences using modals as helping verbs and action verbs.

1. Model sentences using the following modals: **can, could, may, might, must, shall, should, will, would**. Use each modal with one of the following verbs: **coming, finding, finishing, going, hearing, playing, running, seeing, staying, stopping, walking, working**.

   I **can** finish it.
   She **may** play.
   They **should** stop.
   You **will** walk.
   We **could** hear you.
   We **might** run.
   We **shall** stay here.
   You **would** find us.
   They **must** go.

   Have the students repeat each sentence.

2. Model a sentence using one of the action verbs from step 1 without a modal. Follow with a sentence using the same pronoun and action verb, and one of the modals.

   I walk. — I **should** walk.
   They run. — They **might** run.
   She hears you. — She **could** hear you.

   Scramble pronouns, verbs, and modals. Have students repeat each sentence.

3. Provide a simple sentence. Have individual students respond by adding one of the above modals.

   stimulus: You work. — response: *"You (**can** work, **could** work, **might** work)."*
   stimulus: They finished. — response: *"They (**should** finish, **may** finish, **will** finish)."*
   stimulus: We came. — response: *"We (**must** come, **would** come, **shall** come)."*

   Scramble the pronouns, verbs, and modals. Have students repeat each response sentence.

4. Prompt students with an action verb. Have individual students use that verb, along with a modal from step 1, in a complete sentence.

   *"I **can** stay."*
   *"I **should** stay."*
   *"I **may** stay."*
   *"I **could** stay."*
   *"I **will** stay."*
   *"I **might** stay."*
   *"I **shall** stay."*
   *"I **would** stay."*
   *"I **must** stay."*

   Repeat until all the modals are used with each pronoun and verb.

5. Prompt individual students with an action verb from step 1. Have each student create a set of five complete sentences containing the action verb and a modal. Make sure each student has an opportunity to produce at least five different sentences. If a mistake is made, model the correct response and have the student repeat.

6. Encourage students to produce sentences using the modals from this lesson throughout the day.

Lesson 112

Materials: picture cards (action verbs: cooking, cutting, dancing, driving, helping, pushing, reading, running, skating, walking)

In this lesson, students will review forms of **be** (**am, are, is, was, were, be, been, being**) and practice question-statement transformations.

1. Model question-statement transformations using **be** in conjunction with action verbs.

Am I speaking?	I **am** speaking.
Are you dancing?	You **are** dancing.
Is she skating?	She **is** skating.
Was he pushing?	He **was** pushing.
Were they helping?	They **were** helping.

   Have the students repeat each sentence and question.

2. Provide a question using **be** and one of the action verbs from step 1. Elicit a question from the students using the same form of **be** and the action verb.

stimulus: **Is** she pulling?	response: *"She **is** pulling."*
stimulus: **Was** he cooking?	response: *"He **was** cooking."*
stimulus: **Were** they digging?	response: *"They **were** digging."*

   Scramble pronouns, verbs, and verb tenses. Have students repeat each sentence.

3. Provide a statement using **be** and one of the action verbs from step 1. Have students respond with a question, using the same form of **be** and the action verb.

stimulus: I **am** pushing.	response: *"**Am** I pushing?"*
stimulus: You **are** pulling.	response: *"**Are** you pulling?"*
stimulus: He **is** digging.	response: *"**Is** he digging?"*

   Scramble all pronouns and verbs. Have students repeat each response.

4. Pantomime or hold up an action verb picture card. Have individual students create a question and response containing a pronoun, an action verb, and **be** as the helping verb. Have other students generate different questions and responses, scrambling pronouns and verbs until all have been used. Make sure each student creates several questions and responses.

5. Pantomime or hold up a picture card to prompt students with an action verb. Have individual students create a set of five complete sentences containing the action verb and a form of **be**. Make sure each student has an opportunity to produce at least five different sentences. If a mistake is made, model the correct response and have the student repeat.

6. Encourage students to produce question-statement transformations using a form of **be** throughout the day.

Lesson 113

In this lesson, students will review forms of **have** (**have, has, had**) and practice question-statement transformations.

1. Model question-statement transformations using a form of **have** and the following action verbs: **coming, finishing, going, hearing, helping, reading, seeing, speaking, stopping**.

Have I spoken?	I **have** spoken.
Have you gone?	You **have** gone.
Has she finished?	She **has** finished.
Have they gone?	They **have** gone.

   Have the students repeat each sentence and question.

2. Provide a question using a form of **have** and one of the action verbs from step 1. Elicit a response from the students, using the same form of **have** and the action verb.

stimulus: **Have** I spoken?	response: *"I **have** spoken."*
stimulus: **Have** you gone?	response: *"You **have** gone."*
stimulus: **Has** she read?	response: *"She **has** read."*

   Scramble pronouns and verbs. Have students repeat each sentence.

3. Provide a statement using a form of **have** and one of the action verbs from step 1. Have students respond with a question, using the same form of **have** and the action verb.

stimulus: He **has** stopped.	response: *"**Has** he stopped?"*
stimulus: We **had** come.	response: *"**Had** we come?"*
stimulus: You **have** heard.	response: *"**Have** you heard?"*

   Scramble pronouns and verbs. Have students repeat each response.

4. Say an action verb. Have individual students create a question and response containing a pronoun, that action verb, and a form of **have** as the helping verb. Have other students generate different questions and responses. Scramble pronouns and verbs until all have been used. Make sure each student creates several questions and responses.

5. Say an action verb to prompt students. Have individual students create a set of three complete sentences containing the action verb and three forms of **have**. Make sure each student has an opportunity to produce at least three different sentences. If a mistake is made, model the correct response and have the student repeat.

6. Encourage students to produce question-statement transformations using a form of **have** throughout the day.

Lesson 114

Materials: picture cards (action verbs: eating, exercising, helping, jumping, sitting, walking, writing)

Students will review and practice forms of **do** (**do, does, did, do not, did not, does not, don't, didn't, doesn't**) and practice question-negative statement transformations.

1. Model questions followed by negative statements using a form of **do** and the following verbs: **doing, eating, erasing, exercising, hearing, helping, jumping, seeing, sitting, starting, stopping, walking, writing.**

Do you walk to school?	You **do not** walk to school.
Does he sit here?	He **does not** sit here.
Did I help them?	I **did not** help them.

   Have the students repeat each sentence and question.

2. Provide a question using a form of **do** and one of the action verbs from step 1. Elicit a negative response from the students using the same form of **do** and the action verb.

stimulus: **Do** you walk to school?	response: *"You* ***do not*** *walk to school."*
stimulus: **Does** he sit here?	response: *"He* ***does not*** *sit here."*
stimulus: **Did** she erase the board?	response: *"She* ***did not*** *erase the board."*

   Scramble pronouns, verbs, and verb tenses. Have students repeat each sentence.

3. Provide a non-contracted negative statement using a form of **do** and one of the action verbs from step 1. Follow with the contracted form of the original sentence.

You **did not** erase.	You **didn't** erase.
He **does not** sit here.	He **doesn't** sit here.
I **do not** write.	I **don't** write.

   Scramble the pronouns and verbs. Have students repeat each response.

4. Provide a question using **do** and an action verb from step 1. Have individual students respond with a contracted response. Have another student provide the non-contracted, negative response.

stimulus: **Do** you hear?	response: *"You* ***don't*** *hear."*	response: *"You* ***do not*** *hear."*
stimulus: **Did** we see?	response: *"We* ***didn't*** *see."*	response: *"We* ***did not*** *see."*
stimulus: **Does** it stop?	response: *"It* ***doesn't*** *stop."*	response: *"It* ***does not*** *stop."*

5. Hold up a picture card or say an action. Have individual students create a question and response containing a pronoun, that action verb, and a form of **do**. Have other students generate different questions and responses, scrambling pronouns and verbs until all have been used. Have each student create several questions and responses using both the contracted and non-contracted forms of **do**.

6. Encourage students to produce question-negative statement transformations using the contracted and non-contracted forms of **do** throughout the day.

Lesson 115

Materials: picture cards (action verbs: eating, helping, painting, singing, sleeping)

In this lesson, students will create sentences using modals (**can, could, may, might, must, shall, should, will, would**) and practice question-statement transformations.

1. Model questions and responses using modals learned in Lesson 111 with one of the following action verbs: **beginning, catching, coming, crying, eating, flying, going, helping, painting, pitching, singing, sleeping.**

Can you help?	You **can** help.	**Would** they come?	They **would** come.
Shall we eat?	We **shall** eat.	**May** he begin?	He **may** begin.

   Use all verbs and modals. Have the students repeat each sentence and question.

2. Provide a question using a modal and one of the action verbs from step 1. Elicit a response from the students using the same modal and action verb.

   stimulus: **Can** you help? — response: *"You **can** help."*
   stimulus: **Shall** we eat? — response: *"We **shall** eat."*
   stimulus: **Will** she pitch? — response: *"She **will** pitch."*

   Scramble all modals, pronouns, and verbs. Have students repeat each sentence.

3. Provide a statement using one of the modals and an action verb from step 1. Elicit a question from the students using the same modal and action verb.

   Scramble all modals, pronouns, and verbs. Have students repeat each response.

   stimulus: **Shall** we sing? — response: *"We **shall** sing."*
   stimulus: **Might** he paint? — response: *"He **might** paint."*
   stimulus: **Would** you catch? — response: *"You **would** catch."*

4. Provide a simple sentence using an action verb from step 1. Have individual students produce a question by incorporating a modal. Have a second student respond.

   stimulus: I sleep. — response: *"**Should** I sleep?"*
   response: *"I **should** sleep."*

   Have other students generate different questions and responses, scrambling pronouns, verbs, and modals until all have been used. Make sure each student creates several questions and responses.

5. Hold up a picture card or say an action to prompt students. Have individual students create a question using that action verb and one of the modals. Have another student respond. If a mistake is made, model the correct sentence and have the student repeat.

6. Encourage students to produce question-statement transformations using modals throughout the day.

Lesson 116

In this lesson, students will review forms of **be** (**am, are, is, was, were, be, been, being**).

1. Model sentences using the following action verbs with **be** as the helping verb: **calling, finishing, gasping, groaning, hiccupping, laughing, muttering, serving, sneezing, snoring, sobbing, squealing**. Say: I am calling. You are hiccupping. He is sobbing. Scramble pronouns, verbs, and verb tenses. Have students repeat each sentence.

2. Provide a simple sentence. Have individual students respond by adding **be** as the helping verb in any tense.

   stimulus: I call. — response: *"I (**was** calling; **am being** called)."*
   stimulus: He sobs. — response: *"He (**is** sobbing; **has been** sobbing)."*
   stimulus: We gasp. — response: *"We (**were** gasping; **are** gasping)."*

   Repeat with all verbs from step 1. Have students repeat each response sentence.

3. Have individual students provide an action verb. Ask a different student to use that verb in a complete sentence with **be** as the helping verb. Have another student form a different sentence using the same verb, but changing the pronoun or form of the helping verb.

   *"I **am** sneezing."*
   *"She **is** sneezing."*
   *"Last week, they **were** sneezing."*
   *"Tomorrow, they **will be** sneezing."*

4. Provide students with a question containing a pronoun, an action verb, and a form of **be** as the helping verb. Have individual students change the question into a statement.

   stimulus: **Is** she snoring? — response: *"She **is** snoring."*
   stimulus: **Are** you hiccupping? — response: *"You **are** hiccupping."*
   stimulus: **Were** they calling? — response: *"They **were** calling."*

   Scramble verbs, pronouns, and forms of **be**, making sure each student has a chance to respond.

5. Say an action verb. Have individual students create a set of five complete sentences containing that action verb and five forms of **be**. Make sure each student has an opportunity to produce at least five sentences.

6. Encourage students to practice sentences using **be** as a helping verb throughout the day.

Lesson 117

In this lesson, students will review forms of **have** (**have, has, had**).

1. Model sentences using the following action verbs, using a form of **have** as the helping verb: **chuckling, coming, coughing, dreaming, dressing, gasping, giggling, going, groaning, laughing, marching, mixing, mumbling, painting, screaming, serving, sneezing, snoring, sobbing, squealing, starting, talking.** Say: I **have** chuckled. You **have** coughed. He **has** sneezed. Scramble pronouns and use all verbs. Have students repeat each sentence.

2. Provide a simple sentence. Have individual students respond by adding a form of **have** as the helping verb in any tense.

   stimulus: She dreams. — response: *"She (**has** dreamed; **had** dreamed)."*
   stimulus: You cough. — response: *"You (**have** coughed; **had** coughed)."*
   stimulus: I giggle. — response: *"I (**have** giggled; **had** giggled)."*

   Repeat with all verbs from step 1. Have students repeat each response sentence.

3. Have individual students provide an action verb. Ask a different student to use that verb in a complete sentence with **have** as the helping verb. Have another student form a different sentence using the same verb, changing the pronoun or form of the helping verb.

   *"I **have** mumbled."*
   *"I **had** mumbled."*
   *"He **had** mumbled."*

4. Provide students with a question containing a pronoun, an action verb, and a form of **have** as the helping verb. Have individual students change the question into a statement.

   stimulus: **Has** she screamed? — response: *"She **has** screamed."*
   stimulus: **Have** you marched? — response: *"You **have** marched."*
   stimulus: **Had** they come? — response: *"They **had** come."*

   Scramble the verbs, pronouns, and forms of **have**, making sure each student has a chance to respond.

5. Say an action verb to prompt students. Have individual students create a set of three complete sentences containing that action verb and three forms of **have**. Make sure each student has an opportunity to produce at least three sentences.

6. Encourage students to practice sentences using a form of **have** as a helping verb throughout the day.

Lesson 118

In this lesson, students will review three forms of **do** (**do, does, did**).

1. Model sentences using the action verbs from Lessons 116 and 117 (**calling, chuckling, coming, coughing, dreaming, dressing, finishing, gasping, giggling, going, groaning, hiccupping, laughing, marching, mixing, mumbling, muttering, painting, screaming, serving, sneezing, snoring, sobbing, squealing, starting, talking**), using a form of **do** as the helping verb.

   I **do** dream.
   He **does** giggle.
   We **did** serve.

   Scramble all pronouns and verbs. Have students repeat each sentence.

2. Provide a simple sentence. Have individual students respond by adding **do** as the helping verb in any tense.

stimulus: Patty sneezes.	response: *"Patty (**did** sneeze; **does** sneeze)."*
stimulus: They march.	response: *"They (**did** march; **do** march)."*
stimulus: I laugh.	response: *"I (**do** laugh; **did** laugh)."*

   Repeat with all verbs from step 1. Have students repeat each response sentence.

3. Have individual students provide an action verb. Ask a different student to use that verb in a complete sentence with **do** as the helping verb. Have a third student form a different sentence using the same verb, changing the pronoun or form of the helping verb.

"I do talk."	*"I did talk."*	*"You do talk."*	*"You did talk."*	*"She does talk."*
"She did talk."	*"We do talk."*	*"We did talk."*	*"They do talk."*	*"They did talk."*

   Continue to call on students until all possibilities have been generated. Provide a new action verb and repeat.

4. Provide students with a question containing a pronoun, an action verb, and a form of **do** as the helping verb. Have students change the question into a statement.

stimulus: **Did** you finish?	response: *"You **did** finish."*
stimulus: **Does** she snore?	response: *"She **does** snore."*
stimulus: **Do** they paint?	response: *"They **do** paint."*

   Scramble verbs, pronouns, and forms of **do**, making sure each student has a chance to respond.

5. Say an action verb to prompt students. Have individual students create a set of three complete sentences containing that action verb and three forms of **do** (**do, does, did**). Make sure each student has an opportunity to produce at least three sentences.

6. Encourage students to practice sentences using a form of **do** as a helping verb throughout the day.

Lesson 119

In this lesson, students will review modals (**can, could, shall, should, will, would, may, might, must**).

1. Model sentences using the action verbs from Lessons 116–118 (**calling, chuckling, coming, coughing, dreaming, dressing, finishing, gasping, giggling, going, groaning, hiccupping, laughing, marching, mixing, mumbling, muttering, painting, screaming, serving, sneezing, snoring, sobbing, squealing, starting, talking**), using modals as helping verbs.

   They **could** come.
   Leonard **will** mix.
   We **shall** finish.

   Scramble all pronouns, modals, and verbs. Have students repeat each sentence.

2. Provide a simple sentence. Have individual students respond by adding a modal as the helping verb.

   stimulus: They dress. response: *"They (**can; could; will; may; might; must**) dress."*

   Repeat with all verbs from step 1. Have students repeat each response sentence. Make sure all modals are used.

3. Have individual students provide an action verb. Ask a different student to use that verb in a complete sentence, with a modal as the helping verb. Have another student form a different statement using the same verb, changing the helping verb or pronoun.

   *"Kerry **will** talk."*
   *"Kerry **must** talk."*
   *"They **should** talk."*

4. Provide students with a question containing a pronoun, an action verb, and any modal as the helping verb. Have individual students change the question into a statement.

   stimulus: **Should** we serve? response: *"We **should** serve."*
   stimulus: **Would** you start? response: *"You **would** start."*
   stimulus: **May** I paint? response: *"I **may** paint."*

   Scramble verbs, pronouns, and modals, making sure each student has a chance to respond.

5. Say an action verb to prompt students. Have individual students create a set of five complete sentences containing that action verb and five different modals. Make sure each student has an opportunity to produce at least five sentences.

6. Encourage students to practice sentences using modals as helping verbs throughout the day.

Lesson 120

This lesson is a comprehensive review of helping verbs. Use the action verbs from previous lessons to expand this one (**barking, calling, chuckling, cooking, coughing, cutting, crying, dancing, dreaming, driving, exercising, finishing, gasping, giggling, going, groaning, grunting, hearing, helping, hiccupping, humming, laughing, listening, marching, mumbling, muttering, reading, screaming, seeing, serving, singing, sitting, sleeping, sneezing, snoring, sobbing, squealing, standing, starting, staying, stopping, swimming, talking, trying, walking, washing, whining, working**).

1. Model sentences using the forms of **be** (**am, are, is, was, were, be, been, being**). Provide individual students with an action verb. Have individual students produce three complete sentences containing the action verb and three different forms of **be** (e.g., say: Sobbing. The student should respond: *"I am sobbing. She is sobbing. She was sobbing"*). Make sure each student has an opportunity to produce at least three sentences.

2. Model sentences using the forms of **have** (**have, has, had**). Provide individual students with an action verb. Have students produce three complete sentences containing the action verb and three different forms of **have** (e.g., say: Mumbling. The selected student should respond: *"She has mumbled. They have mumbled. You had mumbled"*). Make sure each student has an opportunity to produce at least three sentences.

3. Model sentences using three forms of **do** (**do, does, did**). Provide individual students with an action verb. Have each student produce three complete sentences containing the action verb and three different forms of **do** (e.g., say: Trying. Students should respond: *"He does try. You did try. We do try"*). Make sure each student has an opportunity to produce at least three sentences.

4. Model sentences using the following **modals**: **can, could, shall, should, will, would, may, might, must**. Provide individual students with an action verb. Have each student produce three complete sentences containing the action verb and three different modals (e.g., say: Exercising. Students should respond: *"She should exercise. They will exercise. You might exercise"*). Make sure each student has an opportunity to produce at least three sentences.

5. Have individual students provide a simple sentence using a pronoun and an action verb. Then have each student generate four sentences with the pronoun and action verb, adding a form of **be**, a form of **have**, a form of **do**, and a **modal** as helping verbs. For example, a student should say: *"I sneeze. I am sneezing. I have sneezed. I did sneeze. I might sneeze."* Give each student an opportunity to produce all sentences. If a mistake is made, model the correct response and have the student repeat.

6. Encourage students to continue practicing using helping verbs.

Lesson 121

In this lesson, students will learn indefinite pronouns that stand for people (**somebody, anybody, anyone**) and will recognize contractions.

1. Model questions with **somebody**, **anybody**, or **anyone** as the pronoun, using the past and present tense of the following action verbs: **hammering, helping, juggling, jumping, knocking, talking**. Answer the question in the affirmative, always using **somebody** as the pronoun.

Is somebody knocking?	Yes, somebody is knocking.	Yes, somebody's knocking.
Is anybody knocking?	Yes, somebody is knocking.	Yes, somebody's knocking.
Has anyone knocked?	Yes, somebody has knocked.	Yes, somebody's knocked.

Scramble verbs and verb tenses with the above pronouns. Have students repeat each response.

2. Provide questions using **somebody**, **anybody**, and **anyone**. Have students answer in the affirmative, using **somebody** in a complete sentence. Say: Is anyone juggling? Students should respond: *"Yes, somebody's juggling."* Scramble verbs and verb tenses with the pronouns. Repeat until each student has had a few opportunities to respond.

3. Provide questions using **somebody**, **anybody**, and **anyone**. Have students answer, with the affirmative, using **somebody** in a complete sentence. Have each student respond to several questions containing the same verb before moving on to another student.

stimulus: Is anyone juggling?	response: *"Yes, somebody is juggling."*	response: *"Yes, somebody's juggling."*
stimulus: Is somebody juggling?	response: *"Yes, somebody is juggling."*	response: *"Yes, somebody's juggling."*
stimulus: Has anybody juggled?	response: *"Yes, somebody has juggled."*	response: *"Yes, somebody's juggled."*

Scramble verbs and verb tenses with the above pronouns. Give each student an opportunity to respond.

4. Continue to model questions and responses as in step 1, using the past and present forms of the following verbs: **coming, going, jogging, leaving, running, sleeping**.

Is somebody running?	Yes, somebody is running.	Yes, somebody's running.
Is anybody running?	Yes, somebody is running.	Yes, somebody's running.
Has anyone run?	Yes, somebody has run.	Yes, somebody's run.

Scramble verbs and verb tenses with the above pronouns. Have students repeat each response.

5. Model questions as in step 1, using all verbs in this lesson. Ask individual students several questions before going to another student. Each response should contain **somebody** as the subject. If a mistake is made, model the correct response and have the student repeat.

6. Encourage students to practice these pronouns throughout the day. The subtle differences in meaning and usage of indefinite pronouns make it a difficult concept for English learners. Frequent practice and repetition are necessary for students to master.

Lesson 122

In this lesson, students will learn indefinite pronouns that stand for people (**somebody, someone, anybody, anyone, nobody, no one**).

1. Model questions with **somebody**, **anybody**, **anyone**, or **someone** as the pronoun, using the past and present tense of the following action verbs: **hammering, helping, jumping, juggling, knocking, talking**. Answer the question in the negative, using **nobody** or **no one** as the pronoun.

Is somebody knocking?	No, nobody's knocking.	No, no one's knocking.
Did someone knock?	No, nobody knocked.	No, no one knocked.
Is anybody knocking?	No, nobody's knocking.	No, no one's knocking.
Has anyone knocked?	No, nobody's knocked.	No, no one's knocked.

   Scramble verbs and verb tenses with the above pronouns. Have students repeat each response.

2. Provide questions using **somebody**, **anybody**, **anyone**, and **someone**. Have students answer in the negative, using **nobody** or **no one** in a complete sentence. Say: Is anyone juggling? Students should respond: *"No, nobody's juggling"* or *"No, no one's juggling."* Scramble verbs and verb tenses with the pronouns. Repeat until each student has had a few opportunities to respond.

3. Provide questions using **somebody**, **anybody**, **anyone**, and **someone**. Have students answer in the negative, using **nobody** or **no one** in a complete sentence. Have each student respond to several questions containing the same verb before moving on to another student.

stimulus: Is anyone helping?	response: *"No, no one's helping."*
stimulus: Did anybody help?	response: *"No, no one helped."*
stimulus: Is somebody helping?	response: *"No, no one's helping."*
stimulus: Has someone helped?	response: *"No, no one's helped."*

   Scramble verbs, verb tenses, and pronouns. Give each student an opportunity to respond.

4. Continue to model questions and responses, as in step 1, using the past and present forms of the following verbs: **coming, going, jogging, leaving, running, sleeping**.

Is somebody running?	No, nobody's running.	No, no one's running.
Did someone run?	No, nobody ran.	No, no one ran.
Is anybody running?	No, nobody's running.	No, no one's running.
Has anyone run?	No, nobody's run.	No, no one's run.

   Scramble verbs, verb tenses, and pronouns. Have students repeat each response.

5. Model questions as in step 1 using all verbs in this lesson. Ask individual students several questions before going to another student. Each response should contain **nobody** or **no one** as the subject. If a mistake is made, model the correct response and have the student repeat.

6. Encourage students to continue practicing indefinite pronouns. Frequent practice and repetition are necessary for students to master the subtle differences in meaning and usage.

Lesson 123

In this lesson, students will learn indefinite pronouns that stand for things (**something, anything, nothing**).

1. Model questions with **something** or **anything** as the pronoun, using the past and present tense of the following verbs: **burning, falling, growling, happening, missing, moving**. Model responses in the affirmative and negative, using **something** or **nothing** as the pronoun.

Is something burning?	Yes, something's burning.
Is anything burning?	Yes, something's burning.
Is something missing?	No, nothing's missing.
Is anything missing?	No, nothing's missing.

   Scramble verbs and verb tenses with the above pronouns. Have students repeat each response.

2. Provide questions using **something** or **anything**. Gesture to indicate "yes" or "no" and have students answer using **something** or **nothing** in a complete sentence. Say: Is anything missing? (Nod "yes.") Students should respond: *"Yes, something's missing."* Scramble verbs and verb tenses with the pronouns. Repeat until each student has had a few opportunities to respond.

3. Provide questions using **something** or **anything**. Gesture to indicate "yes" or "no" and have students answer using **something** or **nothing** in a complete sentence. Have each student respond to several questions containing the same verb. For example, have one student answer the following three questions before moving on to another student.

stimulus: Is anything burning?	response: *"Yes, something's burning."*
stimulus: Is something burning?	response: *"No, nothing's burning."*
stimulus: Did something burn?	response: *"No, nothing burned."*

   Scramble verbs, verb tenses, and pronouns. Give each student an opportunity to respond.

4. Continue to model questions and responses, as in step 1, using the past and present forms of the following verbs: **banging, coming, cooking, finishing, going, rapping, ringing, squeaking**.

Is anything banging?	Yes, something's banging.
Is anything banging?	No, nothing's banging.
Is something banging?	No, nothing's banging.

   Scramble verbs and verb tenses with the above pronouns. Have students repeat each response.

5. Model questions as in step 1, using all verbs in this lesson. Ask individual students several questions before going to another student. Each response should contain **something** or **nothing** as the subject. If a mistake is made, model the correct response and have the student repeat.

6. Encourage students to continue practicing indefinite pronouns. Frequent practice and repetition are necessary for students to master the subtle differences in meaning and usage.

Lesson 124

In this lesson, students will learn indefinite pronouns that stand for people and things (**somebody, someone, anybody, anyone, nobody, no one, something, anything, nothing**).

1. Model questions with **somebody**, **someone**, **anybody**, **anyone**, **something**, or **anything** as the pronoun. Model affirmative and negative responses.

Is somebody knocking?	Yes, somebody's knocking.	No, nobody's knocking.
Did someone knock?	Yes, someone knocked.	No, no one knocked.
Is something burning?	Yes, something's burning.	No, nothing's burning.
Did anything burn?	Yes, something burned.	No, nothing burned.

   Scramble verbs and verb tenses with the above pronouns. Have students repeat each response.

2. Provide questions with **somebody**, **anybody**, **anyone**, or **someone** as the pronoun, using the past and present tense of the following action verbs: **hammering, helping, juggling, jumping, knocking, talking**. Have individual students answer with the affirmative. Say: Is anyone hammering? The student should respond: *"Yes, somebody's hammering."* Scramble verbs and verb tenses with the pronouns. Repeat until each student has had a few opportunities to respond.

3. Provide questions with **somebody**, **anybody**, **anyone**, or **someone** as the pronoun, using the verbs from step 2. Have individual students answer with the negative. Say: Is anyone talking? The student should respond: *"No, nobody's talking."* or *"No, no one's talking."* Scramble verbs and verb tenses with the pronouns. Repeat until each student has had a few opportunities to respond.

4. Provide questions with **something** or **anything** as the pronoun, using the past and present forms of the following verbs: **banging, coming, cooking, finishing, going, rapping, ringing, squeaking**. Gesture to indicate "yes" or "no" and have students answer with a complete sentence. Say: Did anything squeak? (No.) Students should respond: *"No, nothing squeaked."* Scramble verbs and verb tenses with the pronouns. Repeat until each student has had a few opportunities to respond.

5. Provide questions with **somebody**, **someone**, **anybody**, **anyone**, **something**, or **anything** as the pronoun, using the verbs from this lesson. Gesture to indicate "yes" or "no" and have students answer with a complete sentence as in step 4. Scramble verbs and verb tenses with each pronoun until each student has had several opportunities to provide correct responses.

6. Encourage students to practice indefinite pronouns throughout the day. The subtle differences in meaning and usage of indefinite pronouns make it a difficult concept for English learners. Frequent practice and repetition are necessary for students to master.

Lesson 125

Materials: picture cards (action verbs: biking, coloring, cooking, dancing, driving, eating, exercising, fishing, helping, juggling, jumping, looking, marching, pushing, reading, running)

In this lesson, students will review indefinite pronouns that stand for people and things (**somebody, someone, anybody, anyone, nobody, no one, something, anything, nothing**).

1. Ask individual students questions containing **somebody**, **someone**, **anybody**, or **anyone** as the subject, using the following verbs: **hammering, helping, juggling, jumping, knocking, running, sleeping, talking**. Prompt an affirmative response. Say: Is somebody talking? (Yes.) The student should respond: *"Yes, somebody's talking."* Scramble pronouns, verbs, and verb tenses. Make sure each student has an opportunity to respond to several questions.

2. Ask individual students questions, following the example from step 1. Prompt a negative response. Say: Did anyone come? (No.) The student should respond: *"No, no one came."* Scramble pronouns, verbs, and verb tenses. Make sure each student has an opportunity to respond to several questions.

3. Ask individual students questions containing **something** or **anything** as the subject, using the following verbs: **banging, burning, coming, cooking, falling, finishing, going, missing, rapping, ringing, squeaking**. Prompt a negative response. Say: Is anything finished? (No.) The student should respond: *"No, nothing's finished."* Scramble pronouns, verbs, and verb tenses. Make sure each student has an opportunity to respond to several questions.

4. Ask individual students questions containing any of the indefinite pronouns, using the following verbs: **biking, coloring, dancing, driving, eating, exercising, fishing, helping, looking, marching, pushing, reading**. Have the student choose a positive or negative response and answer in a complete sentence. Scramble pronouns, verbs, and verb tenses. Make sure each student has an opportunity to respond to several questions.

5. Hold up an action picture card. Have individual students form a question using the displayed verb and one of the indefinite pronouns. Have another student respond. Continue until each student has had several opportunities to form and respond to questions.

6. Encourage students to practice indefinite pronouns throughout the day. The subtle differences in meaning and usage of indefinite pronouns make it a difficult concept for English learners. Frequent practice and repetition are necessary for students to master.

Lesson 126

Materials: picture cards (food: apple, banana, biscuits, burrito, cake, carrots, cherries, chips, cookies, corn, eggs, fajita, grapefruit, grapes, green beans, ham, hamburger, hot dogs, ice cream cone, jam, jelly, juice, lemon, lettuce, lime, milk, nut, onion, orange, oranges, pasta, peach, peanut butter, pear, pie, pineapple, pizza, potato, rice, salad, salt, sandwich, soda, soup, spaghetti, squash, steak, strawberries, taco, tomato, watermelon)

In this lesson, students will learn words representing food.

1. Display and name each picture card. Have the class repeat the name of each food. Review names twice. Finally, use each item in a complete sentence. Say: This is a (cake). This is an (apple). These are (strawberries). Have students repeat each sentence.

2. Divide the class into three groups. Provide each group with an equal number of picture cards. Set the cards in a stack in the middle of the group. *(Note: The side of the card **without** the word should face up.)* In each group, have students take turns identifying the item pictured on the top card, using a complete sentence. If the student names the pictured item correctly, that student keeps the card. If the student incorrectly names the item, the card is placed at the bottom of the stack. Play continues until all cards have been correctly named in a complete sentence. The student with the most cards wins. Note any cards any group is unable to name.

3. Rotate card sets so that each group has a new set of cards and repeat the game. Note any cards any group is unable to name.

4. Rotate card sets once more and repeat the game. If there were any cards any group was unable to name, review with the entire class.

5. Bring the class together and play "Around the World." Play begins with two students standing. Display a card. *(Note: Display the side **without** the word.)* The first student to correctly name the food on the card moves on. The other student sits down. Play continues around the room with the first student to correctly name the food on the next card moving on "around" the class. Review all vocabulary words using this format.

6. Monitor students' oral production in all three groups. If individual students are repeatedly unable to produce names of foods, model and have the student repeat. Encourage students to practice naming foods throughout the day.

Lesson 127

Materials: picture cards (people: boy, carpenter, cook, crossing guard, custodian, dentist, doctor, firefighter, girl, king, librarian, mail carrier, man, mechanic, musician, nurse, painter, police officer, principal, queen, secretary, teacher, vet, woman)

In this lesson, students will learn words representing people.

1. Hold up and name each picture card. Have students repeat each name. Review names twice. Finally, use each item in a complete sentence: This is a (mechanic). Have students repeat each sentence.

2. Divide the class into three groups. Provide each group with an equal number of picture cards. Set the cards in a stack in the middle of the group. *(Note: There should be at least one picture card per student for this exercise. Use cards from Lesson 126 if necessary. The side of the card* ***without*** *the word should face up.)* In each group, have students take turns identifying the item pictured on the top card, using a complete sentence. If the student names the pictured item correctly, that student keeps the card. If the student incorrectly names the item, the card is placed at the bottom of the stack. Play continues until all cards have been correctly named in a complete sentence. The student with the most cards wins. Note any cards any group is unable to name.

3. Rotate card sets so that each group has a new set of cards and repeat the game. Note any cards any group is unable to name.

4. Rotate card sets once more and repeat the game. If there were any cards any group was unable to name, review with the entire class.

5. Bring the class together and play "Around the World." Play begins with two students standing. Display a card. *(Note: Display the side* ***without*** *the word.)* The first student to correctly name the person on the card moves on. The other student sits down. Play continues around the room. Review all vocabulary words using this format.

6. Monitor students' oral production in all three groups. If individual students are repeatedly unable to produce names of people, model and have the student repeat. Encourage students to practice naming people throughout the day.

Lesson 128

Materials: picture cards (food: apple, banana, biscuits, burrito, cake, carrots, cherries, chips, cookies, corn, eggs, fajita, grapefruit, grapes, green beans, ham, hamburger, hot dogs, ice cream cone, jam, jelly, juice, lemon, lettuce, lime, milk, nut, onion, orange, oranges, pasta, peach, peanut butter, pear, pie, pineapple, pizza, potato, rice, salad, salt, sandwich, soda, soup, spaghetti, squash, steak, strawberries, taco, tomato, watermelon; people: boy, carpenter, cook, crossing guard, custodian, dentist, doctor, firefighter, girl, king, librarian, mail carrier, man, mechanic, musician, nurse, painter, police officer, principal, queen, secretary, teacher, vet, woman)

In this lesson, students will review words representing foods and people.

1. Display each food card and have students quickly name each food. Go back through the cards and have students name each food in a complete sentence, using **This/These** sentence construction. Repeat with all people cards.

2. Divide the class into three groups. Provide each group with an equal number of picture cards. Each group should get a mix of food and people cards. Set the cards in a stack in the middle of the group. *(Note: The side of the card **without** the word should face up.)* In each group, have students take turns identifying the item pictured on the top card, using a complete sentence. If the student names the pictured item correctly, that student keeps the card. If the student incorrectly names the item, the card is placed at the bottom of the stack. Play continues until all cards have been correctly named in a complete sentence. The student with the most cards wins. Note any cards any group is unable to name.

3. Rotate card sets so that each group has a new set of cards and repeat the game. Note any cards any group is unable to name.

4. Rotate card sets once more and repeat the game. If there were any cards any group was unable to name, review with the entire class.

5. Bring the class together and play "Around the World." Play begins with two students standing. Display a card. *(Note: Display the side **without** the word.)* The first student to correctly name the picture on the card moves on. The other student sits down. Play continues around the room. Review all vocabulary words using this format.

6. Continue to monitor students' oral production. The goal is automaticity.

Lesson 129

Materials: picture cards (places: barber shop, bridge, bus stop, classroom, dock, farm, forest, highway, hill, island, moon, park, police station, restaurant, stars, sun, swimming pool, train station)

In this lesson, students will learn words representing places.

1. Display and name all of the places on the picture cards. Have the entire group repeat the name of each place. Review names twice. Put place names into complete sentences on the third round: This is an (island). Have students repeat each sentence.

2. Divide the class into three groups. Provide each group with an equal number of picture cards. Set the cards in a stack in the middle of the group. *(Note: There should be at least one picture card per student for this exercise. Use cards from Lesson 128 if you need more cards. The side of the card* ***without*** *the word should face up.)* In each group, have students take turns identifying the object pictured on the top card, using a complete sentence. If the student names the pictured item correctly, that student keeps the card. If the student incorrectly names the item, the card is placed at the bottom of the stack. Play continues until all cards have been correctly named in a complete sentence. The student with the most cards wins. Note any cards any group is unable to name.

3. Rotate card sets so that each group has a new set of cards and repeat the game. Note any cards any group is unable to name.

4. Rotate card sets once more and repeat the game. If there were any cards any group was unable to name, review with the entire class.

5. Bring the class together and play "Around the World." Play begins with two students standing. Display a card. *(Note: Display the side* ***without*** *the word.)* The first student to correctly name the picture on the flashed card moves on. The other student sits down. Play continues around the room with the first student to correctly name the place on the next flashed card moving on "around" the class. Review all vocabulary words using this format.

6. Monitor students' oral production. If individual students are repeatedly unable to produce names of places, model and have the student repeat.

Lesson 130

Materials: picture cards (food: apple, banana, biscuits, burrito, cake, carrots, cherries, chips, cookies, corn, eggs, fajita, grapefruit, grapes, green beans, ham, hamburger, hot dogs, ice cream cone, jam, jelly, juice, lemon, lettuce, lime, milk, nut, onion, orange, oranges, pasta, peach, peanut butter, pear, pie, pineapple, pizza, potato, rice, salad, salt, sandwich, soda, soup, spaghetti, squash, steak, strawberries, taco; tomato, watermelon; people: boy, carpenter, cook, crossing guard, custodian, dentist, doctor, firefighter, girl, king, librarian, mail carrier, man, mechanic, musician, nurse, painter, police officer, principal, queen, secretary, teacher, vet, woman; places: barber shop, bridge, bus stop, classroom, dock, farm, forest, highway, hill, island, moon, park, police station, restaurant, stars, sun, swimming pool, train station)

In this lesson, students will review words representing food, people, and places. Review Lessons 126, 127, and 129.

1. Display each food card and have students quickly name each food. Go back through cards and have students name each food in a complete sentence, using **This/These** sentence construction. Repeat for people and place cards.

2. Divide the class into three groups. Provide each group with an equal number of picture cards. Each group should get a mix of food, place, and people cards. Set the cards in a stack in the middle of the group. *(Note: The side of the card **without** the word should face up.)* In each group, have students take turns identifying the item pictured on the top card, using a complete sentence. If the student names the pictured item correctly, that student keeps the card. If the student incorrectly names the item, the card is placed at the bottom of the stack. Play continues until all cards have been correctly named in a complete sentence. The student with the most cards wins. Note any cards any group is unable to name.

3. Rotate card sets so that each group has a new set of cards and repeat the game. Note any cards any group is unable to name.

4. Rotate card sets once more and repeat the game. If there were any cards any group was unable to name, review with the entire class.

5. Bring the class together and play "Around the World." Play begins with two students standing. Display a card. *(Note: Display the side **without** the word.)* The first student to correctly name the picture on the card moves on. The other student sits down. Play continues around the room. Review all vocabulary words using this format.

6. Continue to monitor students' oral production. The goal is automaticity.

Lesson 131

Materials: picture cards (school things: board, book, book bag, bulletin board, chalk, construction paper, crayons, eraser, globe, glue, ink, locker, map, marker, paints, paper, pen, pencil, pencil sharpener, pencils, ruler, scissors, tape dispenser)

In this lesson, students will learn words representing school things.

1. Display and name all of the school things on the picture cards. Have the entire class repeat the name of each item. Review names twice. Put names of school things into complete sentences on the third round: This is an (eraser). Have students repeat each sentence.

2. Divide the class into three groups. Provide each group with an equal number of picture cards. Set the cards in a stack in the middle of the group. *(Note: There should be at least one picture card per student for this exercise. Use cards from Lesson 130 if you need more cards. The side of the card **without** the word should face up.)* In each group, have students take turns identifying the item pictured on the top card, using a complete sentence. If the student names the pictured item correctly, that student keeps the card. If the student incorrectly names the item, the card is placed at the bottom of the stack. Play continues until all cards have been correctly named in a complete sentence. The student with the most cards wins. Note any cards any group is unable to name.

3. Rotate card sets so that each group has a new set of cards and repeat the game. Note any cards any group is unable to name.

4. Rotate card sets once more and repeat the game. If there were any cards any group was unable to name, review with the entire class.

5. Bring the class together and play "Around the World." Play begins with two students standing. Display a card. *(Note: Display the side **without** the word.)* The first student to correctly name the picture on the flashed card moves on. The other student sits down. Play continues around the room. Review all vocabulary words using this format.

6. Monitor students' oral production in all three groups. If individual students are repeatedly unable to produce names of the pictured items, model and have the student repeat.

Lesson 132

Materials: picture cards (vehicles: ambulance, bicycle, boat, bus, cab, canoe, car, fire engine, garbage truck, helicopter, jet, motorcycle, police car, race car, rowboat, sailboat, ship, spaceship, submarine, train, truck, van)

In this lesson, students will learn words representing vehicles.

1. Display and name all of the vehicles on the picture cards. Have the entire class repeat the name of each item. Review names twice. Put vehicle names into complete sentences on the third round: This is an (ambulance). Have students repeat each sentence.

2. Divide the class into three groups. Provide each group with an equal number of picture cards. Set the cards in a stack in the middle of the group. *(Note: There should be at least one picture card per student for this exercise. Use cards from Lesson 131 if you need more cards. The side of the card **without** the word should face up.)* In each group, have students take turns identifying the item pictured on the top card, using a complete sentence. If the student names the pictured item correctly, that student keeps the card. If the student incorrectly names the item, the card is placed at the bottom of the stack. Play continues until all cards have been correctly named in a complete sentence. The student with the most cards wins. Note any cards any group is unable to name.

3. Rotate card sets so that each group has a new set of cards and repeat the game. Note any cards any group is unable to name.

4. Rotate card sets once more and repeat the game. If there were any cards any group was unable to name, review with the entire class.

5. Bring the class together and play "Around the World." Play begins with two students standing. Display a card. *(Note: Display the side **without** the word.)* The first student to correctly name the picture on the card moves on. The other student sits down. Play continues around the room. Review all vocabulary words using this format.

6. Monitor students' oral production. If individual students are repeatedly unable to produce names of the pictured items, model and have the student repeat.

Lesson 133

Materials: picture cards: (school things: board, book, book bag, bulletin board, chalk, construction paper, crayons, eraser, globe, glue, ink, locker, map, marker, paints, paper, pen, pencil, pencil sharpener, pencils, ruler, scissors, tape dispenser; vehicles: ambulance, bicycle, boat, bus, cab, canoe, car, fire engine, garbage truck, helicopter, jet, motorcycle, police car, race car, rowboat, sail-boat, ship, spaceship, submarine, train, truck, van)

In this lesson, students will review words representing school things and vehicles.

1. Display each card picturing school things and have students quickly name each object. Go back through the cards and have students name each object in a complete sentence, using **This/These** sentence construction. Repeat the exercise, using vehicle picture cards.

2. Divide the class into three groups. Provide each group with an equal number of both school things and vehicle picture cards. Set the cards in a stack in the middle of the group. *(Note: The side of the card **without** the word should face up.)* In each group, have students take turns identifying the item pictured on the top card, using a complete sentence. If the student names the pictured item correctly, that student keeps the card. If the student incorrectly names the item, the card is placed at the bottom of the stack. Play continues until all cards have been correctly named in a complete sentence. The student with the most cards wins. Note any cards any group is unable to name.

3. Rotate card sets so that each group has a new set of cards and repeat the game. Note any cards any group is unable to name.

4. Rotate card sets once more and repeat the game. If there were any cards any group was unable to name, review with the entire class.

5. Bring the class together and play "Around the World." Play begins with two students standing. Display a card. *(Note: Display the side **without** the word.)* The first student to correctly name the picture on the card moves on. The other student sits down. Play continues around the room. Review all vocabulary words using this format.

6. Continue to monitor students' oral production. The goal is automaticity.

Lesson 134

Materials: picture cards (tools: ax, broom, brush, bucket, compass, fire extinguisher, flashlight, glasses, hammer, hose, ladder, microscope, mop, pick, rake, saw, scale, shovel, stapler, telephone, thermometer, yardstick)

In this lesson, students will learn words representing tools for vocabulary expansion.

1. Display and name all tools pictured on the cards. Have the entire class repeat the name of each item. Review names twice. Put tool names into complete sentences on the third round: This is a (hose). Have students repeat each sentence.

2. Divide the class into three groups. Provide each group with an equal number of picture cards. Set the cards in a stack in the middle of the group. *(Note: There should be at least one picture card per student for this exercise. Use cards from Lesson 133 if you need more cards. The side of the card* ***without*** *the word should face up.)* In each group, have students take turns identifying the item pictured on the top card, using a complete sentence. If the student names the pictured item correctly, that student keeps the card. If the student incorrectly names the item, the card is placed at the bottom of the stack. Play continues until all cards have been correctly named in a complete sentence. The student with the most cards wins. Note any cards any group is unable to name.

3. Rotate card sets so that each group has a new set of cards and repeat the game. Note any cards any group is unable to name.

4. Rotate card sets once more and repeat the game. If there were any cards any group was unable to name, review with the entire class.

5. Bring the class together and play "Around the World." Play begins with two students standing. Display a card. *(Note: Display the side* ***without*** *the word.)* The first student to correctly name the picture on the card moves on. The other student sits down. Play continues around the room. Review all vocabulary words using this format.

6. Monitor students' oral production in all three groups. If individual students are repeatedly unable to produce names of the pictured items, model and have the student repeat.

Lesson 135

Materials: picture cards (school things: board, book, book bag, bulletin board, chalk, construction paper, crayons, eraser, globe, glue, ink, locker, map, marker, paints, paper, pen, pencil, pencil sharpener, pencils, ruler, scissors, tape dispenser; tools: ax, broom, brush, bucket, compass, fire extinguisher, flashlight, glasses, hammer, hose, ladder, microscope, mop, pick, rake, saw, scale, shovel, stapler, telephone, thermometer, yardstick; vehicles: ambulance, bicycle, boat, bus, cab, canoe, car, fire engine, garbage truck, helicopter, jet, motorcycle, police car, race car, rowboat, sailboat, ship, spaceship, submarine, train, truck, van)

In this lesson, students will review words representing school things, tools, and vehicles.

1. Display each card of school things and have students quickly name each object. Go back through the cards and have students name each object in a complete sentence, using **This/That** sentence construction. Repeat, using the tool and vehicle picture cards.

2. Divide the class into three groups. Provide each group with an equal number of picture cards, including cards from all three categories. Set the cards in a stack in the middle of the group. *(Note: The side of the card **without** the word should face up.)* In each group, have students take turns identifying the item pictured on the top card, using a complete sentence. If the student names the pictured item correctly, that student keeps the card. If the student incorrectly names the item, the card is placed at the bottom of the stack. Play continues until all cards have been correctly named in a complete sentence. The student with the most cards wins. Note any cards any group is unable to name.

3. Rotate card sets so that each group has a new set of cards and repeat the game. Note any cards any group is unable to name.

4. Rotate card sets once more and repeat the game. If there were any cards any group was unable to name, review with the entire class.

5. Bring the class together and play "Around the World." Play begins with two students standing. Display a card. *(Note: Display the side **without** the word.)* The first student to correctly name the picture on the card moves on. The other student sits down. Play continues around the room. Review all vocabulary words using this format.

6. Continue to monitor students' oral production. These drills can contain nouns from all categories taught up to this point.

Lesson 136

Materials: picture cards (body parts: arm, back, chin, calf, eye, eyebrow, eyelid, face, finger, foot, hand, lap, leg, lip, mouth, neck, nose, shin, shoulder, stomach, thigh, toe, waist)

In this lesson, students will learn words representing body parts.

1. Display and name all of the body parts on the picture cards. Have the entire group repeat the name of each item. Review names twice, then say the name of each body part in a complete sentence, using **This/These** sentence construction. Have students repeat each sentence.

2. Divide the class into three groups. Provide each group with an equal number of picture cards. Set the cards in a stack in the middle of the group. *(Note: There should be at least one picture card per student for this exercise. Use cards from Lesson 135 if you need more cards. The side of the card **without** the word should face up.)* In each group, have students take turns identifying the item pictured on the top card, using a complete sentence. If the student names the pictured item correctly, that student keeps the card. If the student incorrectly names the item, the card is placed at the bottom of the stack. Play continues until all cards have been correctly named in a complete sentence. The student with the most cards wins. Note any cards any group is unable to name.

3. Rotate card sets so that each group has a new set of cards and repeat the game. Note any cards any group is unable to name.

4. Rotate card sets once more and repeat the game. If there were any cards any group was unable to name, review with the entire class.

5. Bring the class together and play "Around the World." Play begins with two students standing. Display a card. *(Note: Display the side **without** the word.)* The first student to correctly name the picture on the card moves on. The other student sits down. Play continues around the room. Review all vocabulary words using this format.

6. Monitor students' oral production in all three groups. If individual students are repeatedly unable to produce names of the pictured items, model and have the student repeat.

Lesson 137

Materials: picture cards (clothing: baseball cap, bib, blouse, boots, cap, coat, collar, dress, gloves, gown, hat, jacket, jeans, mittens, overalls, pajamas, pants, raincoat, shirt, shoes, shorts, skirt, slacks, slippers, sneakers, sock, suit, sweater, swimsuit, tie, vest)

In this lesson, students will learn words representing clothing.

1. Display and name all of the articles of clothing pictured on the cards. Have the entire class repeat the name of each item. Review names twice, then say the name of each article of clothing in a complete sentence, using **This/These** sentence construction. Have students repeat each sentence.

2. Divide the class into three groups. Provide each group with an equal number of picture cards. Set the cards in a stack in the middle of the group. *(Note: There should be at least one picture card per student for this exercise. Use cards from Lesson 136 if you need more cards. The side of the card* ***without*** *the word should face up.)* In each group, have students take turns identifying the item pictured on the top card, using a complete sentence. If the student names the pictured item correctly, that student keeps the card. If the student incorrectly names the item, the card is placed at the bottom of the stack. Play continues until all cards have been correctly named in a complete sentence. The student with the most cards wins. Note any cards any group is unable to name.

3. Rotate card sets so that each group has a new set of cards and repeat the game. Note any cards any group is unable to name.

4. Rotate card sets once more and repeat the game. If there were any cards any group was unable to name, review with the entire class.

5. Bring the class together and play "Around the World." Play begins with two students standing. Display a card. *(Note: Display the side* ***without*** *the word.)* The first student to correctly name the picture on the card moves on. The other student sits down. Play continues around the room. Review all vocabulary words using this format.

6. Monitor students' oral production in all three groups. If individual students are repeatedly unable to produce names of the pictured items, model and have the student repeat.

Lesson 138

Materials: picture cards (body parts: arm, back, chin, calf, eye, eyebrow, eyelid, face, finger, foot, hand, lap, leg, lip, mouth, neck, nose, shin, shoulder, stomach, thigh, toe, waist; clothing: baseball cap, bib, blouse, boots, cap, coat, collar, dress, gloves, gown, hat, jacket, jeans, mittens, overalls, pajamas, pants, raincoat, shirt, shoes, shorts, skirt, slacks, slippers, sneakers, sock, suit, sweater, swimsuit, tie, vest)

In this lesson, students will review words representing body parts and clothing.

1. Display and name all body parts picture cards. Have the entire class repeat the name of each body part. Review names twice, then say the name of each body part in a complete sentence, using **This/These** sentence construction. Have students repeat each sentence. Repeat the exercise, using the pictures of clothing.

2. Divide the class into three groups. Provide each group with an equal number of picture cards, including pictures of body parts and pictures of clothing, in each stack. Set the stack in the middle of the group. *(Note: The side of the card **without** the word should face up.)* In each group, have students take turns identifying the item pictured on the top card, using a complete sentence. If the student names the pictured item correctly, that student keeps the card. If the student incorrectly names the item, the card is placed at the bottom of the stack. Play continues until all cards have been correctly named in a complete sentence. The student with the most cards wins. Note any cards any group is unable to name.

3. Rotate card sets so that each group has a new set of cards and repeat the game. Note any cards any group is unable to name.

4. Rotate card sets once more and repeat the game. If there were any cards any group was unable to name, review with the entire class.

5. Bring the class together and play "Around the World." Play begins with two students standing. Display a card. *(Note: Display the side **without** the word.)* The first student to correctly name the picture on the card moves on. The other student sits down. Play continues around the room. Review all vocabulary words using this format.

6. Continue to monitor students' oral production. The goal is automaticity.

Lesson 139

Materials: picture cards (action verbs: bathing, biking, climbing, closing, coloring, combing, cooking, cutting, dancing, dressing, driving, eating, emptying, exercising, fishing, gluing, helping, hoeing, hugging, jogging, juggling, jumping, keyboarding, kicking, locking, looking, marching, mixing, opening, painting, petting, planting, punching, pushing, raking, reading, riding, running, sharing, singing, sipping, sitting, skating, skipping, sleeping, sliding, sweeping, swimming, walking, writing)

In this lesson, students will learn action verbs.

1. Display and name all action verb picture cards. Have the entire class repeat the name of each action verb. Review names twice, then say the name of each action verb in a complete sentence: This shows (walking). Have students repeat each sentence.

2. Divide the class into three groups. Provide each group with an equal number of picture cards. Set the cards in a stack in the middle of the group. *(Note: The side of the card* ***without*** *the word should face up.)* In each group, have students take turns identifying the action pictured on the top card, using a complete sentence. If the student names the pictured action correctly, that student keeps the card. If the student incorrectly names the action, the card is placed at the bottom of the stack. Play continues until all cards have been correctly named in a complete sentence. The student with the most cards wins. Note any cards any group is unable to name.

3. Rotate card sets so that each group has a new set of cards and repeat the game. Note any cards any group is unable to name.

4. Rotate card sets once more and repeat the game. If there were any cards any group was unable to name, review with the entire class.

5. Bring the class together and play "Around the World." Play begins with two students standing. Display a card. *(Note: Display the side* ***without*** *the word.)* The first student to correctly name the action on the card moves on. The other student sits down. Play continues around the room. Review all action verbs using this format.

6. Monitor students' oral production. If individual students are repeatedly unable to correctly name action verbs, model and have the student repeat.

Lesson 140

Materials: picture cards from Lessons 136–139 (action verbs, body parts, clothing)

In this lesson, students will review words representing body parts, clothing, and action verbs. Review Lessons 136–139.

1. Display and name all picture cards of body parts. Have the entire class repeat the name of each body part. Review names twice, then say the name of each in a complete sentence, using **This/These** sentence construction. Have students repeat each sentence. Repeat the exercise using the pictures of clothing. Repeat the exercise again using action verbs, modeling the sentence using **This shows...** sentence construction.

2. Divide the class into three groups. Provide each group with an equal number of picture cards, including pictures from all three categories. Set the cards in a stack in the middle of the group. *(Note: The side of the card **without** the word should face up.)* In each group, have students take turns identifying the item pictured on the top card, using a complete sentence. If the student names the pictured item correctly, that student keeps the card. If the student incorrectly names the item, the card is placed at the bottom of the stack. Play continues until all cards have been correctly named in a complete sentence. The student with the most cards wins. Note any cards any group is unable to name.

3. Rotate card sets so that each group has a new set of cards and repeat the game. Note any cards any group is unable to name.

4. Rotate card sets once more and repeat the game. If there were any cards any group was unable to name, review with the entire class.

5. Bring the class together and play "Around the World." Play begins with two students standing. Display a card. *(Note: Display the side **without** the word.)* The first student to correctly name the object or action on the card moves on. The other student sits down. Play continues around the room. Review all vocabulary words using this format.

6. Continue to monitor students' oral production and encourage them to continue creating sentences.

Lesson 141

Materials: picture cards (appliances: coffee pot, oven, refrigerator, stove, television, vacuum cleaner; buildings: apartment building, barn, hospital, house, school, shop, silo)

In this lesson, students will learn words representing appliances and buildings for vocabulary expansion.

1. Display and name all appliance picture cards. Have the entire class repeat each name. Review names twice, then say each name in a complete sentence using **This/These** sentence construction. Have students repeat each sentence. Repeat the exercise using the building pictures.

2. Divide the class into three groups. Provide each group with an equal number of both appliance and building picture cards. Set the cards in a stack in the middle of the group. *(Note: There should be at least one picture card per student for this exercise. Use cards that need reinforcement from previous lessons if you need more cards. The side of the card* ***without*** *the word should face up.)* In each group, have students take turns identifying the item pictured on the top card, using a complete sentence. If the student names the pictured item correctly, that student keeps the card. If the student incorrectly names the item, the card is placed at the bottom of the stack. Play continues until all cards have been correctly named in a complete sentence. The student with the most cards wins. Note any cards any group is unable to name.

3. Rotate card sets so that each group has a new set of cards and repeat the game. Note any cards any group is unable to name.

4. Rotate card sets once more and repeat the game. If there were any cards any group was unable to name, review with the entire class.

5. Bring the class together and play "Around the World." Play begins with two students standing. Display a card. *(Note: Display the side* ***without*** *the word.)* The first student to correctly name the picture on the card moves on. The other student sits down. Play continues around the room. Review all vocabulary words using this format.

6. Monitor students' oral production in all three groups. If individual students are repeatedly unable to produce names of appliances or buildings, model and have the student repeat.

Lesson 142

Materials: picture cards (containers: bag, box, can, cup, dish, envelope, garbage can, net, pan, plate, pot, sack, vase; furniture: bed, bookcase, chair, chest, couch, crib, desk, easel, sofa, table)

In this lesson, students will learn words representing containers and furniture for vocabulary expansion.

1. Display and name all of the container picture cards. Have the entire class repeat each name. Review names twice, then say the name of each container in a complete sentence, using **This/These** sentence construction. Have students repeat each sentence. Repeat the exercise using the pictures of furniture.

2. Divide the class into three groups. Provide each group with an equal number of both container and furniture picture cards. Set the cards in a stack in the middle of the group. *(Note: There should be at least one card per student for this exercise. Use picture cards from Lesson 141 if more cards are needed. The side of the card **without** the word should face up.)* In each group, have students take turns identifying the item pictured on the top card, using a complete sentence. If the student names the pictured item correctly, that student keeps the card. If the student incorrectly names the item, the card is placed at the bottom of the stack. Play continues until all cards have been correctly named in a complete sentence. The student with the most cards wins. Note any cards any group is unable to name.

3. Rotate card sets so that each group has a new set of cards and repeat the game. Note any cards any group is unable to name.

4. Rotate card sets once more and repeat the game. If there were any cards any group was unable to name, review with the entire class.

5. Bring the class together and play "Around the World." Play begins with two students standing. Display a card. *(Note: Display the side **without** the word.)* The first student to correctly name the picture on the card moves on. The other student sits down. Play continues around the room. Review all vocabulary words using this format.

6. Monitor students' oral production in all three groups. If individual students are repeatedly unable to produce names of vocabulary words, model and have the student repeat.

Lesson 143

Materials: picture cards (appliances: coffee pot, oven, refrigerator, stove, television, vacuum cleaner; buildings: apartment building, barn, hospital, house, school, shop, silo; containers: bag, box, can, cup, dish, envelope, garbage can, net, pan, plate, pot, sack, vase; furniture: bed, bookcase, chair, chest, couch, crib, desk, easel, sofa, table)

In this lesson, students will review words representing appliances, buildings, containers, and furniture.

1. Display and name all picture cards of appliances. Have the entire class repeat each name. Review names twice, then say the name of each appliance in a complete sentence, using **This/These** sentence construction. Have students repeat each sentence. Repeat the exercise using the pictures of buildings, containers, and furniture.

2. Divide the class into three groups. Provide each group with an equal number of picture cards from all four categories. Set the cards in a stack in the middle of the group. *(Note: The side of the card **without** the word should face up.)* In each group, have students take turns identifying the item pictured on the top card, using a complete sentence. If the student names the pictured item correctly, that student keeps the card. If the student incorrectly names the item, the card is placed at the bottom of the stack. Play continues until all cards have been correctly named in a complete sentence. The student with the most cards wins. Note any cards any group is unable to name.

3. Rotate card sets so that each group has a new set of cards and repeat the game. Note any cards any group is unable to name.

4. Rotate card sets once more and repeat the game. If there were any cards any group was unable to name, review with the entire class.

5. Bring the class together and play "Around the World." Play begins with two students standing. Display a card. *(Note: Display the side **without** the word.)* The first student to correctly name the picture on the card moves on. The other student sits down. Play continues around the room. Review all vocabulary words using this format.

6. Continue to monitor students' oral production. The goal is automaticity.

Lesson 144

Materials: picture cards (machines: computer, fan, fax machine, sewing machine; musical instruments: banjo, bell, clarinet, drum, guitar, piano, sax, tambourine, trombone, trumpet, violin, xylophone)

In this lesson, students will learn words representing machines and musical instruments.

1. Display and name all picture cards of machines. Have the entire class repeat each name. Review names twice, then say each name in a complete sentence, using **This/These** sentence construction. Have students repeat each sentence. Repeat the exercise using the pictures of musical instruments.

2. Divide the class into three groups. Provide each group with an equal number of picture cards, including pictures from both categories. Set the cards in a stack in the middle of the group. *(Note: There should be at least one picture card for each student for this exercise. If more cards are needed, use any cards from previous lessons that need reinforcement. The side of the card* ***without*** *the word should face up.)* In each group, have students take turns identifying the item pictured on the top card, using a complete sentence. If the student names the pictured item correctly, that student keeps the card. If the student incorrectly names the item, the card is placed at the bottom of the stack. Play continues until all cards have been correctly named in a complete sentence. The student with the most cards wins. Note any cards any group is unable to name.

3. Rotate card sets so that each group has a new set of cards and repeat the game. Note any cards any group is unable to name.

4. Rotate card sets once more and repeat the game. If there were any cards any group was unable to name, review with the entire class.

5. Bring the class together and play "Around the World." Play begins with two students standing. Display a card. *(Note: Display the side* ***without*** *the word.)* The first student to correctly name the picture on the card moves on. The other student sits down. Play continues around the room. Review all vocabulary words using this format.

6. Monitor students' oral production. If individual students are repeatedly unable to produce names of vocabulary words, model and have the student repeat.

Lesson 145

Materials: all picture cards from Lessons 126–144

In this lesson, students will review words representing action verbs, appliances, body parts, buildings, clothing, containers, food, furniture, machines, musical instruments, people, places, school things, tools, and vehicles.

1. Keeping cards in their individual category, flash each picture card and have students quickly identify each pictured item.
2. Shuffle all cards together and repeat step 1.
3. Play "Around the World" using pictures from all categories. Start with a pair of students and flash a picture card. The first one to name the picture correctly advances; the other student sits down. Continue in this manner until all cards are reviewed and students are able to name pictures quickly.
4. Display a card and have individual students generate a sentence using the word in context. Have several students provide sentences using the pictured noun or verb before displaying a new card.
5. Pass out at least one card to each student. Have students use the pictured word in a sentence. If a mistake is made, model the correct use of the word and have the student repeat.
6. Encourage students to continue practicing vocabulary.

Lesson 146

Materials: picture cards (insects: ant, bee, beetle, bug, butterfly, caterpillar, dragonfly, grasshopper, ladybug, mosquito, moth, spider, wasp; plants: acorn, bush, daisy, grass, log, mum, pine, plant, rose, tree, vine)

In this lesson, students will learn words representing insects and plants for vocabulary expansion.

1. Display and name all insect picture cards. Have the entire class repeat each name. Review names twice, then say each name in a complete sentence, using **This/These** sentence construction. Have students repeat each sentence. Repeat the exercise using the pictures of plants.

2. Divide the class into three groups. Provide each group with an equal number of both insect and plant picture cards. Set the cards in a stack in the middle of the group. *(Note: There should be at least one card per student for this exercise. Use cards that need reinforcement from previous lessons if you need more cards. The side of the card* ***without*** *the word should face up.)* In each group, have students take turns identifying the item pictured on the top card, using a complete sentence. If the student names the pictured item correctly, that student keeps the card. If the student incorrectly names the item, the card is placed at the bottom of the stack. Play continues until all cards have been correctly named in a complete sentence. The student with the most cards wins. Note any cards any group is unable to name.

3. Rotate card sets so that each group has a new set of cards and repeat the game. Note any cards any group is unable to name.

4. Rotate card sets once more and repeat the game. If there were any cards any group was unable to name, review with the entire class.

5. Bring the class together and play "Around the World." Play begins with two students standing. Display a card. *(Note: Display the side* ***without*** *the word.)* The first student to correctly name the picture on the card moves on. The other student sits down. Play continues around the room. Review all vocabulary words using this format.

6. Monitor students' oral production. If individual students are repeatedly unable to produce vocabulary words, model and have the student repeat.

Lesson 147

Materials: picture cards (money: dime, dollar, nickel, penny, pennies, quarter; shapes [color or outline]: arrow, circle, diamond, heart, hexagon, oval, rectangle, square, star, triangle)

In this lesson, students will learn words representing money and shapes.

1. Display and name all money picture cards. Have the entire class repeat each name. Review names twice, then say each name in a complete sentence, using **This/These** sentence construction. Have students repeat each sentence. Repeat the exercise using the pictures of shapes.

2. Divide the class into three groups. Provide each group with an equal number of both money and shape picture cards. Set the cards in a stack in the middle of the group. *(Note: There should be at least one card for each student. If additional cards are needed, use any cards from previous lessons that need reinforcement. The side of the card* ***without*** *the word should face up.)* In each group, have students take turns identifying the item pictured on the top card, using a complete sentence. If the student names the pictured item correctly, that student keeps the card. If the student incorrectly names the item, the card is placed at the bottom of the stack. Play continues until all cards have been correctly named in a complete sentence. The student with the most cards wins. Note any cards any group is unable to name.

3. Rotate card sets so that each group has a new set of cards and repeat the game. Note any cards any group is unable to name.

4. Rotate card sets once more and repeat the game. If there were any cards any group was unable to name, review with the entire class.

5. Bring the class together and play "Around the World." Play begins with two students standing. Display a card. *(Note: Display the side* ***without*** *the word.)* The first student to correctly name the picture on the card moves on. The other student sits down. Play continues around the room. Review all vocabulary words using this format.

6. Monitor students' oral production. If individual students are repeatedly unable to produce vocabulary words, model and have the student repeat.

Lesson 148

Materials: picture cards (insects: ant, bee, beetle, bug, butterfly, caterpillar, dragonfly, grasshopper, ladybug, mosquito, moth, spider, wasp; money: dime, dollar, nickel, penny, pennies, quarter; plants: acorn, bush, daisy, grass, log, mum, pine, plant, rose, tree, vine; shapes [color or outline]: arrow, circle, diamond, heart, hexagon, oval, rectangle, square, star, triangle)

In this lesson, students will review words representing insects, money, plants, and shapes.

1. Display and name all plant insect cards. Have the entire class repeat each name. Review names twice, then say each name in a complete sentence, using **This/These** construction. Have students repeat each sentence. Repeat the exercise using the pictures of money, plants, and shapes.

2. Divide the class into three groups. Provide each group with an equal number of picture cards, including pictures from all four categories. Set the cards in a stack in the middle of the group. *(Note: The side of the card **without** the word should face up.)* In each group, have students take turns identifying the item pictured on the top card, using a complete sentence. If the student names the pictured item correctly, that student keeps the card. If the student incorrectly names the item, the card is placed at the bottom of the stack. Play continues until all cards have been correctly named in a complete sentence. The student with the most cards wins. Note any cards any group is unable to name.

3. Rotate card sets so that each group has a new set of cards and repeat the game. Note any cards any group is unable to name.

4. Rotate card sets once more and repeat the game. If there were any cards any group was unable to name, review with the entire class.

5. Bring the class together and play "Around the World." Play begins with two students standing. Display a card. *(Note: Display the side **without** the word.)* The first student to correctly name the picture on the card moves on. The other student sits down. Play continues around the room. Review all vocabulary words using this format.

6. Continue to monitor students' oral production. The goal is automaticity.

Lesson 149

Materials: picture cards (animals: ape, bat, bear, beaver, bird, camel, cat, chick, chipmunk, cow, cub, deer, dog, donkey, duck, elephant, fish, fox, frog, giraffe, goat, goose, gorilla, guinea pig, hamster, hen, hippopotamus, horse, kangaroo, lamb, lion, lizard, monkey, mouse, owl, ox, parrot, peacock, penguin, pig, pup, puppy, rabbit, rat, rooster, seal, sheep, skunk, snake, tiger, turkey, turtle, whale, yak, zebra)

In this lesson, students will learn words representing animals.

1. Display picture cards and name all animals. Have the entire class repeat each name. Review names twice, then say each name in a complete sentence, using **This/These** sentence construction. Have students repeat each sentence.

2. Divide the class into three groups. Provide each group with an equal number of picture cards. Set the cards in a stack in the middle of the group. *(Note: The side of the card **without** the word should face up.)* In each group, have students take turns identifying the animal pictured on the top card, using a complete sentence. If the student names the pictured animal correctly, that student keeps the card. If the student incorrectly names the animal, the card is placed at the bottom of the stack. Play continues until all cards have been correctly named in a complete sentence. The student with the most cards wins. Note any animals any group is unable to name.

3. Rotate card sets so that each group has a new set of cards and repeat the game. Note any animals any group is unable to name.

4. Rotate card sets once more and repeat the game. If there were any animals any group was unable to name, review with the entire class.

5. Bring the class together and play "Around the World." Play begins with two students standing. Display a card. *(Note: Display the side **without** the word.)* The first student to correctly name the animal on the card moves on. The other student sits down. Play continues around the room. Review all vocabulary words using this format.

6. Monitor students' oral production. If individual students are repeatedly unable to produce names of animals, model and have the student repeat. Encourage students to generate sentences using animal names throughout the day.

Lesson 150

Materials: picture cards from Lessons 126–149

In this lesson, students will review words representing action verbs, animals, appliances, body parts, buildings, clothing, containers, food, furniture, insects, machines, money, musical instruments, people, places, plants, school things, shapes, tools, and vehicles.

1. Keeping cards in their individual category, flash each picture card and have students quickly identify each pictured item.
2. Shuffle all cards together and repeat step 1. The goal is automaticity.
3. Play "Around the World" using pictures from all categories. Start with a pair of students and flash a picture card. The first one to name the picture correctly advances; the other student sits down. Continue in this manner until all cards are reviewed and students are able to name pictures quickly.
4. Pass out picture cards, one per student. *(Note: The side* ***without*** *the word should face up.)* Have students cover their pictures until they are called on; then, have them look at the picture and make up a sentence using the pictured word as quickly as possible.
5. Pass out a second round of cards and repeat step 4.
6. Continue to monitor students' oral language and encourage students to continue practicing vocabulary.

Lesson 151

In this lesson, students will review personal and objective pronouns, verb phrases, verb forms, subject-verb agreement, and contractions.

1. Model the following questions and responses, gesturing to indicate a positive or negative response. Have students repeat both the question and the responses.

Are the students in their seats?	No, the students **are not** in their seats.
	No, the students **aren't** in their seats.
Have you eaten lunch today?	No, I **have not** eaten lunch today.
	No, I **haven't** eaten lunch today.
Will the boy play the game?	No, the boy **will not** play the game.
	No, the boy **won't** play the game.
Do you think we will finish it on time?	Yes, I think **we will** finish it on time.
	Yes, I think **we'll** finish it on time.
Is it all right if they go with us?	Yes, **it is** all right if they go with us.
	Yes, **it's** all right if they go with us.

2. Repeat questions from step 1. Gesture to indicate a positive or negative response. Have all students respond. Have students answer with the non-contracted verb phrase first and the contracted verb phrase second.

3. Repeat questions from step 1. Gesture to indicate a positive or negative response. Have individual students respond. Have each student answer with both the contracted and non-contracted verb phrase.

4. Provide students with a simple sentence. Have individual students form it into a question. Call on another student to respond. For example, say: Children play. The first student may respond: *"Are the children playing?"* The second student may respond: *"Yes, the children are playing."* Questions and responses will vary; emphasize correct sentence structure.

5. Have individual students form their own questions and call on another student to respond. Make sure each student is able to form questions and answers correctly. If an error is made, model the correct sentence and have the student repeat.

6. Encourage students to practice forming questions and answers throughout the day.

Lesson 152

In this lesson, students will review possessive pronouns, question-statement transformations, contractions, and subject-verb agreement.

1. Model the following questions and responses. Have students repeat both the question and the responses.

Whose pencil is this; is it yours?	Yes, **it is my** pencil. Yes, **it's my** pencil.
Is that Ms. Tucker's car?	No, that **is not** Ms. Tucker's car. No, that **isn't her** car.
Are they bringing his ball?	Yes, **they are** bringing **his** ball. Yes, **they're** bringing **his** ball.
Have you started the picture?	No, I **have not** started the picture. No, I **have not** started **it**.
Did I say I'd give you the book?	Yes, you said **you would** give **me** the book. Yes, you said **you'd** give **me** the book.

2. Repeat questions from step 1. Gesture to indicate a positive or negative response. Have all students respond. Have students answer with the non-contracted verb phrase first and the contracted verb phrase second. Be sure to emphasize pronouns.

3. Repeat questions from step 1. Gesture to indicate a positive or negative response. Have individual students respond. Have each student answer with both the contracted and non-contracted verb phrase.

4. Provide students with a possessive pronoun and noun. Have individual students form it into a question. Call on another student to respond. For example, say: My book. The first student may respond: *"Did you bring my book?"* The second student may respond: *"No, I didn't bring your book."* Questions and responses will vary; emphasize correct sentence structure.

5. Have individual students form a question using a possessive pronoun. Ask another student to respond. Make sure each student is able to form questions and answers correctly. If an error is made, model the correct sentence and have the student repeat.

6. Encourage students to practice forming questions and answers with possessive pronouns throughout the day.

Lesson 153

Materials: picture cards from Lessons 126–149 (action verbs, animals, appliances, body parts, buildings, clothing, containers, food, furniture, insects, machines, money, musical instruments, people, places, plants, school things, shapes, tools, vehicles)

In this lesson, students will review vocabulary, verb phrases, subject-verb agreement, and possessive pronouns.

1. Model the following questions and responses. Have students repeat both the questions and responses.

Are they the new students?	No, they **are not** the new students.
	No, they **aren't** the new students.
Have you done all the exercises?	Yes, **I have** done all the exercises.
	Yes, **I've** done all the exercises.
Did everybody like her?	Yes, everybody **liked** her.

2. Repeat questions from step 1. Gesture to indicate a positive or negative response. Have all students respond. Have students answer with the non-contracted verb phrase first and the contracted verb phrase second.

3. Repeat questions from step 1. Gesture to indicate a positive or negative response. Have individual students respond. Have each student answer with both the contracted and non-contracted verb phrase.

4. Provide students with a noun and an action verb from Lessons 126–149. Have individual students use both to form a question. Call on another student to respond. For example, say: Bell, ringing. The first student may respond: *"Was the bell ringing?"* The second student may respond: *"No, the bell wasn't ringing."* Questions and responses will vary; emphasize correct sentence structure.

5. Prompt students with a picture card. Have individual students form their own questions using that item or action. Ask another student to respond. Make sure each student is able to form questions and answers correctly. If an error is made, model the correct sentence and have the student repeat.

6. Encourage students to practice forming questions and answers throughout the day.

Lesson 154

Materials: picture cards from Lessons 126–149 (action verbs, animals, appliances, body parts, buildings, clothing, containers, food, furniture, insects, machines, money, musical instruments, people, places, plants, school things, shapes, tools, vehicles)

In this lesson, students will review vocabulary, verb phrases, subject-verb agreement, and possessive pronouns.

1. Model the following questions and responses. Have students repeat the questions and responses.

Will the kittens sleep here?	Yes, the **kittens will** sleep here. Yes, **they'll** sleep here.
Were you surprised?	No, I **was not** surprised. No, I **wasn't** surprised.
Has anybody finished this page?	No, **nobody has** finished this page. No, **nobody's** finished this page.
Did the big dog frighten her?	No, the big dog **did not** frighten her. No, the big dog **didn't** frighten her.
Would they like to sit here?	Yes, **they would** like to sit here. Yes, **they'd** like to sit here.

2. Repeat questions from step 1. Gesture to indicate a positive or negative response. Have all students respond. Have students answer with the non-contracted verb phrase first and the contracted verb phrase second.

3. Repeat questions from step 1. Gesture to indicate a positive or negative response. Have individual students respond. Have each student answer with both the contracted and non-contracted verb phrase.

4. Provide students with a noun and an action verb from Lessons 126–149. Have individual students use both to form a question with a pronoun. Call on another student to respond. For example, say: Dog, barking. The first student may respond: *"Did the dog bark at him?"* The second student may respond: *"No, the dog didn't bark at him."* Questions and responses will vary; emphasize correct sentence structure.

5. Prompt students with a picture card. Have individual students form their own questions and call on another student to respond. Make sure each student is able to form questions and answers correctly. If an error is made, model the correct sentence and have the student repeat.

6. Encourage students to practice forming questions and answers using pronouns throughout the day.

Lesson 155

In this lesson, students will review Lessons 151–154.

1. Model questions and responses from step 1 in Lessons 151–154. Have students repeat both the question and the responses.

2. Repeat all questions again. Gesture to indicate a positive or negative response. Have all students respond. Have students answer with the non-contracted verb phrase first and the contracted verb phrase second.

3. Repeat questions a third time. Gesture to indicate a positive or negative response. Have individual students respond. Have each student answer with both the contracted and non-contracted verb phrase.

4. Provide students with a noun and an action verb from Lessons 126–149. Have individual students use both to form a question. Call on another student to respond. For example, say: Banana, eating. The first student may respond: *"Did he eat the banana?"* The second student may respond: *"No, he didn't eat the banana."* Questions and responses will vary; emphasize correct sentence structure.

5. Ask individual students questions about items as they pertain to specific categories (using words from Lessons 126–149). Have students answer in a complete sentence.

   stimulus: Can you name three types of vehicles? — response: *"Three types of vehicles are (a car, a bus, and a van)."*
   stimulus: What three tools did you use in shop? — response: *"I used (a hammer, a saw, and a yardstick)."*

6. Encourage students to practice forming questions and answers throughout the day.

Lesson 156

In this lesson, students will learn to convert grammatically incorrect sentences to grammatically correct sentences.

1. Model grammatically incorrect sentences and follow each with the grammatically correct version. Have students repeat the correct sentence.

Rides he the bus to school.	He rides the bus to school.
I seen the book.	I saw the book.
This is the desk who is broken.	This is the desk that is broken.
Anybody must have helped you.	Somebody must have helped you.
These is no the right ones.	These are not the right ones.

2. Generate grammatically incorrect sentences and have individual students respond with the grammatically correct version. Have all students repeat the correct version.
3. Review each incorrect sentence with students. Have individual students explain why the sentence is incorrect.
4. Ask students to think about a recent episode from class. Have students tell a round-robin story about the episode (i.e., one student begins a story and each student continues it by adding a sentence). Make sure each student contributes at least one sentence to the story.
5. After completing a story, have individual students summarize it in their own words.
6. Monitor students' sentence formation. If errors are made, model and have students repeat the correct sentence.

Lesson 157

Materials: a tall tale to be read aloud

In this lesson, students will learn to convert grammatically incorrect sentences to grammatically correct sentences.

1. Model grammatically incorrect sentences and follow each with the grammatically correct version. Have students repeat the correct sentence.

We drove in these car.	We drove in this car.
Yesterday, I give it to you.	Yesterday, I gave it to you.
You has helped me.	You have helped me.
I sleeped on the couch.	I slept on the couch.
We goed home.	We went home.

2. Generate grammatically incorrect sentences and have individual students respond with the grammatically correct version. Have all students repeat the correct version.

3. Review each incorrect sentence with students. Have individual students explain why the sentence is incorrect.

4. Read a tall tale to the class. Explain that a tall tale is an exaggerated story and is not true. After reading, ask students to identify parts of the story that make it a tall tale.

5. Have students create a round-robin tall tale. Make sure each student contributes at least one sentence. Call on individual students to summarize the tale when the class is finished. Have other students tell the tale with a different ending.

6. Monitor students' sentence formation. If errors are made, model and have students repeat the correct sentence.

Lesson 158

Materials: a realistic short story to be read aloud

In this lesson, students will learn to convert grammatically incorrect sentences to grammatically correct sentences.

1. Model grammatically incorrect sentences and follow each with the grammatically correct version. Have students repeat the correct sentence.

Her reads the story at school.	She reads the story at school.
She seen the movie.	She saw the movie.
Is those new shoes?	Are those new shoes?
I no like her.	I don't like her.
Did you went?	Did you go?

2. Generate grammatically incorrect sentences and have individual students respond with the grammatically correct version. Have all students repeat the correct version.
3. Review each incorrect sentence with students. Have individual students explain why the sentence is incorrect.
4. Read a realistic short story to the class. After reading, ask students to identify parts of the story that could take place.
5. Have students create a realistic, round-robin short story. Make sure each student contributes at least one sentence. When the story is complete, have individual students retell the story, changing any part of it to make it different. Discuss whether the new versions could take place.
6. Monitor students' sentence formation. If errors are made, model and have students repeat the correct sentence.

Lesson 159

Materials: a realistic short story to be read aloud

In this lesson, students will learn to convert grammatically incorrect sentences to grammatically correct sentences.

1. Model grammatically incorrect sentences and follow each with the grammatically correct version. Have students repeat the correct sentence.

Did find you the paper?	Did you find the paper?
My mom cooking.	My mom is cooking.
Can you see man?	Can you see the man?
They readed the story.	They read the story.
She seed us.	She saw us.

2. Generate grammatically incorrect sentences and have individual students respond with the grammatically correct version. Have all students repeat the correct version.

3. Review each incorrect sentence with students. Have individual students explain why the sentence is incorrect.

4. Read a realistic short story to the class. After reading, ask students to identify parts of the story that could take place.

5. Have students create a realistic, round-robin short story. Make sure each student contributes at least one sentence. When the story is complete, have individual students retell the story in their own words. Have other students retell it with a new ending. Discuss whether the new endings could happen.

6. Monitor students' sentence formation. If errors are made, model and have students repeat the correct sentence.

Lesson 160

In this lesson, students will practice converting grammatically incorrect sentences to grammatically correct sentences.

1. Model grammatically incorrect sentences and follow each with the grammatically correct version. Have students repeat the correct sentence.

Anybody must have helped you.	Somebody must have helped you.
We drove in these car.	We drove in (this, his, her, their, our) car.
You has helped me.	You have helped me.
I sleeped on the couch.	I slept on the couch.
Is those new shoes?	Are those new shoes?
Did you went?	Did you go?
Did find you the paper?	Did you find the paper?
My mom cooking.	My mom is cooking.

2. Have individual students generate a grammatically incorrect sentence. Have a second student respond with the grammatically correct version. Ask the first to tell what was wrong with their sentence. Repeat until each student has an opportunity to do both of the above instructions.

3. Have individual students generate a grammatically incorrect sentence. Have the same student correct it and explain what was wrong with the original version. Repeat until each student has had a few opportunities to participate.

4. Have students create a round-robin tall tale. Make sure each student contributes at least one sentence. When it is complete, have students identify the parts of the story that could not really happen.

5. Have students create a realistic, round-robin short story. Make sure each student contributes at least one sentence. Make sure students understand that the story is not supposed to be true, but should be possible. When it is complete, have students identify the parts that could really happen.

6. Monitor students' sentence formation. If errors are made, model and have students repeat the correct sentence.

Lesson 161

In this lesson, students will practice converting grammatically incorrect sentences to grammatically correct sentences.

1. Model grammatically incorrect sentences and follow each with the grammatically correct version. Have students repeat the correct sentence.

She will walking.	She will be walking. She will walk.
Her gave it to me.	She gave it to me.
These is not enough.	This is not enough. These are not enough.
Did anybody happen to you?	Did anything happen to you?
We need both of this.	We need both of these.

2. Generate grammatically incorrect sentences and have individual students respond with the grammatically correct version. Have all students repeat the correct version.
3. Review each incorrect sentence with students. Have individual students explain why the sentence is incorrect.
4. Review stories from Lessons 157–159. Generate a discussion based on differences students noticed between the short stories and the tall tale. Ask students to change the tall tale in a way that would make it more believable. *(Note: Depending on the class and class size, this exercise could be done as a brainstorming session where students all generate different ideas together, or by having individual students come up with at least one idea. Use the model that will generate the most participation.)*
5. Ask each student to describe a recent lesson or incident from school. Allow students to take their time and be as precise as possible. Make sure each student has an opportunity to share with the class.
6. Encourage students to think about a story to tell in class. They may want to ask friends outside of class for a story.

Lesson 162

In this lesson, students will practice converting grammatically incorrect sentences to grammatically correct sentences.

1. Model grammatically incorrect sentences and follow each with the grammatically correct version. Have students repeat the correct sentence.

All of the bus are here.	All of the buses are here.
Me and her can help you.	She and I can help you.
Me and my friends are going.	My friends and I are going.
Him and me played ball.	He and I played ball.
This are Sondra's sweater.	This is Sondra's sweater.

2. Generate grammatically incorrect sentences and have individual students respond with the grammatically correct version. Have all students repeat the correct version.

3. Review each incorrect sentence with students. Have individual students explain why the sentence is incorrect.

4. Review stories from Lessons 157–159. Ask students to change the short stories in ways that would make them more like tall tales. *(Note: Depending on the class and class size, this exercise could be done as a brainstorming session where students all generate different ideas together, or by having individual students come up with at least one idea. Use the model that will generate the most participation.)*

5. Ask students to share stories they have heard or read. Allow students to take their time and be as precise as possible. Make sure each student has an opportunity to share with the class.

6. Monitor students' sentence formation. Provide needed assistance, but allow each student ample production time.

Lesson 163

Materials: a short story to be read aloud

In this lesson, students will practice converting grammatically incorrect sentences to grammatically correct sentences.

1. Model grammatically incorrect sentences and follow each with the grammatically correct version. Have students repeat the correct sentence.

He football plays.	He plays football.
They is swimming.	They are swimming.
Did she came with you?	Did she come with you?
Us won the game.	We won the game.
Have you rode in his car?	Have you ridden in his car?

2. Generate grammatically incorrect sentences and have individual students respond with the grammatically correct version. Have all students repeat the correct version.

3. Review each incorrect sentence with students. Have individual students explain why the sentence is incorrect.

4. Read a fictional short story to the class. Ask individual students to retell it using their own words. Ask students to identify parts of the story that could happen. Focus more on sentence structure than answer content. Make sure each student has an opportunity to contribute.

5. Generate a discussion about the story. Have students discuss specific actions the characters did that could or could not happen. Ask students to identify which parts of the story are more likely to occur than others. Encourage all students to engage in discussion. Allow students to take their time and be as precise as possible. Make sure each student has an opportunity to share with the class.

6. Monitor students' sentence formation. Provide needed assistance, but allow each student ample production time.

Lesson 164

Materials: short story from Lesson 163

In this lesson, students will practice converting grammatically incorrect sentences to grammatically correct sentences.

1. Model grammatically incorrect sentences and follow each with the grammatically correct version. Have students repeat the correct sentence.

She sing with her friends.	She sings with her friends.
My mother pretty.	My mother is pretty. My mother's pretty.
Have you think about it?	Have you thought about it?
Luis play on the team.	Luis plays on the team.
Anita go with us.	Anita goes with us. Anita went with us.

2. Generate grammatically incorrect sentences and have individual students respond with the grammatically correct version. Have all students repeat the correct version.

3. Review each incorrect sentence with students. Have individual students explain why the sentence is incorrect.

4. Have individual students summarize the story from Lesson 163. Ask students to change it into a tall tale. *(Note: Depending on the class and class size, this exercise could be done as a brainstorming session where students all generate different ideas together, or taking turns with each student creating at least one idea. Use the model that will generate the most participation.)*

5. Ask students to think about the main characters and their actions. Create a discussion by asking students what they would do differently if they were among the characters. Allow students to take their time and be as precise as possible. Make sure each student has an opportunity to share with the class.

6. Monitor students' sentence formation. Provide needed assistance, but allow each student ample production time.

Lesson 165

In this lesson, students will practice converting grammatically incorrect sentences to grammatically correct sentences.

1. Generate grammatically incorrect stimulus sentences. Have individual students provide the correct version. Use prompts from Lessons 161–164. Make sure all students generate a corrected version.

stimulus: She will walking.	response: *"She will walk."*
stimulus: These is not enough.	response: *"These are not enough."*
stimulus: We need both of this.	response: *"We need both of these."*
stimulus: All of the bus are here.	response: *"All of the buses are here."*
stimulus: Him and me played ball.	response: *"He and I played ball."*
stimulus: This are her sweater.	response: *"This is her sweater."*
stimulus: Have you rode in his car?	response: *"Have you ridden in his car?"*
stimulus: He football plays.	response: *"He plays football."*
stimulus: Us won the game.	response: *"We won the game."*
stimulus: She sing with her friends.	response: *"She sings with her friends."*
stimulus: Have you think about it?	response: *"Have you thought about it?"*
stimulus: Box is full.	response: *"The box is full."*

2. Have individual students generate a grammatically incorrect sentence. Have a second student respond with the grammatically correct version. Ask the first student to tell what was wrong with the sentence. Repeat until each student has done both of the above instructions.

3. Have individual students generate a grammatically incorrect sentence. Have the same student correct it and explain what was wrong with the original version. Repeat until each student has had a few opportunities to participate.

4. Have students create a round-robin tall tale. When it is complete, have students identify the parts of the story that could not really happen.

5. Have students create a round-robin realistic story. Make sure each student contributes at least one sentence. Make sure students understand that the story is not supposed to be true, but should be possible.

6. Initiate and involve all students in conversation about how English works. Do not recite rules; rather, let students explain in their own words.

Lesson 166

In this lesson, students will discuss how sentence meaning changes with slight word variations.

1. Model the following sentences and have students repeat. Ask students to explain how the sentences differ in meaning. If necessary, help them distinguish the subtle differences.

   They walk home.
   They can walk home.
   They will walk home.

2. Model the following sentences and have students repeat. Ask students to explain how the sentences differ in meaning. If necessary, help them distinguish the subtle differences.

   Juanita walked in.
   Juanita walked out.
   Juanita walked there.

3. Model the following sentences and have students repeat. Ask students to explain how the sentences differ in meaning. If necessary, help them distinguish the subtle differences.

   It smells good.
   It smells funny.
   It smells wonderful.

4. Model the following sentences and have students repeat. Ask students to explain how the sentences differ in meaning. If necessary, help them distinguish the subtle differences.

   The paper was burned.
   He burned the paper.
   He was burning the paper.

5. Provide further practice by modifying the subject and predicate of each of the sentences from steps 1–4. Ask students to explain how each change affects the meaning of the sentence.

6. Ensure that all students have ample opportunity for verbal input. Monitor student understanding of this concept and provide individual help when needed.

Lesson 167

In this lesson, students will discuss how sentence meaning changes with slight word variations.

1. Model the following sentences and have students repeat. Ask students to explain how the sentences differ in meaning. If necessary, help them distinguish the subtle differences.

   The ice cream melted.
   The ice cream is melting.
   The ice cream might melt.

2. Model the following sentences and have students repeat. Ask students to explain how the sentences differ in meaning. If necessary, help them distinguish the subtle differences.

   Big trucks drive on this street.
   Big trucks drive on that street.
   Big trucks drive on her street.

3. Model the following sentences and have students repeat. Ask students to explain how the sentences differ in meaning. If necessary, help them distinguish the subtle differences.

   The students have to get in line.
   The students should get in line.
   The students could get in line.

4. Model the following sentences and have students repeat. Ask students to explain how the sentences differ in meaning. If necessary, help them distinguish the subtle differences.

   He had a dog.
   He has a dog.
   He wants a dog.

5. Provide further practice by modifying the subject and predicate of each of the sentences from steps 1–4. Ask students to explain how each change affects the meaning of the sentence.

6. Ensure that all students have ample opportunity for verbal input. Monitor student understanding of this concept and provide individual help when needed.

Lesson 168

In this lesson, students will discuss how sentence meaning changes with slight word variations.

1. Model the following sentences and have students repeat. Ask students to explain how the sentences differ in meaning. If necessary, help them distinguish the subtle differences.

   Were you at home?
   Are you at home?
   Will you be at home?

2. Model the following sentences and have students repeat. Ask students to explain how the sentences differ in meaning. If necessary, help them distinguish the subtle differences.

   The table was here.
   The table was there.
   The table was moved.

3. Model the following sentences and have students repeat. Ask students to explain how the sentences differ in meaning. If necessary, help them distinguish the subtle differences.

   This is a banana.
   These are bananas.
   Those are bananas.

4. Model the following sentences and have students repeat. Ask students to explain how the sentences differ in meaning. If necessary, help them distinguish the subtle differences.

   Give me a pencil.
   Give me the pencil.
   Give me that pencil.

5. Provide further practice by asking individual students to provide a simple sentence. Have two other students change its meaning by altering one or two words, as shown in the previous steps. Call on other students to explain how the sentences differ in meaning. If students have difficulty with this, modify the subject and predicate of each of the sentences from steps 1–4. Ask students to explain how each change affects the meaning of the sentence.

6. Ensure that all students have ample opportunity for verbal input. Monitor student understanding of this concept and provide individual help when needed.

Lesson 169

In this lesson, students will discuss how sentence meaning changes with slight word variations.

1. Model the following sentences and have students repeat. Ask students to explain how the sentences differ in meaning. If necessary, help them distinguish the subtle differences.

   He was there.
   He came there.
   He stayed there.

2. Model the following sentences and have students repeat. Ask students to explain how the sentences differ in meaning. If necessary, help them distinguish the subtle differences.

   Did something happen to you?
   Is something happening to you?
   Will something happen to you?

3. Model the following sentences and have students repeat. Ask students to explain how the sentences differ in meaning. If necessary, help them distinguish the subtle differences.

   We saw our friends.
   You saw our friends.
   She saw our friends.

4. Model the following sentences and have students repeat. Ask students to explain how the sentences differ in meaning. If necessary, help them distinguish the subtle differences.

   We made some sandwiches.
   We ate some sandwiches.
   We packed some sandwiches.

5. Provide further practice by asking individual students to provide a simple sentence. Have two other students change its meaning by altering one word, as shown in the previous steps. Call on other students to explain how the sentences differ in meaning. If students have difficulty with this, modify the subject and predicate of each of the sentences from steps 1–4. Ask students to explain how each change affects the meaning of the sentence.

6. Ensure that all students have ample opportunity for verbal input. Monitor student understanding of this concept and provide individual help when needed.

Lesson 170

In this lesson, students will review how sentence meaning changes with slight word variations.

1. Have students repeat sentence patterns from steps 1–4 of Lessons 166–169. Discuss how the sentence meanings differ with slight variations. Be sure each student is able to explain differences in meaning for at least one example.

2. Model the following challenge set of sentences (in which differences result from participle forms) and have students repeat. Ask students to explain how the sentences differ. Make sure students correlate the difference between the past and present participle forms.

   Mother gave me some money.
   Mother had given me some money.
   Mother has given me some money.

3. Model another challenge set of sentences and have students repeat. Ask students to explain how the sentences differ. Make sure students correlate the difference between the past and present participle forms.

   Our teacher walked with us.
   Our teacher has walked with us.
   Our teacher had walked with us.

4. Use sentence sets above and change the tense to the present and future. Have students repeat each new sentence. Discuss the difference between changing the meaning and changing the tense of a sentence.

5. Call on individual students and provide a simple sentence. Have each student change the tense using present participle (has) and past participle (had). Ask a different student to explain how this affects the meaning.

6. Ensure that all students have ample opportunity for verbal input. Monitor student understanding of this concept and provide individual help when needed.

Lesson 171

In this lesson, students will discuss how sentence meaning changes with slight word variations.

1. Model the following sentences and have students repeat. Ask students to explain how the sentences differ in meaning. If necessary, help them distinguish the differences.

   He felt sick.
   He looked sick.
   He was sick.

2. Model the following sentences and have students repeat. Ask students to explain how the sentences differ in meaning. If necessary, help them distinguish the differences.

   What does she drive?
   What does she sail?
   What does she fly?

3. Model the following sentences and have students repeat. Ask students to explain how the sentences differ in meaning. If necessary, help them distinguish the differences.

   It tastes good.
   It looks good.
   It smells good.

4. Model the following sentences and have students repeat. Ask students to explain how the sentences differ in meaning. If necessary, help them distinguish the differences.

   Li can swim.
   Li might swim.
   Li must swim.

5. Provide further practice by modifying the subject and predicate of each of the sentences from steps 1–4. Ask students to explain how each change affects the meaning of the sentence.

6. Ensure that all students have ample opportunity for verbal input. Monitor student understanding of this concept and provide individual help when needed.

Lesson 172

In this lesson, students will discuss how sentence meaning changes with slight word variations.

1. Model the following sentences and have students repeat. Ask students to explain how the sentences differ in meaning. If necessary, help them distinguish the differences.

   The fire engine raced past.
   The fire engine drove past.
   The fire engine paraded past.

2. Model the following sentences and have students repeat. Ask students to explain how the sentences differ in meaning. If necessary, help them distinguish the differences.

   Big trucks drive on this street.
   Big trucks drive on that street.
   Big trucks drive on her street.

3. Model the following sentences and have students repeat. Ask students to explain how the sentences differ in meaning. If necessary, help them distinguish the differences.

   The ship arrived.
   The ship sailed.
   The ship docked.

4. Model the following sentences and have students repeat. Ask students to explain how the sentences differ in meaning. If necessary, help them distinguish the differences.

   My books are here.
   Our books are here.
   Your books are here.

5. Provide further practice by modifying the subject and predicate of each of the sentences from steps 1–4. Ask students to explain how each change affects the meaning of the sentence.

6. Ensure that all students have ample opportunity for verbal input. Monitor student understanding of this concept and provide individual help when needed.

Lesson 173

In this lesson, students will discuss how sentence meaning changes with slight word variations.

1. Model the following sentences and have students repeat. Ask students to explain how the sentences differ in meaning. If necessary, help them distinguish the differences.

   This is the one.
   That is the one.
   Those are the ones.

2. Model the following sentences and have students repeat. Ask students to explain how the sentences differ in meaning. If necessary, help them distinguish the differences.

   These chips are crispy.
   These chips are stale.
   These chips are soggy.

3. Model the following sentences and have students repeat. Ask students to explain how the sentences differ in meaning. If necessary, help them distinguish the differences.

   Someone hit the car.
   Something hit the car.
   Nothing hit the car.

4. Model the following sentences and have students repeat. Ask students to explain how the sentences differ in meaning. If necessary, help them distinguish the differences.

   Show us a book bag.
   Show us the book bag.
   Show us that book bag.

5. Provide further practice by asking individual students to provide a simple sentence. Have two other students change its meaning by altering one or two words, as shown in the previous steps. Call on other students to explain how the sentences differ in meaning. Give each student an opportunity to both produce a simple sentence and alter a different one.

6. Ensure that all students have ample opportunity for verbal input. Monitor student understanding of this concept and provide individual help when needed.

Lesson 174

In this lesson, students will discuss how sentence meaning changes with slight word variations.

1. Model the following sentences and have students repeat. Ask students to explain how the sentences differ in meaning. If necessary, help them distinguish the differences.

   Maria was here.
   Maria came here.
   Maria stayed here.

2. Model the following sentences and have students repeat. Ask students to explain how the sentences differ in meaning. If necessary, help them distinguish the differences.

   Did anything cause this?
   Did anyone cause this?
   Did anybody cause this?

3. Model the following sentences and have students repeat. Ask students to explain how the sentences differ in meaning. If necessary, help them distinguish the differences.

   We played in the game.
   You played in the game.
   She played in the game.

4. Model and have students repeat another set of sentences. Ask students to explain how the sentences differ in meaning. If necessary, help them distinguish the differences.

   I need some new shoes.
   I want some new shoes.
   I have some new shoes.

5. Provide further practice by asking individual students to provide a simple sentence. Have two other students change its meaning by altering one word, as shown in the previous steps. Call on other students to explain how the sentences differ in meaning. Give each student an opportunity to both produce a simple sentence and alter another one.

6. Ensure that all students have ample opportunity for verbal input. Monitor student understanding of this concept and provide individual help when needed.

Lesson 175

In this lesson, students will review how sentence meaning changes with slight word variations.

1. Have students repeat sentence patterns from steps 1–4 of Lessons 171–174. Discuss how the sentence meanings differ with slight variations. Be sure each student is able to explain differences in meaning for at least one example.

2. Model the following challenge set of sentences and have students repeat. Ask students to explain how the sentences differ. Make sure students correlate the difference between the past and present participle forms.

   Kareem put it away.
   Kareem has put it away.
   Kareem had put it away.

3. Model another challenge set of sentences and have students repeat. Ask students to explain how the sentences differ. Make sure students correlate the difference between the past and present participle forms.

   Martina waited for them to get here.
   Martina has waited for them to get here.
   Martina had waited for them to get here.

4. Use sentence sets above and change the tense to the present and future. Have students repeat each new sentence. Discuss the difference between changing the meaning and changing the tense of a sentence.

5. Call on individual students and provide a simple sentence. Have each student change the tense using present participle (has) and past participle (had). Ask a different student to explain how this affects the meaning.

6. Ensure that all students have ample opportunity for verbal input. Monitor student understanding of this concept and provide individual help when needed.

Lesson 176

In this lesson, students will learn expository speaking.

1. Choose several of the following topics and demonstrate short speeches for students to model.

   My favorite zoo animal is _______ because...
   My favorite pet animal is _______ because...
   My favorite school subject is _______ because...
   My favorite adult is _______ because...
   My favorite day of the week is _______ because...
   My favorite place is _______ because...
   My favorite color is _______ because...
   My favorite vehicle is _______ because...
   My favorite sport is _______ because...
   My favorite food is _______ because...

2. Divide the class into small groups. Give each group a different topic from step 1. Have students take turns expanding on the selected topic. Have students generate a short speech to share with the whole class.

3. Bring the students back together. Have students take turns speaking about their assigned topic. Make this as comfortable as possible. If the classroom structure is flexible, create a big circle and allow students to remain seated while they speak. Note areas in which students need practice.

4. After each student speaks, have other students ask questions. Make sure each student asks a few questions throughout the class.

5. Encourage speakers to respond in complete sentences. Allow students to take their time as they formulate their thoughts.

6. Monitor speeches, providing nurturing assistance and encouragement.

Lesson 177

In this lesson, students will learn expository speaking.

1. Choose several of the following topics and demonstrate short speeches for students to model.

   The funniest TV show is _______ because...
   My favorite thing to cook is _______ because...
   My favorite story is _______ because...
   The hardest thing for me is...
   Next summer, I'd like to...
   I wish that my mother or father could...
   If I won a million dollars, I would...
   When I am alone, I like to...
   To help our school, we need...

2. Divide the class into small groups. Give each group a different topic from step 1. Have students take turns expanding on the selected topic. Have students generate a short speech to share with the whole class.

3. Bring the students back together. Have students take turns speaking about their assigned topic. Make this as comfortable as possible. If the classroom structure is flexible, create a big circle and allow students to remain seated while they speak. Note areas in which students need practice.

4. After each student speaks, have other students ask questions. Make sure each student asks a few questions throughout the class.

5. Encourage speakers to respond in complete sentences. Allow students to take their time as they formulate their thoughts.

6. Monitor speeches, providing nurturing assistance and encouragement.

Lesson 178

In this lesson, students will learn expository speaking.

1. Choose several of the following topics and demonstrate short speeches for students to model.

   One thing I want to learn about is…
   I was so tired because…
   One sport I like to watch on TV is…
   One day, I hope I can…
   Some people are so lucky that they can…
   If I could give somebody a present, I…
   My family's favorite holiday is…
   Once I had a dream about…
   The time I was most scared was when…
   The chores I have to do at home are…

2. Divide the class into small groups. Give each group a different topic from step 1. Have students take turns expanding on the selected topic. Have students generate a short speech to share with the whole class.

3. Bring the students back together. Have students take turns speaking about their assigned topic. Make this as comfortable as possible. If the classroom structure is flexible, create a big circle and allow students to remain seated while they speak. Note areas in which students need practice.

4. After each student speaks, have other students ask questions. Make sure each student asks a few questions throughout the class.

5. Encourage speakers to respond in complete sentences. Allow students to take their time as they formulate their thoughts.

6. Monitor speeches, providing nurturing assistance and encouragement.

Lesson 179

In this lesson, students will learn expository speaking.

1. Choose several of the following topics and demonstrate short speeches for students to model.

    I wish somebody could help me…
    The instrument I would like to play is the…
    I have never ridden on a/an…
    I wish that I could take a trip to…
    The thing that makes me really mad is…
    When I was really little, I would…
    My mother doesn't like…
    A funny thing that happened at school was…
    I wish that doctors could…
    A funny thing that happened at home was…

2. Divide the class into small groups. Give each group a different topic from step 1. Have students take turns expanding on the selected topic. Have students generate a short speech to share with the whole class.

3. Bring the students back together. Have students take turns speaking about their assigned topic. Make this as comfortable as possible. If the classroom structure is flexible, create a big circle and allow students to remain seated while they speak. Note areas in which students need practice.

4. After each student speaks, have other students ask questions. Make sure each student asks a few questions throughout the class.

5. Encourage speakers to respond in complete sentences. Allow students to take their time as they formulate their thoughts.

6. Monitor speeches, providing nurturing assistance and encouragement.

Lesson 180

In this lesson, students will learn expository speaking.

1. Choose several of the following topics and demonstrate short speeches for students to model.

   Tomorrow, I hope that we can…
   On holidays, my family likes to eat…
   If I were a grandmother/father, I would…
   If I could have a garden, I would plant….
   I wish I had a house that was…
   The person who makes me laugh the most is…
   My mother doesn't like it if…
   I like/don't like babies because…
   On my first day of school, I thought…
   If I could be anybody on TV, I would be…

2. Divide the class into small groups. Give each group a different topic from step 1. Have students take turns expanding on the selected topic. Have students generate a short speech to share with the whole class.

3. Bring the students back together. Have students take turns speaking about their assigned topic. Make this as comfortable as possible. If the classroom structure is flexible, create a big circle and allow students to remain seated while they speak. Note areas in which students need practice.

4. After each student speaks, have other students ask questions. Make sure each student asks a few questions throughout the class.

5. Encourage speakers to respond in complete sentences. Allow students to take their time as they formulate their thoughts.

6. Monitor speeches, providing nurturing assistance and encouragement.

Lesson 181

Materials: index cards

In this lesson, students will learn additional indefinite pronouns (**a lot, all, both, each, either, few, lots, many, neither, one, several, some**).

1. Model the following sentences and have students repeat. Choose specific students to stand after each sentence to demonstrate meaning.

Either of us will stand.	All of us will stand.	Several of us will stand.
Neither of us will stand.	Some of us will stand.	One of us will stand.
Each of us will stand.	Many of us will stand.	Lots of us will stand.
Both of us will stand.	Few of us will stand.	A lot of us will stand.

2. Divide the class into small groups. Model the sentences from step 1. Have each group demonstrate the meaning while repeating each sentence.

3. Repeat the sentences from step 1 using the modal: **must** (e.g., say: Either of us must stand). Have students repeat new sentences. Emphasize the difference in meaning that results from changing the helping verb.

4. Say: A few of you must stand. Few of you must stand. Model several sentences using **few** and **a few**. Have students repeat. Point out the difference between **few** and the other indefinite pronouns. Explain that English speakers do **not** say "a neither," "a many," "an all," but "a few" is correct.

5. Review previously taught indefinite pronouns (**anybody, anyone, anything, no one, nobody, nothing, somebody, someone, something**) and the ones learned in this lesson by writing all 21 indefinite pronouns on individual index cards. Hold up cards and say each word aloud. Have students repeat each indefinite pronoun. Distribute cards; ask all students to generate a sentence with the indefinite pronoun shown on their cards. If an error is made, model the correct production and have students repeat. Save the index cards for use in subsequent lessons.

6. Encourage students to continue practicing usage of indefinite pronouns.

Lesson 182

Materials: index cards from Lesson 181

In this lesson, students will review indefinite pronouns (**a lot, all, anybody, anyone, anything, both, each, either, few, lots, many, neither, no one, nobody, nothing, one, several, some, somebody, someone, something**).

1. Model the following sentences and have students repeat.

   Either of us can wave.
   Neither of us can wave.
   Each of us can wave.
   Both of us can wave.
   All of us can wave.
   Some of us can wave.
   Many of us can wave.
   Few of us can wave.
   Several of us can wave.
   One of us can wave.
   Lots of us can wave.
   A lot of us can wave.

2. Divide the class into small groups. Model the sentences from step 1. Have each group demonstrate the meaning while repeating each sentence.

3. Model the following sentences and have students repeat.

   Either of them will sit.
   Neither of them will sit.
   Each of them will sit.
   Both of them will sit.
   All of them will sit.
   Some of them will sit.
   Many of them will sit.
   Few of them will sit.
   Several of them will sit.
   One of them will sit.
   Lots of them will sit.
   A lot of them will sit.

   Emphasize the difference in meaning between these sentences and the sentences modeled in step 1 that results from changing the helping verb and the pronoun.

4. Say: Few of you can wave. Have students repeat. Next, say: A few of you can wave. Have students repeat. Discuss the differences in these two statements. Emphasize **limitation** for the former and **permission** for the latter. Generate several more examples to illustrate the difference in meaning.

5. Review all indefinite pronouns by holding up the index cards created for Lesson 181 and saying each word aloud. Have students repeat each indefinite pronoun. Distribute cards; ask all students to generate a sentence with the indefinite pronoun shown on their cards. If an error is made, model the correct production and have students repeat.

6. Encourage students to continue practicing usage of indefinite pronouns.

Lesson 183

Materials: index cards from Lesson 181

In this lesson, students will review indefinite pronouns (**a lot, all, anybody, anyone, anything, both, each, either, few, lots, many, neither, no one, nobody, nothing, one, several, some, somebody, someone, something**).

1. Model the following sentences and have students repeat.

   Either of us could read.
   Neither of us could read.
   Each of us could read.
   Both of us could read.
   All of us could read.
   Some of us could read.
   Many of us could read.
   Few of us could read.
   Several of us could read.
   One of us could read.
   Lots of us could read.
   A lot of us could read.

2. Divide the class into small groups. Model the sentences from step 1. Have each group demonstrate the meaning while repeating each sentence.

3. Model the following sentences and have students repeat.

   Either of us would write.
   Neither of us would write.
   Each of us would write.
   Both of us would write.
   All of us would write.
   Some of us would write.
   Many of us would write.
   Few of us would write.
   Several of us would write.
   One of us would write.
   Lots of us would write.
   A lot of us would write.

   Discuss the difference in meaning between **could** and **would**.

4. Generate examples to illustrate the difference in meaning between **could** and **would**. Ask students to explain the difference in the examples.

5. Review all indefinite pronouns by holding up the index cards created for Lesson 181 and saying each word aloud. Have students repeat each indefinite pronoun. Distribute cards; ask all students to generate a sentence with the indefinite pronoun shown on their cards. If an error is made, model the correct production and have students repeat.

6. Encourage students to continue practicing usage of indefinite pronouns.

Lesson 184

Materials: index cards from Lesson 181

In this lesson, students will review indefinite pronouns (**a lot, all, anybody, anyone, anything, both, each, either, few, lots, many, neither, no one, nobody, nothing, one, several, some, somebody, someone, something**).

1. Model the following sentences and have students repeat.

   Either of us should turn.
   Neither of us should turn.
   Each of us should turn.
   Both of us should turn.
   All of us should turn.
   Some of us should turn.
   Many of us should turn.
   Few of us should turn.
   Several of us should turn.
   One of us should turn.
   Lots of us should turn.
   A lot of us should turn.

2. Divide the class into small groups. Model the sentences from step 1. Have each group demonstrate the meaning while repeating each sentence.

3. Model the following sentences and have students repeat.

   Either of them will eat.
   Neither of them will eat.
   Each of them will eat.
   Both of them will eat.
   All of them will eat.
   Some of them will eat.
   Many of them will eat.
   Few of them will eat.
   Several of them will eat.
   One of them will eat.
   Lots of them will eat.
   A lot of them will eat.

   Emphasize the difference in meaning between these sentences and the sentences modeled in step 1 that results from changing the helping verb and the pronoun.

4. Generate examples to illustrate the difference in meaning between **should** and **will**. Have students repeat and explain the difference between the paired sentences.

5. Review all indefinite pronouns by holding up the index cards created for Lesson 181 and saying each word aloud. Have students repeat each indefinite pronoun. Distribute cards; ask all students to generate a sentence with the indefinite pronoun shown on their cards. If an error is made, model the correct production and have students repeat.

6. Encourage students to continue practicing usage of indefinite pronouns.

Lesson 185

Materials: index cards from Lesson 181

In this lesson, students will review indefinite pronouns (**a lot, all, anybody, anyone, anything, both, each, either, few, lots, many, neither, no one, nobody, nothing, one, several, some, somebody, someone, something**).

1. Use index cards from Lesson 181 to review indefinite pronouns. Say each pronoun and have students repeat.
2. Hold up two cards at a time. Call on individual students to explain the differences between the two indefinite pronouns shown. Repeat until each student has had an opportunity to explicate.
3. Use index cards to prompt individual students to generate sentences containing indefinite pronouns. Make sure students use the pronouns correctly. If errors are made in production, model correct sentence formation and have students repeat.
4. Use index cards to prompt individual students to generate questions containing indefinite pronouns. Have another student respond. Make sure questions are answered with the correct form of the indefinite pronoun and helping verb. Give each student an opportunity to form a question and a response.
5. Use index cards to prompt individual students to generate questions and answers containing indefinite pronouns. Have students answer their own questions. Make sure students use pronouns correctly in sentences. Give each student an opportunity to form a question and a response.
6. Encourage students to continue practicing usage of indefinite pronouns.

Lesson 186

Materials: common objects (e.g., desks, notebooks, pencils, sweaters)

In this lesson, students will learn positive, comparative (**-er**), and superlative (**-est**) adjective inflections.

1. Model a sentence using a comparative adjective (e.g., say: This pencil is shorter than that one). Next, model a sentence using the superlative form of the same adjective (e.g., say: That pencil is the shortest). Have students repeat each sentence. Model several sets of sentences; use objects to help demonstrate.

2. Model sentences using the positive, comparative, and superlative adjective sets below. Have students repeat each sentence.

   safe, safer, safest
   new, newer, newest
   red, redder, reddest
   warm, warmer, warmest
   plain, plainer, plainest
   old, older, oldest
   cold, colder, coldest
   hot, hotter, hottest

3. Ask students to name nouns the following adjectives could be describing: **big, dark, early, late, light, little, narrow, short, tall, wide**. Make a list of the nouns generated and post the list where all students can read it.

4. Have students produce sentences using the adjectives from step 3 in either the positive, comparative, or superlative form. Encourage students to use the list of nouns generated in step 3 to help them. Demonstrate the use of any adjectives the students are having a difficult time using correctly.

5. Using the following list, ask individual students to pick one adjective and generate a set of three sentences using the positive, comparative, and superlative forms: **funny, hard, large, loud, mean, pretty, quiet, sad, small, soft, strong, sweet, ugly, weak**. If students are having a difficult time creating sentences, encourage them to use the nouns generated in step 3 as the subjects. Be sure that all students are able to generate several sentences using positive, comparative, and superlative adjectives.

6. Encourage students to practice using positive, comparative, and superlative adjective forms throughout the day.

Lesson 187

In this lesson, students will reinforce learning of positive, comparative (**-er**), and superlative (**-est**) adjective inflections.

1. Model a sentence using an adjective (e.g., say: Maria is short). Form a sentence with the comparative form of the same adjective (e.g., say: Maria is shorter than Dominic). Next, model a sentence using the superlative form of the same adjective (e.g., say: Maria is the shortest girl in her family). Have students repeat each sentence. Model several sets of sentences.

2. Model sentences using the positive, comparative, and superlative adjective sets below. Have students repeat each sentence.

   wide, wider, widest
   cool, cooler, coolest
   great, greater, greatest
   young, younger, youngest
   lovely, lovelier, loveliest
   warm, warmer, warmest
   tame, tamer, tamest
   wild, wilder, wildest

3. Ask students to name nouns the following adjectives could be describing: **bright, clear, dull, happy, lazy, pure, quick, ripe, slim, slow, wise**. Make a list of the nouns generated and post the list where all students can read it.

4. Have students produce sentences using the adjectives from step 3 in either the positive, comparative, or superlative form. Encourage students to use the list of nouns generated in step 3 to help them. Demonstrate the use of any adjectives the students are having a difficult time using correctly.

5. Using the following list, ask individual students to pick one adjective and generate a set of three sentences using the positive, comparative, and superlative forms: **cute, deep, high, kind, long, low, plain, proud, rare, steep**. If students are having a difficult time creating sentences, encourage them to use the nouns generated in step 3 as subjects. Be sure that all students are able to generate several sentences using positive, comparative, and superlative adjectives.

6, Encourage students to practice using positive, comparative, and superlative adjective forms throughout the day.

Lesson 188

In this lesson, students will learn how to create comparative and superlative adjective inflections using **more** and **most**.

1. Explain to the class that an adjective having more than two syllables (and sometimes only two syllables) requires the use of **more** and **most** to create comparative and superlative adjective inflections. Model sentences using the positive, comparative, and superlative forms of the following adjectives: **beautiful, common, courteous, famous, generous, numerous** (e.g., say: Lee is a courteous student. Lee is more courteous than Paul. Lee is the most courteous person I know). Have students repeat each sentence using all adjectives. Continue to model sentences.

2. Model sentences using the positive, comparative, and superlative forms of the following adjectives: **dependable, helpful, interesting, reliable, thoughtful, valuable,** as in step 1. Have students repeat each sentence.

3. Review monosyllabic adjectives. Provide students with adjectives from Lessons 186 or 187. Have students take turns generating sentences using either the positive, comparative, or superlative form of each adjective. Each student should have an opportunity to create and share several different sentences.

4. Provide students with an adjective from Lessons 186 or 187 (**big, bright, clear, cold, cool, cute, dark, deep, dull, early, funny, great, happy, hard, high, hot, kind, large, late, lazy, light, little, long, loud, lovely, low, mean, narrow, new, old, plain, pretty, proud, pure, quick, quiet, rare, red, ripe, sad, safe, short, slim, slow, small, soft, steep, strong, sweet, tall, tame, ugly, warm, weak, wide, wild, wise, young**). Have students take turns generating sentence sets using the positive, comparative, and superlative forms of each adjective. Each student should create and share at least three sets of sentences.

5. Provide students with three adjectives from steps 1 or 2. Have students take turns generating sentence sets using the positive, comparative, and superlative forms of each adjective. Each student should create and share at least one set of sentences.

6. Encourage students to practice using positive, comparative, and superlative adjective forms throughout the day.

Lesson 189

In this lesson, students will learn about irregular inflections for comparative and superlative forms of adjectives.

1. Model sentences using the positive, comparative, and superlative forms of the following irregular adjective sets: **bad, worse, worst; good, better, best; little, less, least; many, more, most.** Have students repeat each sentence.
2. Have individual students generate sentence sets using each of the adjectives in step 1. Prompt each student by modeling a new sentence (e.g., say: He is a good soccer player.). Then call on each student to form two sentences, one with the comparative form and one with the superlative form of that adjective. Make sure each student creates two sentences for each adjective.
3. Review adjectives requiring **more** and **most** for comparative and superlative forms. Have students generate a list of adjectives that require **more** and **most**.
4. Model sentences using the positive, comparative, and superlative forms of the following adjectives: **beautiful, common, courteous, dependable, famous, generous, helpful, interesting, numerous, reliable, thoughtful, valuable.** Have students repeat each sentence.
5. Have students generate sentences using the positive, comparative, and superlative forms of the adjectives listed in step 4. Make sure each student creates at least four different sets.
6. Be sure each student is able to generate several sentences using the positive, comparative, and superlative forms, both regular and irregular. Encourage students to produce sentences using all forms of adjectives throughout the day.

Lesson 190

In this lesson, students will review positive, comparative, and superlative adjective inflection forms (both regular and irregular).

1. Call on individual students to generate a set of sentences that contains all three inflection forms of the following adjectives: **big, cute, deep, early, hard, high, kind, late, little, long, low, plain, proud, rare, soft, steep, sad, wide**. Make sure each student has an opportunity to create at least two sets of sentences.

2. Call on individual students to generate a set of sentences that contains all three inflection forms of the following adjectives: **bright, clear, dark, dull, happy, large, lazy, light, loud, pretty, pure, quick, quiet, ripe, short, slim, slow, small, tall, ugly, wise**. Give each student an opportunity to demonstrate mastery.

3. Call on individual students to generate a set of sentences that contains all three inflection forms of the following adjectives: **beautiful, common, courteous, dependable, famous, generous, helpful, interesting, numerous, reliable, thoughtful, valuable**. Make sure each student understands the use of **more** and **most** with these adjectives. Give each student an opportunity to demonstrate mastery.

4. Call on individual students to generate sentence sets that contain all three inflection forms using the following adjectives: **bad, good, little, many**. Make sure each student has an opportunity to use all four adjectives in a set of sentences. Repetition is important to grasp irregular adjective forms.

5. Prompt students with an adjective from steps 1–4. Call on individual students to generate sentence sets containing the positive, comparative, and superlative forms. Be sure to mix the order of the adjectives. If students use an adjective incorrectly, model the correct sentence construction and have students repeat.

6. Encourage students to practice making comparisons during the school day and using these adjective forms to create sentences.

Lesson 191

Materials: picture cards (vehicles: airplane, ambulance, bicycle, boat, bus, cab, canoe, car, fire engine, garbage truck, helicopter, jet, motorcycle, police car, race car, rowboat, sailboat, ship, spaceship, submarine, train, truck, van)

In this lesson, students will learn how prepositional phrases modify nouns and pronouns.

1. Each of the following sentence fragments demonstrates how prepositional phrases act as adjectives by modifying the object that precedes it. Read the fragments aloud and prompt students with the question that follows. Have students answer the question with the correct prepositional phrase.

stimulus: the flowers **in the yard**; which flowers?	response: *"in the yard"*
stimulus: the students **in the class**; which students?	response: *"in the class"*
stimulus: the girl **on the boat**; which girl?	response: *"on the boat"*
stimulus: the house **down the street**; which house?	response: *"down the street"*
stimulus: the story **of his life**; which story?	response: *"of his life"*

2. Read the following fragments aloud to show how prepositional phrases begin with a preposition and end with the object of the preposition. Prompt students with the question that the phrase answers.

stimulus: the desk **beside me**; which desk?	response: *"beside me"*
stimulus: the gift **from them**; which gift?	response: *"from them"*
stimulus: the girl **between us**; which girl?	response: *"between us"*
stimulus: the books **near her**; which books?	response: *"near her"*
stimulus: the story **about him**; which story?	response: *"about him"*

3. Hold up a picture card and provide a prepositional phrase. Have students generate a sentence using the vehicle as the subject and a prepositional phrase as the modifier, (e.g., hold up the **boat** and say: On the water. Students may respond: *"The boat sails on the water")*. Have students repeat each sentence. Use all picture cards; give each student several opportunities to form sentences. If a mistake is made, model the correct production and have students repeat.

4. Hold up a picture card and provide several prepositional phrases. Have individual students generate several sentences using that vehicle with each prepositional phrase.

stimulus: in the yard	response: *"We have a car in the yard."*
stimulus: on the street	response: *"There is a car on the street."*
stimulus: next to the garage	response: *"There is a car next to the garage."*

   Have students repeat each sentence. Give each student several opportunities to form sentences.

5. Hold up a picture card and ask a student to provide a prepositional phrase. Have another student generate a sentence with the vehicle as the subject and the prepositional phrase as the modifier. Give each student several opportunities to generate prepositional phrases and sentences.

6. Have students practice creating sentences with prepositional phrases throughout the day.

Lesson 192

Materials: picture cards (tools: ax, broom, brush, bucket, compass, fire extinguisher, flashlight, glasses, hammer, hose, ladder, microscope, mop, pick, rake, saw, scale, shovel, stapler, telephone, thermometer, yardstick)

In this lesson, students will learn how prepositional phrases modify verbs.

1. The prepositional phrases in the following sentences modify the verbs by telling **how**, **when**, **where**, or **why** the action is happening. Read the sentence aloud and prompt students with the question each phrase answers. Have the class respond with the prepositional phrase.

   stimulus: I read with help. How? — response: *"with help"*
   stimulus: I read before noon. When? — response: *"before noon"*
   stimulus: I read under the tree. Where? — response: *"under the tree"*
   stimulus: I read with the class. How? — response: *"with the class"*
   stimulus: I read during recess. When? — response: *"during recess"*
   stimulus: I read for fun. Why? — response: *"for fun"*

2. Continue demonstrating how prepositional phrases act as adjectives. (*Note: When the object is a pronoun, an objective pronoun is used.*) Read each sentence aloud and prompt students with the question each phrase answers. Have the class respond with the prepositional phrase.

   stimulus: I left after school. When? — response: *"after school"*
   stimulus: Dad sat between us. Where? — response: *"between us"*
   stimulus: It crept under us. Where? — response: *"under us"*

3. Hold up tool picture cards and provide several prepositional phrases. Have individual students generate several sentences using the same tool with different prepositional phrases.

   stimulus: on the desk — response: *"I see the stapler on the desk."*
   stimulus: in her hand — response: *"She has a stapler in her hand."*

   Have all students repeat the sentence. Make sure each student has several opportunities to create sentences.

4. Continue to supply prepositional phrases while holding up tool picture cards. Have individual students use both elements to generate a sentence. Make sure all students are able to create complete sentences using prepositional phrases.

5. Continue to supply prepositional phrases while holding up tool picture cards. Have individual students use both elements to generate a sentence. Have the class repeat each sentence created. Ask what question is answered by the phrase (**how, when, where, why**). Focus on fluent sentence production. Make sure all students are able to create complete sentences using prepositional phrases.

6. Encourage students to practice creating sentences with prepositional phrases throughout the day.

Lesson 193

Materials: picture cards (sports equipment: arrows, baseball, basketball, bat, fin, football, glove [baseball], skateboard, soccer ball)

In this lesson, students will continue learning about prepositional phrases as modifiers.

1. Each of the following prepositional phrases tells **how, how many, what kind of, when, where, which,** or **why** about the action or subject. Read the sentence aloud and prompt students with the questions that follow. Have students answer with the correct prepositional phrase.

   stimulus: She succeeded by hard work. How? response: *"by hard work"*
   stimulus: He planted about a dozen trees. How many? response: *"about a dozen"*
   stimulus: I like gum with sugar. What kind of gum? response: *"with sugar"*
   stimulus: We bought the car on sale. Which car? response: *"on sale"*
   stimulus: I walked after sunset. When? response: *"after sunset"*
   stimulus: Li goes into the house. Where? response: *"into the house"*

2. Review how prepositional phrases begin with a preposition and end with the object of the preposition. (*Note: When the object is a pronoun, an objective pronoun is used.*) Prompt students with sentences containing prepositional phrases. Have students repeat each sentence. Ask students to identify the prepositional phrase and the question that each phrase answers. For example, say: He looks above me. Students should say: *"above me"* (for the prepositional phrase) and *"where"* (for the question it answers). Use different prepositional phrases, giving each student several opportunities to identify them.

3. Hold up a picture card and provide a prepositional phrase. Have individual students generate a sentence using the pictured object as the subject and the given prepositional phrase as the modifier. Have students repeat each sentence. Scramble picture cards and prepositional phrases. Give each student several opportunities to form sentences. If a mistake is made, model the correct production and have students repeat.

4. Hold up a picture card and provide several prepositional phrases. Have individual students generate several sentences using the pictured object with each prepositional phrase. Have all students repeat each sentence. Scramble picture cards and prepositional phrases. Give each student several opportunities to create sentences.

5. Hold up a card and ask a student to provide a prepositional phrase. Have a different student create a sentence using the pictured object as the subject and the given prepositional phrase as the modifier. After each sentence, ask students what question the prepositional phrase answers. Make sure each student can create sentences with prepositional phrases. Focus on rapid, fluent sentence production.

6. Encourage students to practice creating sentences with prepositional phrases throughout the day.

Lesson 194

Materials: magazines and books with pictures

In this lesson, students will practice prepositional phrases demonstrating **how, how many, what kind of, when, where, which,** and **why**.

1. Display pictures from magazines or books. Ask students to name the objects in the picture. Call on individual students to generate a sentence containing two of the objects, one as the subject and one as the object of the preposition (e.g., "*The woman is standing near the house*").

2. Provide a few stimulus prepositions. (*Note: See Appendix F for a list of prepositions.*) Have students generate a list of prepositions to help with sentence construction. Write out the list where students can refer to it.

3. Have students select three pictures from any book or magazine. Call on individual students to share sentences containing prepositional phrases describing the pictures. Refer students to the preposition list from step 2, if needed. If students generate a sentence without a prepositional phrase, model the sentence correctly and have students repeat.

4. Have students choose three more pictures and create more sentences. Each sentence should contain a prepositional phrase showing the relationship between objects in the picture. Refer students to the preposition list, if needed. Help students identify which question is answered by their prepositional phrases.

5. Focus on rapid, fluent sentence generation. Make sure all students are able to create complete sentences using prepositional phrases.

6. Encourage students to practice creating sentences with prepositional phrases throughout the day.

Lesson 195

Materials: picture cards from Lessons 191–193 (sports equipment; tools; vehicles)

In this lesson, students will review prepositional phrases that demonstrate **how, how many, what kind of, when, where, which,** and **why**. Use the list of prepositions from Appendix F to extend the review.

1. Review all the questions prepositional phrases can answer. Prompt individual students with a prepositional phrase and have them respond with the question it answers. Then, ask them to use that phrase in a sentence. Repeat until each student has had several opportunities to form sentences.

2. Read the following sentence fragments and have individual students identify the prepositional phrase in each, then use the prepositional phrase in a complete sentence. Emphasize that each phrase answers **which**.

the flowers in the yard	the students in the class	the girl on the boat
the problem on the board	the house down the street	the story of his life
the desk beside me	the gift from them	the girl between us
the books near her	the story about him	the seat by you

3. Provide individual students with one of the following or other prepositional phrases and have them use the phrases in a sentence. Ask the student what question the phrase answers. Repeat until each student has had several opportunities to form sentences with prepositional phrases.

with help	before noon	behind the door
near Denver	on the desk	with the class
for my brother	in the winter	around the bend

4. Provide individual students with one of the following or other prepositional phrases and have them use the phrases in a sentence. Ask different students what question the phrase answers. Repeat until each student has had several opportunities to form sentences with prepositional phrases.

above the building	in the class	on the dock
against the rules	after the movie	during our break
about nine	before art class	near my bike
behind the garage	with great sadness	by my cat

5. Distribute picture cards of sports equipment, tools, and vehicles to each student. Have students describe their pictures by generating a sentence containing a prepositional phrase. Have different students tell what question the phrase answers. Continue until all students show comprehension of prepositional phrases.

6. Encourage students to practice creating sentences with prepositional phrases throughout the day.

Lesson 196

In this lesson, students will learn reflexive pronouns (**herself, himself, itself, myself, ourselves, themselves, yourself, yourselves**).

1. Model the following sentences and have students repeat.

    I blamed myself.
    She hid herself.
    It stopped itself.
    You saved yourselves.
    You helped yourself.
    He stopped himself.
    We drew ourselves.
    They saw themselves.

2. Use the sentences from step 1 to demonstrate how sentences can be expanded by adding prepositional phrases. Have students repeat each new sentence.

    I blamed myself **for the trouble**.
    She hid herself **from others**.
    It stopped itself **from flooding**.
    You saved yourselves **from work**.
    You helped yourself **to water**.
    He stopped himself **in time**.
    We drew ourselves **in art class**.
    They saw themselves **in the photo**.

3. Prompt students with a prepositional phrase. Have individual students generate sentences with that prepositional phrase. Ask different students what question that phrase answers. Give each student an opportunity to produce a sentence.

4. List the reflexive pronouns where students can read them. Prompt students with a prepositional phrase. Ask individual students to generate sentences containing the prompted prepositional phrase and a reflexive pronoun.

    stimulus: in the morning — response: *"She dressed **herself** in the morning."*
    stimulus: with hard work — response: *"We taught **ourselves** with hard work."*
    stimulus: on the boat — response: *"He injured **himself** on the boat."*

    Answers will vary. Focus on correct use of reflexive pronouns and prepositions. Make sure each student has several opportunities to generate a sentence.

5. Have individual students create complete sentences using prepositional phrases and reflexive pronouns. Refer students to the list of reflexive pronouns. Have all students repeat sentences. Make sure each student has several opportunities to generate a sentence.

6. Encourage students to use reflexive pronouns throughout the day.

Lesson 197

In this lesson, students will practice reflexive pronouns (**herself, himself, itself, myself, ourselves, themselves, yourself, yourselves**).

1. Model the following sentences and have students repeat.

   I broke myself.
   You hit yourself.
   They gave themselves.
   We taught ourselves.
   You found yourselves.
   She invited herself.
   He led himself.
   It lent itself.

2. Use the sentences from step 1 to demonstrate how sentences can be expanded by adding prepositional phrases. Have students repeat each new sentence.

   I broke myself **of the habit**.
   You hit yourself **in the arm**.
   They gave themselves **as an example**.
   We taught ourselves **from the video**.
   You found yourselves **at the museum**.
   She invited herself **to the party**.
   He led himself **off the mountain**.
   It lent itself **to a smile**.

3. Prompt students with a prepositional phrase. Have individual students generate sentences with that prepositional phrase. Ask different students what question that phrase answers. Give each student an opportunity to produce a sentence.

4. List the reflexive pronouns where students can read them. Prompt students with a prepositional phrase. Ask individual students to generate sentences containing the prompted prepositional phrase and a reflexive pronoun.

   stimulus: between us — response: *"They found **themselves** between us."*
   stimulus: after sunset — response: *"She covered **herself** after sunset."*
   stimulus: before school — response: *"He bathed **himself** before school."*

   Answers will vary. Focus on correct use of reflexive pronouns and prepositions. Make sure each student has several opportunities to generate sentences.

5. Have individual students create complete sentences using prepositional phrases and reflexive pronouns. Refer students to the list of reflexive pronouns. Have all students repeat sentences. Make sure each student has several opportunities to generate sentences.

6. Encourage students to use reflexive pronouns throughout the day.

Lesson 198

In this lesson, students will learn intensive pronouns (**herself, himself, itself, myself, ourselves, themselves, yourself, yourselves**). (*Note: The words appear in the same form as the reflexive pronouns. Focus on the difference in* ***function*** *throughout the lesson. Students need to be able to produce sentences with the correct use of both reflexive and intensive pronouns.*)

1. Model the following sentences and have students repeat.

   I myself wrote this.
   He himself was the one.
   You yourselves saw it.
   She herself has it.
   You yourself earned this.
   It itself stopped ringing.
   They themselves did it.
   We ourselves are responsible.

2. Prompt individual students with the sentences from step 1. Ask each student to expand the sentence by adding a prepositional phrase. Have all students repeat each sentence. Allow each student an opportunity to expand a sentence using a prepositional phrase.

3. Model the following sentences and have students repeat.

   You yourselves saw it before school.
   He himself was the one in red.
   You yourself earned this for us.
   She herself has it with her.
   She herself grew these at home.
   They themselves did it in fun.
   I myself wrote this for class.
   We ourselves are on time.

   Prompt students with one of the sentences and have individual students form a new sentence by changing the verb and prepositional phrase. Give each student an opportunity to produce a new sentence.

4. Prompt students with pronoun pairs (e.g., I, myself). Ask individual students to generate sentences containing an intensive pronoun and a prepositional phrase. Focus on correct use of intensive pronouns and prepositions. Make sure each student has several opportunities to generate a sentence.

5. Prompt students with a pronoun. Have individual students create a complete sentence containing the pronoun as the subject, a prepositional phrase, and an intensive pronoun. Have a list of intensive pronouns in front of the class to which students may refer. Have all students repeat each sentence. Make sure each student has several opportunities to generate sentences.

6. Encourage students to use intensive pronouns throughout the day.

Lesson 199

In this lesson, students will practice intensive pronouns (**herself, himself, itself, myself, ourselves, themselves, yourself, yourselves**).

1. Model the following sentences and have students repeat.

   I myself ate this.
   He himself laughed.
   You yourselves swam.
   She herself finished the book.
   You yourself stayed until the end.
   It itself fell apart.
   They themselves fell down.
   We ourselves found the prize.

2. Prompt individual students with the sentences from step 1. Ask each to expand the sentence by adding a prepositional phrase. Have all students repeat each sentence. Allow each student an opportunity to expand a sentence using a prepositional phrase.

3. Model the following sentences and have students repeat.

   You yourselves played before lunch.
   He himself read it to you.
   She herself sang in the auditorium.
   We ourselves did it for him.
   They themselves had one for dinner.
   She herself gave it to me.
   You yourself stayed until the end.
   I myself carried it to school.

   Prompt students with one of the sentences and have individual students form a new sentence by changing the verb and prepositional phrase. Give each student an opportunity to produce a new sentence.

4. Prompt students with pronoun pairs (e.g., I, myself). Ask individual students to generate sentences containing an intensive pronoun and a prepositional phrase. Focus on correct use of intensive pronouns and prepositions. Make sure each student has several opportunities to generate sentences.

5. Prompt students with a pronoun. Have individual students create a complete sentence containing the pronoun as the subject, a prepositional phrase, and an intensive pronoun. Have a list of intensive pronouns in front of the class to which students may refer. Have all students repeat sentences. Make sure each student has several opportunities to generate sentences.

6. Encourage students to use intensive pronouns throughout the day.

Lesson 200

In this lesson, students will practice reflexive and intensive pronouns (**herself, himself, itself, myself, ourselves, themselves, yourself, yourselves**). *(Note: Both pronouns appear in the same form. Be sure to emphasize the difference in* ***function*** *between reflexive and intensive pronouns.)*

1. Model the following sentences and have students repeat.

   I myself wrote this story for class.
   He himself stayed at home.
   You yourselves saw it from here.
   She herself has been near it.
   You helped yourself to a drink.
   They themselves sat under it.
   I blamed myself for the trouble.
   She herself cooked these in her oven.
   You yourself earned this for us.
   It stopped itself from flooding.
   They themselves did it without help.
   We ourselves will try for it.
   He stopped himself on time.
   She hid herself from her friend.
   We drew ourselves in art class.
   You left yourselves in danger.

2. Prompt individual students with sentences from step 1 and a pronoun. Ask each to create a new sentence by using the new pronoun. For example, say: He stopped himself on time. They.... The student should respond: *"They stopped themselves on time."* Have all students repeat the new sentence. Scramble pronouns with each sentence and repeat until each student has several opportunities to create new sentences.

3. List the reflexive pronouns where students can read them. Prompt students with a prepositional phrase. Ask individual students to generate sentences containing the prompted prepositional phrase and a reflexive pronoun.

   stimulus: in the morning — response: *"She dressed **herself** in the morning."*

4. List the intensive pronouns where students can read them. Prompt students with a sentence fragment. Ask individual students to generate sentences containing the prompted sentence fragment and an intensive pronoun.

   stimulus: are responsible — response: *"We **ourselves** are responsible."*

5. Have individual students create complete sentences containing reflexive and intensive pronouns. Refer students to the lists, if needed. Have all students repeat each sentence. Make sure each student has several opportunities to generate sentences.

6. Encourage students to use reflexive and intensive pronouns throughout the day.

Lesson 201

In this lesson, students will learn adverbs of time.

1. Explain to students that adverbs can modify verbs by describing **how, how little, how much, when,** and **where**. Model the following adverbs that tell **when: again, already, always, before, early, ever, first, frequently, immediately, late, never, now, occasionally, often, seldom, sometimes, soon**. Use each adverb in a sentence and have students repeat.

2. Ask students to name some things they **always** do. Have each student generate a sentence using **always**. Have the class repeat each sentence. Make sure every student produces at least one sentence.

3. Repeat the exercise outlined in step 2 for each adverb listed in step 1. Make sure students understand the meaning of the adverb before asking them to generate sentences. Have the class repeat each sentence. If a student makes a mistake, model the correct sentence and have the student repeat. Focus on correct use of adverbs, rather than prescriptive grammar rules.

4. Prompt students with adverbs from step 1. Have individual students use the adverbs in complete sentences. Scramble adverbs; make sure each student has a few opportunities to form sentences.

5. Prompt students with **when** questions. Have each student answer using an adverb in a complete sentence. List adverbs where students can read them.

stimulus: When do you like to wake up?	response: *"I like to wake up late."*
stimulus: When do you watch television?	response: *"I never watch television."*
stimulus: How often do you go to the movies?	response: *"I go to the movies often."*

   *(Note: In Lessons 192 and 193, students learned ways in which prepositional phrases function like adverbs. Steer questions away from answers with prepositional phrases. If a student does answer with a prepositional phrase, emphasize the difference between a prepositional phrase and the adverbs listed in step 1. Give examples of words that function as adverbs and prepositions, such as **before**.)*

6. Encourage students to frequently ask themselves **when** questions throughout the day and generate sentences using adverbs from this lesson.

Lesson 202

In this lesson, students will learn adverbs of place.

1. Remind students that adverbs can modify verbs by describing **how, how little, how much, when,** and **where**. Model the following adverbs that tell **where: above, around, away, back, below, beyond, down, far, forth, forward, here, in, inside, out, outside, there, up, within**. Use each adverb in a sentence and have students repeat.

2. Ask students to name things they do **outside**. Have each student generate a sentence using **outside**. Have the class repeat each sentence. Make sure every student produces at least one sentence.

3. Repeat the exercise outlined in step 2 for each adverb listed in step 1. Make sure students understand the meaning of the adverb before asking them to generate sentences. Have the class repeat each sentence. If a student makes a mistake, model the correct sentence and have the student repeat. Focus on the correct use of adverbs, rather than prescriptive grammar rules.

4. Prompt students with adverbs from step 1. Have individual students use the given adverb in a complete sentence. Scramble adverbs; make sure each student has a few opportunities to form sentences.

5. Prompt students with **where** questions. Have each student answer using an adverb in a complete sentence. Have a list of the adverbs in front of the class to which students may refer.

stimulus: Where do you study?	response: *"I study here."*
stimulus: Where is his book?	response: *"His book is inside."*
stimulus: Where do you eat lunch?	response: *"I eat lunch outside."*

   (Note: In Lessons 192 and 193, students learned ways in which prepositional phrases function like adverbs. Steer questions away from answers with prepositional phrases. If a student does answer with a prepositional phrase, emphasize the difference between a prepositional phrase and the adverbs listed in step 1. Give examples of words that function as adverbs and prepositions, such as ***in.****)*

6. Encourage students to frequently ask themselves **where** questions throughout the day and generate sentences using adverbs from this lesson.

Lesson 203

In this lesson, students will learn adverbs of manner.

1. Remind students that adverbs can modify verbs by describing **how, how little, how much, when,** and **where**. Model the following adverbs that tell **how: bravely, carefully, cheerfully, easily, eagerly, expertly, fast, happily, hard, honestly, politely, quickly, quietly, seriously, slowly, smoothly, softly, well**. Use each adverb in a sentence and have students repeat.

2. Have students discuss what it means to be **honest**. Ask students to name things that can be done honestly. Have each student generate a sentence using **honest**. Have the class repeat each sentence. Make sure every student produces at least one sentence.

3. Repeat the exercise outlined in step 2 for each adverb listed in step 1. Make sure students understand the meaning of the adverb before asking them to generate sentences. Have the class repeat each sentence. If a student makes a mistake, model the correct sentence and have the student repeat. Focus on correct use of adverbs, rather than prescriptive grammar rules.

4. Prompt students with adverbs from step 1. Have individual students use the given adverb in a complete sentence. Scramble adverbs; make sure each student has a few opportunities to form sentences.

5. Prompt students with **how** questions. Have each student answer using an adverb in a complete sentence. Have a list of the adverbs in front of the class to which students may refer.

   stimulus: How do you study? — response: *"I study quietly."*
   stimulus: How is your class? — response: *"My class is hard."*
   stimulus: How does she talk? — response: *"She talks softly."*

6. Encourage students to frequently ask themselves **how** questions throughout the day and generate sentences using adverbs from this lesson.

Lesson 204

In this lesson, students will learn adverbs of degree.

1. Remind students that adverbs can modify verbs by describing **how, how little, how much, when,** and **where**. Model the following adverbs that tell **how much** or **how little: almost, barely, fully, greatly, hardly, little, merely, much, nearly, partially, partly, quite, rather, scarcely, sufficiently, too, very**. Use each adverb in a sentence and have students repeat.

2. Have students discuss what it means to have a "close call." Ask students to generate sentences using **nearly**. Have the class repeat each sentence. Make sure every student produces at least one sentence.

3. Repeat the exercise outlined in step 2 for each adverb listed in step 1. Make sure students understand the meaning of the adverb before asking them to generate sentences. Have the class repeat each sentence. If a student makes a mistake, model the correct sentence and have the student repeat. Focus on the correct use of adverbs, rather than prescriptive grammar rules.

4. Prompt students with adverbs from step 1. Have individual students use the given adverb in a complete sentence. Scramble adverbs and make sure each student has a few opportunities to form sentences.

5. Prompt students with **how little** and **how much** questions. Have each student answer using an adverb in a complete sentence. Have a list of the adverbs in front of the class to which students may refer.

   stimulus: How much do you study? response: *"I scarcely study."*
   stimulus: How much does she swim? response: *"She hardly swims."*

6. Encourage students to frequently ask themselves **how much** or **how little** questions throughout the day and generate sentences with adverbs from this lesson.

Lesson 205

In this lesson, students will review adverbs from Lessons 201–204.

1. Model adverbs of time (**again, already, always, before, early, ever, first, frequently, immediately, late, never, now, occasionally, often, seldom, sometimes, soon**). Have students repeat. Prompt individual students with an adverb of time and have each student produce a sentence. Have all students repeat. Scramble adverbs; make sure each student produces at least one sentence.

2. Model adverbs of place (**above, around, away, back, below, beyond, down, far, forth, forward, here, in, inside, out, outside, there, up, within**). Have students repeat. Prompt individual students with an adverb of place and have each student produce a sentence. Have all students repeat. Scramble adverbs; make sure each student produces at least one sentence.

3. Model adverbs of manner (**bravely, carefully, cheerfully, easily, eagerly, expertly, fast, happily, hard, honestly, politely, quickly, quietly, seriously, slowly, smoothly, softly, well**). Have students repeat. Prompt individual students with an adverb of manner and have each student produce a sentence. Have all students repeat. Scramble adverbs; make sure each student produces at least one sentence.

4. Model adverbs of degree (**almost, barely, fully, greatly, hardly, little, merely, much, nearly, partially, partly, quite, rather, scarcely, sufficiently, too, very**). Have students repeat. Prompt individual students with an adverb of degree and have each student produce a sentence. Have all students repeat. Scramble adverbs; make sure each student produces at least one sentence.

5. Prompt students with **how, how little, how much, when,** and **where** questions. Have each student answer using an adverb from steps 1–4 in a complete sentence. Have a list of the adverbs in front of the class to which students may refer. *(Note: In Lessons 192 and 193, students learned ways in which prepositional phrases function like adverbs. Steer questions away from answers with prepositional phrases. If a student does answer with a prepositional phrase, emphasize the difference between a prepositional phrase and an adverb. Give examples of words that function as adverbs and prepositions.)*

6. Encourage students to practice forming sentences with adverbs throughout the day.

Lesson 206

Materials: index cards or squares of paper

In this lesson, students will review indefinite pronouns.

1. Have students work in pairs and write the following pronouns on index cards: **a lot, all, anybody, anyone, anything, both, each, either, few, lots, many, neither, no one, nobody, nothing, one, several, some, somebody, someone, something**.

2. Have student pairs drill each other for pronoun recognition. Each student should read all pronouns aloud correctly.

3. Have students take turns generating sentences with their partners, using each pronoun in a complete sentence. The teacher should monitor pairs and provide assistance when necessary.

4. Have students discuss the use of these pronouns with their partners. Have pairs create a list of "tips" to be shared with the class that will help determine how and when they are used. Ask students to include tips on ways to remember the pronouns.

5. Bring the class back together. Use the set of index cards to drill the entire group. Review each word again and encourage students to share their "tips" generated in step 4.

6. Repeat exercises as necessary until all students have mastered indefinite pronouns. Encourage students to generate sentences with indefinite pronouns throughout the day.

Lesson 207

Materials: index cards or squares of paper

In this lesson, students will review reflexive and intensive pronouns.

1. Have students work in pairs and write the following pronouns on index cards: **herself, himself, itself, myself, ourselves, themselves, yourself, yourselves**.
2. Have student pairs drill each other for pronoun recognition. Each student should read all pronouns aloud correctly.
3. Have students take turns generating sentences with their partners, using each pronoun in a complete sentence. Ask students to generate two sentences for each pronoun, making it reflexive in one and intensive in the other. For example, hold up **ourselves**. Say: We washed ourselves. We ourselves ate the pie. The teacher should monitor pairs and provide assistance when necessary.
4. Have students discuss the use of reflexive and intensive pronouns with their partners. Have pairs create a list of "tips" to be shared with the class that will help determine how and when they are used. Ask students to include tips on ways to remember the pronouns.
5. Bring the class back together. Use the set of index cards to drill the entire group. Review each word again and encourage students to share their "tips" generated in step 4.
6. Repeat exercises as necessary until all students have mastered reflexive and intensive pronouns. Encourage students to generate sentences with these pronouns throughout the day.

Lesson 208

In this lesson, students will review prepositional phrases functioning as adjectives.

1. Each of the following sentence fragments demonstrates how prepositional phrases act as adjectives by modifying the object that precedes it. Read the fragments aloud and prompt students with the successive question. Have students answer the question with the correct prepositional phrase.

   stimulus: the car **in the driveway**; which car? response: *"in the driveway"*
   stimulus: the girls **on the team**; which girls? response: *"on the team"*
   stimulus: the panda **at the zoo**; which panda? response: *"at the zoo"*
   stimulus: the sentence **on the board**; which sentence? response: *"on the board"*
   stimulus: the man **with the truck**; which man? response: *"with the truck"*
   stimulus: the leg **of the table**; which leg? response: *"of the table"*

2. Read the following sentence fragments aloud to demonstrate how prepositional phrases begin with a preposition and end with the object of the preposition. Prompt students with the question that the prepositional phrase answers.

   stimulus: the lamp **beside us**; which lamp? response: *"beside us"*
   stimulus: the books **from them**; which books? response: *"from them"*
   stimulus: the pillow **between us**; which pillow? response: *"between us"*
   stimulus: the picture **near her**; which picture? response: *"near her"*
   stimulus: the lesson **for him**; which lesson? response: *"for him"*
   stimulus: the one **from them**; which one? response: *"from them"*

3. Repeat prepositional phrases from steps 1 and 2. Ask students to identify the preposition. Discuss the words that make up prepositional phrases. Make sure students understand that every prepositional phrase ends with a noun or pronoun called the object of the preposition. Reread the prepositional phrases and have students identify the **object of the preposition**.

4. Prompt students with a preposition. *(Note: See Appendix F for a list of prepositions.)* Have individual students generate a sentence using the preposition. Ask another student to identify the object of the preposition in that sentence. Repeat until each student has had several opportunities to create a sentence. If an error is made in sentence construction, model the correct sentence and have students repeat.

5. Continue prompting students with prepositions. Have individual students generate a sentence that contains the preposition. Ask another student to identify the prepositional phrase and what question it answers. Repeat until each student has had several opportunities to create a sentence.

6. Encourage students to practice creating sentences with prepositional phrases throughout the day. Ask them to practice determining what question the prepositional phrase answers.

Lesson 209

In this lesson, students will review adverbs and prepositional phrases functioning as adverbs.

1. Model the following adverbs and have students repeat: **already, back, below, beyond, bravely, carefully, eagerly, easily, fast, first, forward, fully, hard, hardly, here, near, never, now, partially, partly, quite, scarcely, seldom, slowly, sometimes, then, there, today, too, very, well**. Ask students what question each adverb answers (e.g., **how, how little, how much, when, where**).

2. Prompt students with an adverb from step 1. Have individual students generate a sentence using that adverb. Repeat until each student has had several opportunities to produce sentences.

3. Remind students that prepositional phrases can modify verbs by telling **how, when, where,** or **why** the action is happening. Read the following sentences aloud and prompt students with the question each phrase answers. Have the class respond with the prepositional phrase.

stimulus: I finished it in pain. How?	response: *"in pain"*
stimulus: I finished it with the group. How?	response: *"with the group"*
stimulus: I finished it around ten. When?	response: *"around ten"*
stimulus: I finished it on the table. Where?	response: *"on the table"*
stimulus: I finished it for my sister. Why?	response: *"for my sister"*
stimulus: I finished it in the morning. When?	response: *"in the morning"*
stimulus: I finished it near Miami. Where?	response: *"near Miami"*

4. Use the following sentences to review the elements of a prepositional phrase. Remind students that each begins with a preposition and ends with the preposition's object (i.e., the word to which it relates). When the object is a pronoun, an **object pronoun** is used. Have students repeat the following sentences. Call on individual students to identify the prepositional phrase, the preposition, and the object of the preposition.

   He left before us. She voted for you. It flew above us. Dad stayed near us.

   Repeat this exercise using the sentences from step 3. Make sure each student has an opportunity to identify all three elements named above.

5. Prompt students with a preposition. *(Note: See Appendix F for a list of prepositions.)* Have individual students generate a sentence using the preposition. Ask other students to identify the question the preposition is answering. Repeat until each student has had several opportunities to create sentences. If an error is made in sentence construction, model the correct sentence and have students repeat.

6. Encourage students to practice creating sentences containing a prepositional phrase throughout the day.

Lesson 210

This lesson is a comprehensive review of Lessons 206–209.

1. Have students generate sentences with the following indefinite pronouns: **a lot, all, anybody, anyone, anything, both, each, either, few, lots, many, neither, no one, nobody, nothing, one, several, some, somebody, someone, something**. Make sure each student has an opportunity to produce a few sentences.

2. Have students generate sentences with the following reflexive and intensive pronouns: **herself, himself, itself, myself, ourselves, themselves, yourself, yourselves**. Make sure each student is able to produce sentences with the words as reflexive pronouns and intensive pronouns.

3. Remind students that prepositional phrases can act as adjectives by modifying the object that precedes it. Read the fragments aloud and prompt students with the successive question. Have students answer the question with the correct prepositional phrase.

stimulus: the car **in the driveway**; which car?	response: *"in the driveway"*
stimulus: the girls **on the team**; which girls?	response: *"on the team"*
stimulus: the panda **at the zoo**; which panda?	response: *"at the zoo"*
stimulus: the sentence **on the board**; which sentence?	response: *"on the board"*
stimulus: the man **with the truck**; which man?	response: *"with the truck"*
stimulus: the leg **of the table**; which leg?	response: *"of the table"*
stimulus: the lamp **beside us**; which lamp?	response: *"beside us"*
stimulus: the books **from them**; which books?	response: *"from them"*
stimulus: the pillow **between us**; which pillow?	response: *"between us"*
stimulus: the picture **near her**; which picture?	response: *"near her"*
stimulus: the lesson **for him**; which lesson?	response: *"for him"*
stimulus: the one **from them**; which one?	response: *"from them"*

4. Repeat the sentence fragments from step 3. Ask individual students to identify the prepositional phrase, the preposition, and the question it answers.

5. Prompt students with a preposition. *(Note: See Appendix F for a list of prepositions.)* Have individual students generate a sentence using the preposition. Ask another student to identify the question the preposition is answering. Repeat until each student has had several opportunities to create a sentence. If an error is made in sentence construction, model the correct sentence and have students repeat.

6. Encourage students to practice creating sentences containing prepositional phrases as adjectives and adverbs throughout the day.

Lesson 211

In this lesson, students will learn formation, use, and meaning of phrasal verbs.

1. Say each of the following phrasal verbs and have students repeat: **act like, act up, add up, add up to, ask out, back down, back off, back up, beg off, blow up, bone up on, break down, break in, break into, break up, bring back, bring off, bring up, brush up on, build up**. Create a brief scenario to illustrate the use and meaning of each phrasal verb. Be sure to use each verb in a sentence.

2. Discuss the meanings of each phrasal verb. Give special attention to those whose meanings are not literal.

3. Take the phrasal verbs apart. Discuss the meanings of the separate words, then the meaning of the phrase (e.g., talk about the meaning of "act," "up," and "act up").

4. List the phrasal verbs from step 1 where students can read them. Call on individual students to generate a sentence containing a phrasal verb. Repeat until each student has had several opportunities to produce a sentence. If students use a phrasal verb incorrectly, model the correct use and have students repeat.

5. Separate students into pairs. Divide verbs from step 1 evenly between each pair. Have students create and deliver short dialogues using as many of these phrasal verbs as possible. Listen carefully to students' oral output, providing definitions and assistance as necessary.

6. Encourage students to listen for phrasal verbs. Have them practice using the phrasal verbs from this lesson throughout the day.

Lesson 212

In this lesson, students will learn formation, use, and meaning of phrasal verbs.

1. Say each of the following phrasal verbs and have students repeat: **burn down, burn up, butt in, butter up, call off, call on, calm down, care for, catch on, catch up, catch up with, check in, check into, check off, check out, check out of, cheer up, chew out, chicken out, chip in**. Create a brief scenario to illustrate the use and meaning of each phrasal verb. Be sure to use each verb in a sentence.

2. Discuss the meanings of each phrasal verb. Give special attention to those whose meanings are not literal.

3. Take the phrasal verbs apart. Discuss the meanings of the separate words, then the meaning of the phrase (e.g., talk about the meaning of "call," "off," and "call off").

4. List the phrasal verbs from step 1 where students can read them. Call on individual students to generate a sentence containing a phrasal verb. Repeat until each student has had several opportunities to produce sentences. If a student uses a phrasal verb incorrectly, model the correct use and have the student repeat.

5. Separate students into pairs. Divide verbs from step 1 evenly between each pair. Have students create and deliver short dialogues using as many of these phrasal verbs as possible. Monitor students' oral output, providing definitions and assistance as necessary.

6. Encourage students to listen for phrasal verbs. Have them practice using the phrasal verbs from this lesson throughout the day.

Lesson 213

In this lesson, students will learn formation, use, and meaning of phrasal verbs.

1. Say each of the following phrasal verbs and have students repeat: **clam up, come across, come down on, come to, count on, crack down, crack down on, cross out, cut back, cut back on, do in, do over, drag on, draw up, drop by, drop in, drop in on, drop out, drop out of, drop off**. Create a brief scenario to illustrate the use and meaning of each phrasal verb. Be sure to use each verb in a sentence.

2. Discuss the meanings of each phrasal verb. Give special attention to those whose meanings are not literal.

3. Take the phrasal verbs apart. Discuss the meanings of the separate words, then the meaning of the phrase (e.g., talk about the meaning of "clam," "up," and "clam up").

4. List the phrasal verbs from step 1 where students can read them. Call on individual students to generate a sentence containing a phrasal verb. Repeat until each student has had several opportunities to produce sentences. If a student uses a phrasal verb incorrectly, model the correct use and have the student repeat.

5. Separate students into pairs. Divide verbs from step 1 evenly between each pair. Have students create and deliver short dialogues using as many of these phrasal verbs as possible. Monitor students' oral output, providing definitions and assistance as necessary.

6. Encourage students to listen for phrasal verbs. Have them practice using the phrasal verbs from this lesson throughout the day.

Lesson 214

In this lesson, students will learn formation, use, and meaning of phrasal verbs.

1. Say each of the following phrasal verbs and have students repeat: **draw out, eat out, egg on, end up, face up to, fall through, feel up to, figure out, fill in, fill in for, fill out, find out, find out about, get across, get along with, get around, get around to, get by, get in, get on**. Create a brief scenario to illustrate the use and meaning of each phrasal verb. Be sure to use each verb in a sentence.

2. Discuss the meanings of each phrasal verb. Give special attention to those whose meanings are not literal.

3. Take the phrasal verbs apart. Discuss the meanings of the separate words, then the meaning of the phrase (e.g., talk about the meaning of "fall," "through," and "fall through").

4. List the phrasal verbs from step 1 where students can read them. Call on individual students to generate a sentence containing a phrasal verb. Repeat until each student has had several opportunities to produce a sentence. If a student uses a phrasal verb incorrectly, model the correct use and have the student repeat.

5. Separate students into pairs. Divide verbs from step 1 evenly between each pair. Have students create and deliver short dialogues using as many of these phrasal verbs as possible. Monitor students' oral output, providing definitions and assistance as necessary.

6. Encourage students to listen for phrasal verbs. Have them practice using the phrasal verbs from this lesson throughout the day.

Lesson 215

In this lesson, students will learn formation, use, and meaning of phrasal verbs.

1. Say each of the following phrasal verbs and have students repeat: **get off, get out of, get over, get rid of, get up, give up, go out with, go with, goof off, grow up, hand in, hand out, hang up, have to do with, hold up, iron out, jack up, jump all over, keep at, keep on**. Create a brief scenario to illustrate the use and meaning of each phrasal verb. Be sure to use each verb in a sentence.

2. Discuss the meanings of each phrasal verb. Give special attention to those whose meanings are not literal.

3. Take the phrasal verbs apart. Discuss the meanings of the separate words, then the meaning of the phrase (e.g., talk about the meaning of "iron," "out," and "iron out").

4. List the phrasal verbs from step 1 where students can read them. Call on individual students to generate a sentence containing a phrasal verb. Repeat until each student has had several opportunities to produce a sentence. If a student uses a phrasal verb incorrectly, model the correct use and have the student repeat.

5. Separate students into pairs. Divide verbs from step 1 evenly between each pair. Have students create and deliver short dialogues using as many of these phrasal verbs as possible. Monitor students' oral output, providing definitions and assistance as necessary.

6. Encourage students to listen for phrasal verbs. Have them practice using the phrasal verbs from this lesson throughout the day.

Lesson 216

In this lesson, students will learn formation, use, and meaning of phrasal verbs.

1. Say each of the following phrasal verbs and have students repeat: **kick out, knock out, lay off, leave out, let down, let up, look back on, look down on, look forward to, look in on, look into, look like, look over, look up, look up to, luck out, make fun of, make up, make up with**. Create a brief scenario to illustrate the use and meaning of each phrasal verb. Be sure to use each verb in a sentence.

2. Discuss the meanings of each phrasal verb. Give special attention to those whose meanings are not literal.

3. Take the phrasal verbs apart. Discuss the meanings of the separate words, then the meaning of the phrase (e.g., talk about the meaning of "kick," "out," and "kick out").

4. List the phrasal verbs from step 1 where students can read them. Call on individual students to generate a sentence containing a phrasal verb. Repeat until each student has had several opportunities to produce a sentence. If a student uses a phrasal verb incorrectly, model the correct use and have the student repeat.

5. Separate students into pairs. Divide verbs from step 1 evenly between each pair. Have students create and deliver short dialogues using as many of these phrasal verbs as possible. Monitor students' oral output, providing definitions and assistance as necessary.

6. Encourage students to listen for phrasal verbs. Have them practice using the phrasal verbs from this lesson throughout the day.

Lesson 217

In this lesson, students will learn formation, use, and meaning of phrasal verbs.

1. Say each of the following phrasal verbs and have students repeat: **make for, mark down, mark up, mix up, nod off, pan out, pass away, pass out, pick on, pick out, pick up for, pitch in, pull off, pull over, put away, put in, put off, put on, put up, put up with**. Create a brief scenario to illustrate the use and meaning of each phrasal verb. Be sure to use each verb in a sentence.

2. Discuss the meanings of each phrasal verb. Give special attention to those whose meanings are not literal.

3. Take the phrasal verbs apart. Discuss the meanings of the separate words, then the meaning of the phrase (e.g., talk about the meaning of "mark," "down," and "mark down").

4. List the phrasal verbs from step 1 where students can read them. Call on individual students to generate a sentence containing a phrasal verb. Repeat until each student has had several opportunities to produce a sentence. If a student uses a phrasal verb incorrectly, model the correct use and have the student repeat.

5. Separate students into pairs. Divide verbs from step 1 evenly between each pair. Have students create and deliver short dialogues using as many of these phrasal verbs as possible. Monitor students' oral output, providing definitions and assistance as necessary.

6. Encourage students to listen for phrasal verbs. Have them practice using the phrasal verbs from this lesson throughout the day.

Lesson 218

In this lesson, students will learn formation, use, and meaning of phrasal verbs.

1. Say each of the following phrasal verbs and have students repeat: **put back, rip off, round off, run into, run out of, set back, set up, show up, slip up, stand for, stand out, stand up, take after, take back, take care of, take off, tell off, throw away, throw off, tick off.** Create a brief scenario to illustrate the use and meaning of each phrasal verb. Be sure to use each verb in a sentence.

2. Discuss the meanings of each phrasal verb. Give special attention to those whose meanings are not literal.

3. Take the phrasal verbs apart. Discuss the meanings of the separate words, then the meaning of the phrase (e.g., talk about the meaning of "show," "up," and "show up").

4. List the phrasal verbs from step 1 where the students can read them. Call on individual students to generate a sentence containing a phrasal verb. Repeat until each student has had several opportunities to produce a sentence. If a student uses a phrasal verb incorrectly, model the correct use and have the student repeat.

5. Separate students into pairs. Divide verbs from step 1 evenly between each pair. Have students create and deliver short dialogues using as many of these phrasal verbs as possible. Monitor students' oral output, providing definitions and assistance as necessary.

6. Encourage students to listen for phrasal verbs. Have them practice using the phrasal verbs from this lesson throughout the day.

Lesson 219

In this lesson, students will learn formation, use, and meaning of phrasal verbs.

1. Say each of the following phrasal verbs and have students repeat: **throw out, throw up, try on, try out, try out for, turn around, turn down, turn in, turn off, turn on, turn up, wait on, wake up, watch out for, wear out, work out, wrap up, write down, write up, zonk out**. Create a brief scenario to illustrate the use and meaning of each phrasal verb. Be sure to use each verb in a sentence.

2. Discuss the meanings of each phrasal verb. Give special attention to those whose meanings are not literal.

3. Take the phrasal verbs apart. Discuss the meanings of the separate words, then the meaning of the phrase (e.g., talk about the meaning of "turn," "up," and "turn up").

4. List the phrasal verbs from step 1 where students can read them. Call on individual students to generate a sentence containing a phrasal verb. Repeat until each student has had several opportunities to produce a sentence. If a student uses a phrasal verb incorrectly, model the correct use and have the student repeat.

5. Separate students into pairs. Divide verbs from step 1 evenly between each pair. Have students create and deliver short dialogues using as many of these phrasal verbs as possible. Monitor students' oral output, providing definitions and assistance as necessary.

6. Encourage students to listen for phrasal verbs. Have them practice using the phrasal verbs from this lesson throughout the day.

Lesson 220

This lesson is a comprehensive review of 180 phrasal verbs from Lessons 211–219.

1. Have students repeat each of the following phrasal verbs: **act like, act up, add up, add up to, ask out, back down, back off, back up, beg off, blow up, bone up on, break down, break in, break into, break up, bring back, bring off, bring up, brush up on, build up, burn down, burn up, butt in, butter up, call off, call on, calm down, care for, catch on, catch up, catch up with, check in, check into, check off, check out, check out of, cheer up, chew out, chicken out, chip in**. Prompt students with one of the phrasal verbs. Have individual students generate a sentence containing the prompted verb. Scramble verbs and repeat until each student has had several opportunities to produce a sentence. Keep track of any verbs with which students have trouble.

2. Repeat step 1 using the following phrasal verbs: **clam up, come across, come down on, come to, count on, crack down, crack down on, cross out, cut back, cut back on, do in, do over, drag on, draw up, drop by, drop in, drop in on, drop out, drop out of, drop off, draw out, eat out, egg on, end up, face up to, fall through, feel up to, figure out, fill in, fill in for, fill out, find out, find out about, get across, get along with, get around, get around to, get by, get in, get on**.

3. Repeat step 1 using the following phrasal verbs: **get off, get out of, get over, get rid of, get up, give up, go out with, go with, goof off, grow up, hand in, hand out, hang up, have to do with, hold up, iron out, jack up, jump all over, keep at, keep on, kick out, knock out, lay off, leave out, let down, let up, look back on, look down on, look forward to, look in on, look into, look like, look over, look up, look up to, luck out, make fun of, make up, make up with**. Include any verbs from steps 1 and 2 with which students have had trouble.

4. Repeat step 1 using the following phrasal verbs: **make for, mark down, mark up, mix up, nod off, pan out, pass away, pass out, pick on, pick out, pick up for, pitch in, pull off, pull over, put away, put back, put in, put off, put on, put up, put up with, rip off, round off, run into, run out of, set back, set up, show up, slip up, stand for, stand out, stand up, take after, take back, take care of, take off, tell off, throw away, throw off, tick off**.

5. Repeat step 1 using the following phrasal verbs: **throw out, throw up, try on, try out, try out for, turn around, turn down, turn in, turn off, turn on, turn up, wait on, wake up, watch out for, wear out, work out, wrap up, write down, write up, zonk out**. Include any verbs from steps 1 through 4 with which students have had trouble.

6. Focus on students' oral output, rather than abstract explanations of how each phrasal verb is used. Phrasal verbs are difficult for many English learners. Keep a list of phrasal verbs with which students have had trouble for ongoing review.

Lesson 221

In this lesson, students will learn present, past, and past participle forms of irregular verbs.

1. Model the present, past, and past participle forms of the following irregular verbs. Have students repeat.

Present	Past	Past Participle (need helping verb)
am, is, are	was, were	been
awake	awoke	awakened
beat	beat	beaten

2. Emphasize that all English verbs consist of three principal forms, or tenses: present, past, and past participle. Name each verb from step 1 and use in a sentence. Prompt students with the present tense of each verb and have individual students produce a sentence with it.

3. Scramble verb forms from step 1 and prompt students. Have each student create sentences using all three forms of each verb (i.e., each student should produce nine different sentences). If a mistake is made, model the correct production and have students repeat.

4. Model the present, past, and past participle of the following irregular verbs. Have students repeat. Use each verb form in a sentence and have students repeat. Next, scramble all forms of the following verbs. Prompt students with a verb form and have individual students use it in a sentence. Have each student create sentences using all three forms of each verb (i.e., each student should produce nine different sentences).

Present	Past	Past Participle (need helping verb)
bend	bent	bent
bet	bet	bet
bind	bound	bound

5. Repeat the exercise outlined in step 4 using the following irregular verbs.

Present	Past	Past Participle (need helping verb)
bite	bit	bitten
blow	blew	blown
break	broke	broken

6. Encourage students to practice using the present, past, and past participle forms of these irregular verbs throughout the day.

Lesson 222

In this lesson, students will learn present, past, and past participle forms of irregular verbs.

1. Model the present, past, and past participle forms of the following irregular verbs. Have students repeat.

Present	**Past**	**Past Participle** (need helping verb)
bring	brought	brought
build	built	built
burn	burned	burned

2. Emphasize that all English verbs consist of three principal forms, or tenses: present, past, and past participle. Name each verb from step 1 and use in a sentence. Prompt students with the present tense of each verb and have individual students produce a sentence with it.

3. Scramble verb forms from step 1 and prompt students. Have each student create sentences using all three forms of each verb (i.e., each student should produce nine different sentences). If a mistake is made, model the correct production and have students repeat.

4. Model the present, past, and past participle of the following irregular verbs. Have students repeat. Use each verb form in a sentence and have students repeat. Next, scramble all forms of the following verbs. Prompt students with a verb form and have individual students use it in a sentence. Have each student create sentences using all three forms of each verb (i.e., each student should produce nine different sentences).

Present	**Past**	**Past Participle** (need helping verb)
burst	burst	burst
catch	caught	caught
choose	chose	chosen

5. Repeat the exercise outlined in step 4 using the following irregular verbs.

Present	**Past**	**Past Participle** (need helping verb)
come	came	come
do	did	done
draw	drew	drawn

6. Encourage students to practice using the present, past, and past participle forms of these irregular verbs throughout the day.

Lesson 223

In this lesson, students will learn present, past, and past participle forms of irregular verbs.

1. Model the present, past, and past participle forms of the following irregular verbs. Have students repeat.

Present	**Past**	**Past Participle** (need helping verb)
dream	dreamed, dreamt	dreamed, dreamt
drink	drank	drunk
drive	drove	driven

2. Emphasize that all English verbs consist of three principal forms, or tenses: present, past, and past participle. Name each verb from step 1 and use in a sentence. Prompt students with the present tense of each verb and have individual students produce a sentence with it.

3. Scramble verb forms from step 1 and prompt students. Have each student create sentences using all three forms of each verb (i.e., each student should produce nine different sentences). If a mistake is made, model the correct production and have students repeat.

4. Model the present, past, and past participle of the following irregular verbs. Have students repeat. Use each verb form in a sentence and have students repeat. Next, scramble all forms of the following verbs. Prompt students with a verb form and have individual students use it in a sentence. Have each student create sentences using all three forms of each verb (i.e., each student should produce nine different sentences).

Present	**Past**	**Past Participle** (need helping verb)
eat	ate	eaten
fall	fell	fallen
find	found	found

5. Repeat the exercise outlined in step 4 using the following irregular verbs.

Present	**Past**	**Past Participle** (need helping verb)
fly	flew	flown
forget	forgot	forgotten
freeze	froze	frozen

6. Encourage students to practice using the present, past, and past participle forms of these irregular verbs throughout the day.

Lesson 224

In this lesson, students will learn present, past, and past participle forms of irregular verbs.

1. Model the present, past, and past participle forms of the following irregular verbs. Have students repeat.

Present	Past	Past Participle (need helping verb)
give	gave	given
go	went	gone
grow	grew	grown

2. Emphasize that all English verbs consist of three principal forms, or tenses: present, past, and past participle. Name each verb from step 1 and use in a sentence. Prompt students with the present tense of each verb and have individual students produce a sentence with it.

3. Scramble verb forms from step 1 and prompt students. Have each student create sentences using all three forms of each verb (i.e., each student should produce nine different sentences). If a mistake is made, model the correct production and have students repeat.

4. Model the present, past, and past participle of the following irregular verbs. Have students repeat. Use each verb form in a sentence and have students repeat. Next, scramble all forms of the following verbs. Prompt students with a verb form and have individual students use it in a sentence. Have each student create sentences using all three forms of each verb (i.e., each student should produce nine different sentences).

Present	Past	Past Participle (need helping verb)
hang	hung	hung
have, has	had	had
hear	heard	heard

5. Repeat the exercise outlined in step 4 using the following irregular verbs.

Present	Past	Past Participle (need helping verb)
hide	hid	hidden
hold	held	held
hurt	hurt	hurt

6. Encourage students to practice using the present, past, and past participle forms of these irregular verbs throughout the day.

Lesson 225

In this lesson, students learn will present, past, and past participle forms of irregular verbs.

1. Model the present, past, and past participle forms of the following irregular verbs. Have students repeat.

Present	Past	Past Participle (need helping verb)
keep	kept	kept
kneel	kneeled, knelt	kneeled, knelt
know	knew	known

2. Emphasize that all English verbs consist of three principal forms, or tenses: present, past, and past participle. Name each verb from step 1 and use in a sentence. Prompt students with the present tense of each verb and have individual students produce a sentence with it.

3. Scramble verb forms from step 1 and prompt students. Have each student create sentences using all three forms of each verb (i.e., each student should produce nine different sentences). If a mistake is made, model the correct production and have students repeat.

4. Model the present, past, and past participle of the following irregular verbs. Have students repeat. Use each verb form in a sentence and have students repeat. Next, scramble all forms of the following verbs. Prompt students with a verb form and have individual students use it in a sentence. Have each student create sentences using all three forms of each verb (i.e., each student should produce nine different sentences).

Present	Past	Past Participle (need helping verb)
lay	laid	laid
leave	left	left
lend	lent	lent

5. Repeat the exercise outlined in step 4 using the following irregular verbs.

Present	Past	Past Participle (need helping verb)
let	let	let
lie (recline)	lay	lain
lose	lost	lost

6. Encourage students to practice using the present, past, and past participle forms of these irregular verbs throughout the day.

Lesson 226

In this lesson, students will learn present, past, and past participle forms of irregular verbs.

1. Model the present, past, and past participle forms of the following irregular verbs. Have students repeat.

Present	**Past**	**Past Participle** (need helping verb)
make	made	made
mean	meant	meant
meet	met	met

2. Emphasize that all English verbs consist of three principal forms, or tenses: present, past, and past participle. Name each verb from step 1 and use in a sentence. Prompt students with the present tense of each verb and have individual students produce a sentence with it.

3. Scramble verb forms from step 1 and prompt students. Have each student create sentences using all three forms of each verb (i.e., each student should produce nine different sentences). If a mistake is made, model the correct production and have students repeat.

4. Model the present, past, and past participle of the following irregular verbs. Have students repeat. Use each verb form in a sentence and have students repeat. Next, scramble all forms of the following verbs. Prompt students with a verb form and have individual students use it in a sentence. Have each student create sentences using all three forms of each verb (i.e., each student should produce nine different sentences).

Present	**Past**	**Past Participle** (need helping verb)
read	read	read
ride	rode	ridden
ring	rang	rung

5. Repeat the exercise outlined in step 4 using the following irregular verbs.

Present	**Past**	**Past Participle** (need helping verb)
rise	rose	risen
run	ran	run
say	said	said

6. Encourage students to practice using the present, past, and past participle forms of these irregular verbs throughout the day.

Lesson 227

In this lesson, students will learn present, past, and past participle forms of irregular verbs.

1. Model the present, past, and past participle forms of the following irregular verbs. Have students repeat.

Present	Past	Past Participle (need helping verb)
see	saw	seen
shake	shook	shaken
sing	sang	sung

2. Emphasize that all English verbs consist of three principal forms, or tenses: present, past, and past participle. Name each verb from step 1 and use in a sentence. Prompt students with the present tense of each verb and have individual students produce a sentence with it.

3. Scramble verb forms from step 1 and prompt students. Have each student create sentences using all three forms of each verb (i.e., each student should produce nine different sentences). If a mistake is made, model the correct production and have students repeat.

4. Model the present, past, and past participle of the following irregular verbs. Have students repeat. Use each verb form in a sentence and have students repeat. Next, scramble all forms of the following verbs. Prompt students with a verb form and have individual students use it in a sentence. Have each student create sentences using all three forms of each verb (i.e., each student should produce nine different sentences).

Present	Past	Past Participle (need helping verb)
sink	sank	sunk
sit	sat	sat
speak	spoke	spoken

5. Repeat the exercise outlined in step 4 using the following irregular verbs.

Present	Past	Past Participle (need helping verb)
spin	spun	spun
stand	stood	stood
steal	stole	stolen

6. Encourage students to practice using the present, past, and past participle forms of these irregular verbs throughout the day.

Lesson 228

In this lesson, students will learn present, past, and past participle forms of irregular verbs.

1. Model the present, past, and past participle forms of the following irregular verbs. Have students repeat.

Present	**Past**	**Past Participle** (need helping verb)
stick	stuck	stuck
swim	swam	swum
swing	swung	swung

2. Emphasize that all English verbs consist of three principal forms, or tenses: present, past, and past participle. Name each verb from step 1 and use in a sentence. Prompt students with the present tense of each verb and have individual students produce a sentence with it.

3. Scramble verb forms from step 1 and prompt students. Have each student create sentences using all three forms of each verb (i.e., each student should produce nine different sentences). If a mistake is made, model the correct production and have students repeat.

4. Model the present, past, and past participle of the following irregular verbs. Have students repeat. Use each verb form in a sentence and have students repeat. Next, scramble all forms of the following verbs. Prompt students with a verb form and have individual students use it in a sentence. Have each student create sentences using all three forms of each verb (i.e., each student should produce nine different sentences).

Present	**Past**	**Past Participle** (need helping verb)
teach	taught	taught
tear	tore	torn
throw	threw	thrown

5. Repeat the exercise outlined in step 4 using the following irregular verbs.

Present	**Past**	**Past Participle** (need helping verb)
wear	wore	worn
write	wrote	written

6. Encourage students to practice using the present, past, and past participle forms of these irregular verbs throughout the day.

Lesson 229

This is a comprehensive review of present, past, and past participle forms of irregular verbs.

1. Use each of the following verb forms in a sentence and have students repeat. Prompt individual students with verb forms and have them generate sentences. Have each student create several sentences.

Present	Past	Past Participle (need helping verb)	Present	Past	Past Participle (need helping verb)
am, is, are	was, were	been	bind	bound	bound
awake	awoke	awakened	bite	bit	bitten
beat	beat	beaten	blow	blew	blown
bend	bent	bent	break	broke	broken
bet	bet	bet	bring	brought	brought

2. Repeat step 1 using the following verb forms.

Present	Past	Past Participle (need helping verb)	Present	Past	Past Participle (need helping verb)
build	built	built	choose	chose	chosen
burn	burned	burned	come	came	come
burst	burst	burst	do	did	done
catch	caught	caught	draw	drew	drawn

3. Repeat step 1 using the following verb forms.

Present	Past	Past Participle (need helping verb)	Present	Past	Past Participle (need helping verb)
dream	dreamed, dreamt	dreamed, dreamt	find	found	found
drink	drank	drunk	fly	flew	flown
drive	drove	driven	forget	forgot	forgotten
eat	ate	eaten	freeze	froze	frozen
fall	fell	fallen	give	gave	given

4. Repeat step 1 using the following verb forms.

Present	Past	Past Participle (need helping verb)	Present	Past	Past Participle (need helping verb)
go	went	gone	hear	heard	heard
grow	grew	grown	hide	hid	hidden
hang	hung	hung	hold	held	held
have, has	had	had	hurt	hurt	hurt

5. Remind students that all English verbs consist of these three principal forms, or tenses. Prompt students with the present tense forms of the above verbs and have them provide the past and past participle forms. Repeat until all verbs have been reviewed.

6. Encourage students to practice using the present, past, and past participle forms of these irregular verbs throughout the day. Review until mastery is achieved.

Lesson 230

This is a comprehensive review of present, past, and past participle forms of irregular verbs.

1. Use each of the following verb forms in a sentence and have students repeat. Scramble verbs, prompt students with a verb form, and have them generate sentences. Have each student create several sentences.

Present	Past	Past Participle (need helping verb)	Present	Past	Past Participle (need helping verb)
keep	kept	kept	lend	lent	lent
kneel	kneeled, knelt	kneeled, knelt	let	let	let
know	knew	known	lie (recline)	lay	lain
lay	laid	laid	lose	lost	lost
leave	left	left	make	made	made

2. Repeat step 1 using the following verb forms.

Present	Past	Past Participle (need helping verb)	Present	Past	Past Participle (need helping verb)
mean	meant	meant	ring	rang	rung
meet	met	met	rise	rose	risen
read	read	read	run	ran	run
ride	rode	ridden	say	said	said

3. Repeat step 1 using the following verb forms.

Present	Past	Past Participle (need helping verb)	Present	Past	Past Participle (need helping verb)
see	saw	seen	speak	spoke	spoken
shake	shook	shaken	spin	spun	spun
sing	sang	sung	stand	stood	stood
sink	sank	sunk	steal	stole	stolen
sit	sat	sat	stick	stuck	stuck

4. Repeat step 1 using the following verb forms.

Present	Past	Past Participle (need helping verb)	Present	Past	Past Participle (need helping verb)
swim	swam	swum	throw	threw	thrown
swing	swung	swung	wear	wore	worn
teach	taught	taught	write	wrote	written
tear	tore	torn			

5. Remind students that all English verbs consist of these three principal forms, or tenses. Prompt students with the present tense forms of the above verbs and have them provide the past and past participle forms. Repeat until all verbs have been reviewed.

6. Encourage students to practice using the present, past, and past participle forms of these irregular verbs throughout the day. Review until mastery is achieved.

Lesson 231

Materials: noun picture cards

In this lesson, students will learn to form compound subjects using **and** and **or**.

1. Read each sentence aloud and make two simple sentences out of each sentence. For example, say: Rashad and Ennis took the test. Rashad took the test. Ennis took the test. Have students repeat all three sentences. Ask students to generate the original sentence.

   Rashad and Ennis took the test.
   Plants and flowers grew in the yard.
   Cartoons or game shows were on TV.
   Dogs and cats like to play with balls.
   Computers and telephones are necessary.
   Paper and pencils will be provided.
   The Saints or the Rams will win the title.
   She and I tried hard to do this homework.
   Dinner and a movie would be a treat.
   Apples or bananas make a good snack.
   Mothers and fathers love their children.
   Students and teachers worked at the game.
   Photographs and paintings filled the room.
   Either Naomi or Martha will go with you.
   Sunrise and sunset are my favorite times.
   Somebody or something is responsible.
   Books and newspapers covered the chairs.
   Gabriella and Danielle speak fluent Italian.

2. Provide students with two noun picture cards. Have students use them to create three sentences, two with a simple subject and one with a compound subject. Have a different student create three different sentences using the same two nouns. Make sure students use **and** or **or** in their sentences containing a compound subject.

3. Emphasize that sentences with a compound subject have only one predicate but two nouns as the subject. Repeat the sentences from step 1, having students name the subject in each one. Say: Plants and flowers grew in the yard. Students should respond: *"Plants and flowers."*

4. Ask students how sentence meaning differs when compound subjects are connected by **and** as opposed to **or**. Hold up two noun picture cards and have individual students generate a sentence using **or**. Have a different student say the same sentence with the conjunction **and**. Have students explain the different meanings between the two sentences. Repeat until each student has had several opportunities to produce a sentence.

5. Using the noun picture cards, continue to have students create sentences that have a compound subject containing **and** or **or**, as described in step 2.

6. Encourage students to practice generating sentences with compound subjects throughout the day.

Lesson 232

Materials: action picture cards

In this lesson, students will learn to form compound predicates using **and** and **or**.

1. Read each sentence aloud and make two simple sentences out of each sentence. For example, say: We'll bake chicken or fry fish for dinner. We'll bake chicken for dinner. We'll fry fish for dinner. Have students repeat all three sentences. Ask students to generate the original sentence.

   We'll bake chicken or fry fish for dinner.
   I do homework or play ball after school.
   My cat sat and purred in the sunshine.
   You helped us and gave us hope.
   The nurse works nights and sleeps days.
   He bakes or buys cookies on Saturdays.
   Roberto fell and hurt himself.
   They'll win or lose the title tonight.
   People screamed and yelled at her.
   Do you walk or ride to school?
   I heard fire engines and police sirens.
   Al listens and remembers what he hears.
   Carmelita studied and passed the test.
   Astronauts train hard and work long hours.
   Should we stop and start again?
   I can't think or get anything done today.
   Mr. Lopez plays the piano and sings.
   I thought about it and changed my mind.

2. Provide students with two action picture cards. Have students use them to create three sentences, two with a simple predicate and one with a compound predicate. Have a different student create three different sentences using the same two verbs. Make sure students use **and** or **or** in their sentences containing a compound predicate.

3. Explain that a sentence with a compound subject has two nouns joined together by a conjunction, and a sentence with a compound predicate has two actions joined together by a conjunction. Use the following sentences to illustrate: Photographs and paintings filled the room. (Two nouns.) We'll bake chicken or fry fish for dinner. (Two actions.)

4. Ask students how sentence meaning differs when compound predicates are connected by **and** as opposed to **or**. Hold up two action picture cards and have individual students generate a sentence using **or**. Have a different student say the same sentence with the conjunction **and**. Have students explain the different meanings between the two sentences. Repeat until each student has had several opportunities to produce a sentence.

5. Using the action picture cards, continue to have students create sentences that have a compound predicate containing **and** or **or**, as described in step 2.

6. Encourage students to practice generating sentences with compound predicates throughout the day.

Lesson 233

Materials: noun and action picture cards

In this lesson, students will learn to form compound subjects and compound predicates using **and**, **but**, and **or**.

1. Read these simple sentences and have students repeat.

   Ed drank milk.
   Ambulances shrieked.
   Sharon gave instructions.
   Our class saw a play.
   Mario rents the uniforms.
   The House passed a bill.
   Liz found the information.
   Doctors rushed to the accident scene.
   Mr. Perez finished it.
   My house looks old.

2. Prompt students with a simple sentence from step 1. Have students change the simple subject to a compound subject using **and** or **or**. For example, students may respond:

   "Ed or Sam drank the milk."
   "Liz or Pat found the information."
   "Doctors and nurses rushed to the scene."
   "Mario or Jack rents the uniforms."
   "The House and Senate passed a bill."
   "Sharon or Tony gave instructions."
   "Our class and their class saw a play."
   "My house and your house look old."

3. Prompt students with a simple sentence from step 1. Have students change the simple predicate to a compound predicate using **and**, **but**, or **or**. For example, students may respond:

   "Ed drank milk and ate graham crackers."
   "Ambulances shrieked and warned us."
   "My house looks but doesn't feel old."
   "Mr. Perez finished it but started over."
   "The House passed and published a bill."
   "Liz found the information and copied it."
   "Our class saw a play and wrote a review."
   "Mario selects the uniforms or buys them."

4. Prompt students with a simple sentence from step 1. Have students change both the simple subject and predicate to a compound subject and a compound predicate using **and**, **but**, or **or**. For example, students may respond:

   "Ed and Sam drank milk and ate crackers."
   "Our class and Lee's class saw a play but didn't write a review."
   "Ambulances or police sirens shrieked and warned us."

5. Prompt students with the noun and action picture cards. Have students create sentences that have compound subjects and/or compound predicates containing **and**, **but** or **or**, as described in step 4. Make sure each student produces several sentences.

6. Encourage students to practice generating sentences with compound subjects and compound predicates throughout the day.

Lesson 234

Materials: noun and action picture cards; strips of paper

In this lesson, students will learn to form compound sentences using **and**, **but**, and **or**.

1. Write the following sentences on sentence strips and read aloud.

   Dan will skate to the park.
   Luke will ride with Paolo.
   Maria will walk back.
   Phil will go to the store.
   Shane won't go to the dance.
   Anna will drive home.
   Carlos will stay at school.
   George will go to soccer practice.
   Leeta will watch the game.
   Roberta won't talk to Marc.

2. Explain to students that compound sentences can be made by joining two simple sentences with a conjunction. Demonstrate this by holding up two sentence strips at a time and reading aloud with **and**, **but**, or **or** as the coordinating conjunction (e.g., say: Luke will ride with Paolo, but Maria will walk back). Discuss how sentence meaning changes when **and** or **or** is substituted for **but**.

3. Pass out sentence strips. Have students work in pairs to create compound sentences by joining their strips with **and**, **but**, or **or**. Have students work independently, making up their own sentences to join with the one on their strips. Have students share the compound sentence created.

4. Ask each student to create at least three compound sentences with the sentence strips. Be sure to emphasize use of **and**, **but**, or **or**; have students use one conjunction in each sentence. Each compound sentence should have a different conjunction **(and, but, or**). Ask students to share compound sentences with the class.

5. Pass out noun and action picture cards and have students use them to create compound sentences. Have students share their sentences with the class. Continue until each student has created several compound sentences. Be sure that each student comprehends the difference between **and**, **but**, and **or** in sentence formation.

6. Monitor students' oral output. Encourage students to practice compound sentences throughout the day.

Lesson 235

Materials: sentence strips from Lesson 234

In this lesson, students will review compound subjects and compound predicates.

1. Read each of the following sentences aloud. Have students break them down into simple sentences (without compound subjects).

   Rashad and Ennis took the test.
   Plants and flowers grew in the yard.
   Either Naomi or Martha will go with you.
   Sunrise and sunset are my favorite times.
   She and I tried hard to do this homework.
   Dinner and a movie would be a treat.
   Apples or bananas make a good snack.
   Photographs and paintings filled the room.
   Paper and pencils will be provided.
   Somebody or something is responsible.
   Books and newspapers covered the chairs.
   Gabriella and Danielle speak fluent Italian.

2. Read each of the following sentences aloud. Have students break them down into simple sentences (without compound predicates).

   We'll bake chicken or fry fish for dinner.
   I do homework or play ball after school.
   My cat sat and purred in the sunshine.
   The nurse works nights and sleeps days.
   He bakes or buys cookies on Saturdays.
   I can't think or get anything done today.
   Mr. Lopez plays the piano and sings.
   Do you walk or ride to school?
   I heard fire engines and police sirens.
   Carmelita studied and passed the test.
   Astronauts train hard and work long hours.
   Roberto fell and hurt himself.
   They'll win or lose the title tonight.
   I thought about it and changed my mind.

3. Read the following simple sentences. Have students produce compound subjects, using and or or as conjunctions (e.g., say: Ed drank milk. Students may respond: *"Ed and Sue drank milk"*).

   Ed drank milk.
   Ambulances shrieked.
   Sharon gave instructions.
   Our class saw a play.
   Mario selects the uniforms.
   The House passed a bill.
   Liz found the information.
   Doctors rushed to the accident scene.
   Mr. Perez finished it.
   My house looked old.

4. Read the simple sentences from step 3. Have students produce compound subjects and compound predicates using **and**, **but**, or **or**. For example, say: Liz found the information. Students may respond: *"Liz and Jose found the information and sold it."*

5. Hold up a sentence strip from Lesson 234. Have students form compound sentences by joining the prompted sentence with one of their own. Make sure **and**, **but**, or **or** is used in each formation. Encourage students to make compound sentences containing compound subjects and compound predicates (e.g., students may say: *"Dr. Lee **and** her assistant pulled my tooth **and** filled a cavity"*).

6. Encourage students to practice compound sentences throughout the day.

Lesson 236

In this lesson, students will learn to form relative clauses using the relative pronoun **who.**

1. Read each of the following sentences and have students repeat. Ask the students to listen for a pattern in the sentences.

   He is the student who won the prize.
   The one who teaches math is Mr. Lee.
   He who hesitates is lost.
   She knows the girl who drives.
   I preferred the candidate who lost.
   Do you know the man who won?
   It was Edison who invented the lightbulb.
   Dr. King, who had the dream, led us.
   Grant, who led the Union, won.
   Eva was the student who helped me.
   Steve is the student who finished first.
   We looked for the person who drove that cab.
   Is she the one who brought the gifts for us?
   They who plant seeds reap rewards.
   Lee, who led the Confederacy, lost.
   You are the one who helped me.

2. Read sentences from step 1. After each sentence, prompt students with a question to elicit the relative clause (e.g., say: He is the student who won the prize. Which student? Students should respond: *"Who won the prize"*).

3. Read each sentence from step 1 with and without the relative clause. Explain that the sentence without the relative clause is the **base** sentence (e.g., say: He is the student who won the prize. He is the student Ø).

4. Say each sentence from step 1. Have students identify the base sentences of each.

   stimulus: He is the student who won the prize. — response: *"He is the student Ø."* response: *"He Ø won the prize."*
   stimulus: He who hesitates is lost. — response: *"He Ø hesitates."* response: *"He Ø is lost."*

5. Provide two base sentences and ask students to combine them using **who**. Be sure that each student generates a sentence containing a relative clause. Repeat until each student has had several opportunities to create sentences containing a relative clause.

   stimulus: He is the boy. He writes well. — response: *"He is the boy who writes well."*
   stimulus: She knows the girl. The girl drives. — response: *"She knows the girl who drives."*

6. Encourage students to listen for **who** relative clauses throughout the day.

Lesson 237

In this lesson, students will learn to form relative clauses using the relative pronoun **that**.

1. Read each of the following sentences and have students repeat. Ask the students to listen for a pattern in the sentences. Note that **that** sets off an essential relative clause.

   This is the story that we read.
   The watch that is broken is mine.
   The lamp that fell was not damaged.
   I loved the poem that you wrote.
   The box that we opened was empty.
   Is this the book that you needed?
   Cities that are exciting attract tourists.
   I lost the pencil that had a good eraser.
   The family that came from Austin moved in.
   The team that won was Los Angeles.
   The injury that I suffered caused me pain.
   Science is a subject that interests me.
   Habits that we have are hard to break.
   A mystery is something that is unknown.

2. Read the sentences from step 1. After each sentence, prompt students with a question to elicit the relative clause. For example, say: This is the story that we read. Which story? Students should respond: *"that we read."* Point out to students that **who** refers to people and **that** refers to people, animals, or things.

3. Read each sentence from step 1 and then repeat it without the relative clause. Explain that the sentence without the relative clause is the **base** sentence (e.g., say: Science is a subject that interests me. Science is a subject Ø).

4. Say each sentence from step 1. Have students identify the base sentence of each.

   stimulus: The watch that is broken is mine. response: *"The watch Ø is mine."*
   stimulus: The box that we opened was empty. response: *"The box Ø was empty."*

5. Provide two base sentences and ask students to combine them using **that**. Be sure that each student generates a sentence containing a relative clause. Repeat until each student has had several opportunities to create sentences containing a relative clause.

   stimulus: Here is the canvas. I need to paint. response: *"Here is the canvas that I need to paint."*

6. Encourage students to listen for **that** relative clauses throughout the day.

Lesson 238

In this lesson, students will learn to form relative clauses using the relative pronoun **which**.

1. Read each of the following sentences and have students repeat. Ask the students to listen for a pattern in the sentences. Note that **which** sets off a nonessential relative clause.

   Anchorage is in Alaska, which is a big state.
   I live in New Mexico, which is bilingual.
   The cats, which sat there, were beautiful.
   We like San Diego, which has much history.
   Atlanta, which is Georgia's capital, is hot.
   I enjoyed the meal, which you prepared.
   Canaries, which sing sweetly, are yellow.
   The dogs, which had been fed, slept.
   Honolulu, which attracts tourists, is lovely.
   Miami, which is subtropical, is in Florida.
   They came from Arizona, which is dry.
   These are the apples, which we bought yesterday.
   Here are the towels, which we folded.
   It was explained in a letter, which I read.
   We ate lunch, which was served here.
   These are the tools, which they used.

2. Read sentences from step 1. After each sentence, prompt students with a question to elicit the relative clause. For example, say: Anchorage is in Alaska, which is a big state. What about Alaska? Students should respond: *"which is a big state."* Remind students that **who** refers to people and **that** refers to people, animals, or things. Emphasize that **which** refers to animals or things.

3. Read each sentence from step 1. Ask students to identify the base sentence (e.g., say: The dogs, which had been fed, slept. Students should respond: *"The dogs Ø slept"*).

4. Read each sentence from step 1. Have students identify the base sentence and the relative clause. Ask individual students to form a new sentence using the same relative clause with a new base sentence. For example, say: The cats, which sat there, were beautiful. Students may respond: *"The cats Ø were beautiful"* (base sentence); *"which sat there"* (relative clause); *"The animals, which sat there, looked hungry."*

5. Prompt students with a base sentence, using the sentences in step 1. Have students use the prompt to generate a sentence containing a relative clause. Repeat until each student has had several opportunities to create sentences containing a relative clause.

   stimulus: We ate lunch. response: *"We ate lunch, which was delicious."*

6. Encourage students to listen for **which** relative clauses throughout the day.

Lesson 239

In this lesson, students will learn to form relative clauses using the relative pronoun **what**.

1. Read each of the following sentences and have students repeat. Ask the students to listen for a pattern in the sentences.

   Is this what you wanted?
   We try to do what is right.
   We cannot change what is done.
   I don't know what he did.
   Do you know what is finished?
   It was not what we thought.
   He told us what we should do.
   I can't think what we might need.
   He asked what Sam had brought.
   Mothers know what is best for their children.
   I loved what we heard.
   We wondered what became of her.
   What happened was a mystery.
   What a cool car you bought!

2. Read sentences from step 1. After each sentence, prompt students with a question to elicit the relative clause. For example, say: It was not what we thought. It was not what? Students should respond: *"what we thought."* Remind students that **who** refers to people; **that** refers to people, animals, or things; and **which** refers to animals or things. Indicate that **what** means "that which" or "the thing which."

3. Read each sentence from step 1. Ask students to identify the base sentence. For example, say: I loved what we heard. Students should respond: *"I loved Ø."*

4. Say each sentence from step 1. Have students identify the relative clause of each. For example:

   stimulus: He told us what we should do. response: *"what we should do"*
   stimulus: We wondered what became of her. response: *"what became of her"*

5. Prompt students with a base sentence, using the sentences in step 1. Have students use the prompt to generate a sentence containing a relative clause. Repeat until each student has had several opportunities to create sentences containing a relative clause.

   stimulus: He told us. response: *"He told us what a cold day it would be."*

6. Encourage students to listen for **what** relative clauses throughout the day.

Lesson 240

In this lesson, students will review ways to form relative clauses using the relative pronouns **who**, **that**, **which**, and **what**.

1. Review with students that **who** refers to people; **that** refers to people, animals, or things; **which** refers to animals or things; and **what** means "that which" or "the thing which."

2. Read each of the following sentences and have students repeat.

   He is the player who won the game.
   She explained what we needed to know.
   Did you find the paper that you needed?
   I don't know what he did.
   He told us what we should do.
   I fed the animals, which were very hungry.
   The children, who live here, are relatives.
   I should thank the person who did this.
   I can't think what we might need.
   The principal knows who did it.
   Can you see the person who is in back?
   This is the new car that my sister bought.
   She couldn't decide what she should do.
   He longs for his home, which is far away.
   The girl who played the flute was Mia.
   What was the movie that you saw?

3. Read sentences from step 1. Ask students if another relative pronoun can be substituted. If so, have them demonstrate. Have students repeat the sentence with the new relative pronoun. For example, say: He is the player who won the game. Students should respond: *"He is the player that won the game."* (Point out that "which" would be incorrect, as it is referring to a person.)

4. Begin a round-robin story with one of the sentences from step 1. Have each student add a sentence to the story. Continue using sentences from step 1 to create other stories. Encourage students to use relative clauses in their sentences. Make sure each student has several opportunities to produce sentences.

5. Provide students with a base sentence and a relative clause. Have students use the prompt to generate a sentence containing both elements. Have another student use the same base sentence with a new relative clause. Repeat until each student has had several opportunities to create sentences containing a relative clause.

6. Encourage students to listen for **who, that, which,** and **what** relative clauses throughout the day.

Lesson 241

In this lesson, students will learn sentence expansion with adverbial clauses using conjunctive adverbs. Adverbial clauses modify verbs, adjectives, and other adverbs.

1. Expand the base sentences provided using the following conjunctive adverbs: **after, as, before, since, until, when, where, while** (e.g., say: I want to see you. I want to see you after they go home.). Have students repeat each sentence.

Sailboats raced.	I want to see you.	We stood in line.
Pete bought some stamps.	The band played.	Al bought this book.
We began in October.	The books arrived.	Dogs barked.
Spring had ended.	Anita waited.	Janet answered.
You should enter.	We tried everything.	Her pictures were developed.
We finished the project.	The bell rang.	The silence ended.
The milk spilled.	I dropped the papers.	I read the book.

2. Have students form sentences with adverbial clauses. Post a list of the conjunctive adverbs from step 1 in the front of the class. Prompt students with a base sentence from step 1 and have individual students expand it using a conjunctive adverb. Continue until each student has had a few opportunities to expand sentences. *(Note: Focus on sentence expansion; grammatical terms do not need to be emphasized.)*

   stimulus: We tried everything. response: *"We tried everything while we waited for him."*

3. Demonstrate how sentence structure can be reversed by switching the base sentence with the adverbial clause (e.g., say: The silence ended when the bell rang. When the bell rang, the silence ended). Provide several examples and have students repeat.

4. Prompt students with a sentence containing an adverbial clause. (Each adverbial clause should begin with one of the conjunctive adverbs listed in step 1.) Have individual students change the position of the adverbial clause as shown in step 3. Make sure each student has a few opportunities to rearrange sentences. If an error is made, model the correct sentence construction and have student repeat.

5. Prompt students with a conjunctive adverb. Have individual students generate a sentence with the given adverb. Then have students reverse the positions of the base sentence and the adverbial clause (e.g., say: When. Students may respond: *"I run when I have to. When I have to, I run"*). Ask all students to repeat both sentences. Give each student an opportunity to generate a sentence.

6. Encourage students to create sentences with adverbial clauses by using **after, as, before, since, until, when, where,** and **while** throughout the day.

Lesson 242

In this lesson, students will practice sentence expansion with adverbial clauses using conjunctive adverbs.

1. Expand the base sentences provided using the following conjunctive adverbs: **after, as, before, since, until, when, where, while**. For example, say: I was really scared. I was really scared before you came here. Have students repeat each sentence.

She opened her package.	The bell rang.	She started to cry.
Let's see a movie.	I was really scared.	They tried to tell her.
We can fix it.	My mom was happy.	Collect the papers.
People were running.	We thought about it.	Please pass out these books.
Our teacher helped him.	Can you give it to her?	The playground was quiet.
One night, he left.	Can you come?	My friend came.
Could you stay?	The car stopped.	He sailed the boat.

2. Have students form sentences with adverbial clauses. Post a list of the conjunctive adverbs from step 1 in the front of the class. Prompt students with a base sentence from step 1 and have individual students expand it using a conjunctive adverb. Continue until each student has a few opportunities to expand sentences. *(Note: Focus on sentence expansion; grammatical terms do not need to be emphasized.)*

3. Demonstrate how sentence structure can be reversed by switching the base sentence with the adverbial clause. Say: The bell rang as we left. As we left, the bell rang. We left as the bell rang. Provide several examples and have students repeat.

4. Prompt students with a sentence containing an adverbial clause. (Each adverbial clause should begin with one of the conjunctive adverbs listed in step 1.) Have individual students change the position of the adverbial clause as shown in step 3. Make sure each student has a few opportunities to rearrange sentences. If an error is made, model the correct sentence construction and have student repeat.

5. Prompt students with a conjunctive adverb. Have individual students generate a sentence with the given adverb. Then have students reverse the positions of the base sentence and the adverbial clause. Ask all students to repeat both sentences. Give each student an opportunity to generate a sentence.

6. Encourage students to create sentences with adverbial clauses by using **after, as, before, since, until, when, where,** and **while** throughout the day.

Lesson 243

In this lesson, students will practice sentence expansion with subordinate clauses using subordinate conjunctions.

1. Expand the base sentences provided using the following subordinate conjunctions: **as, as if, because, for, if, provided, since, so that, than, until, where, while**. For example, say: We left yesterday. We left yesterday so that we wouldn't have to drive in the snow. Have students repeat each sentence.

I waited in the gym.	We left yesterday.	My sister made a salad.
You can't imagine it.	People left the stadium.	I wrote my report.
Our team was not ready.	Liz went to the party.	We read this for history.
Mom helped me.	I washed the towels.	We arrived from Russia.
Let's go together.	He thanked us.	My father was born in Mexico.
Jim smelled the flowers.	You should try it.	My mother left Saigon.
Her little sister was sick.	They lived in China.	My father couldn't find his razor.

2. Have students form sentences with subordinate clauses. Post a list of the subordinate conjunctions from step 1 in the front of the class. Prompt students with a base sentence from step 1 and have individual students expand it using a subordinate conjunction. Continue until each student has a few opportunities to expand sentences. *(Note: Focus on sentence expansion; grammatical terms do not need to be emphasized.)*

3. Demonstrate how sentence structure can be reversed by switching the base sentence with the subordinate clause. Say: I waited in the gym because she was late. Because she was late, I waited in the gym. Provide several examples and have students repeat.

4. Prompt students with a sentence containing a subordinate clause. (Each subordinate clause should begin with one of the subordinate conjunctions listed in step 1.) Have individual students change the position of the subordinate clause as shown in step 3. Make sure each student has a few opportunities to rearrange sentences. If an error is made, model the correct sentence construction and have student repeat.

5. Prompt students with a subordinate conjunction. Have individual students generate a sentence with the given conjunction. Then have students reverse the positions of the base sentence and the subordinate clause. Ask all students to repeat both sentences. Give each student an opportunity to generate a sentence.

6. Encourage students to create sentences with subordinate clauses by using **as, as if, because, for, if, provided, since, so that, than, until, where,** and **while** throughout the day.

Lesson 244

In this lesson, students will practice sentence expansion using subordinate conjunctions.

1. Using the base sentences provided, demonstrate how subordinate conjunctions (**as, as if, because, for, if, provided, since, so that, than, until, where, while**) can be used to create one complex sentence. For example, say: We found a public park. We ate lunch. We found a public park where we ate lunch. Have students repeat each sentence.

We found a public park.	They'll be here.	There is a lot of work to do.
She has to get back here.	They challenged us.	I might do it.
He stayed indoors.	The teacher helped us.	Sari tried to start the car.
Some of us stayed.	We ate lunch.	Kim left after school.
Tran gave Mr. Myers her report.	Our lunch was gone.	There isn't enough money.
We watched the game.	The crowd loved him.	Karen will be first.
My mother fixed it.	Her house is beautiful.	I'd like to have some ice cream.

2. Post a list of the subordinate conjunctions from step 1 in the front of the class. Prompt students with two simple sentences. Have students form complex sentences using subordinate conjunctions. Continue until each student has a few opportunities to form complex sentences. *(Note: Focus on sentence expansion; grammatical terms do not need to be emphasized.)*

3. Demonstrate how sentence structure can be reversed by switching the base sentence with the subordinate clause. Say: He stayed indoors while his ankle was broken. While his ankle was broken, he stayed indoors. Provide several examples and have students repeat.

4. Prompt students with a sentence containing a subordinate clause. (Each subordinate clause should begin with one of the subordinate conjunctions listed in step 1.) Have individual students change the position of the subordinate clause as shown in step 3. Make sure each student has a few opportunities to rearrange sentences. If an error is made, model the correct sentence construction and have student repeat.

5. Prompt students with a subordinate conjunction. Have individual students generate a complex sentence with the given subordinate conjunction. Then have the students reverse the positions of the base sentence and the subordinate clause. Ask all students to repeat both sentences. Give each student an opportunity to generate a sentence.

6. Encourage students to create sentences with subordinate clauses by using **as, as if, because, for, if, provided, since, so that, than, until, where,** and **while** throughout the day.

Lesson 245

This lesson is a comprehensive review of sentence expansion using conjunctive adverbs and subordinate conjunctions.

1. Prompt students with a base sentence and a conjunctive adverb (**after, as, before, since, until, when, where, while**). Have individual students expand sentences.

   stimulus: Pete bought some stamps **when**… response: *"he went to the post office."*
   stimulus: We began in October **before**… response: *"the winter season arrived."*
   stimulus: We stood in line **while**… response: *"we waited for everyone else."*

   Answers will vary. Focus on sentence expansion, not grammatical terms. *(Note: For a list of stimulus sentences, see Lessons 241–244.)*

2. Prompt students with a base sentence and a subordinate conjunction (**as, as if, because, for, if, provided, since, so that, than, until, where, while**). Have individual students expand sentences.

   stimulus: Let's go together **since**… response: *"we live on the same street."*
   stimulus: You should try it **while**… response: *"you still have some time."*
   stimulus: They lived in China **until**… response: *"I was born."*

   Answers will vary. Focus on proper sentence construction. Repeat until each student has had several opportunities to expand a sentence.

3. Provide complex sentences and have individual students demonstrate their knowledge of syntax by switching the positions of the base sentence and the adverbial clause.

   stimulus: We stood **when** she entered. response: *"**When** she entered, we stood."*
   stimulus: The band played **as** she entered. response: *"**As** she entered, the band played."*
   stimulus: We left **after** the show ended. response: *"**After** the show ended, we left."*

4. Provide complex sentences and have individual students demonstrate their knowledge of syntax by switching the positions of the base sentence and the subordinate clause.

   stimulus: We saw a park **as** we drove by. response: *"**As** we drove by, we saw a park."*
   stimulus: Let's go together **since** we live on the same street. response: *"**Since** we live on the same street, let's go together."*

5. Prompt students with a base sentence a conjunction from steps 1 or 2. Have students create complex sentences using the base sentence and an adverbial clause, beginning with the prompted conjunction.

   stimulus: The milk spilled **when**… response: *"**when** she dropped her glass."*
   stimulus: Janet answered **since**… response: *"**since** she was the first to raise her hand."*
   stimulus: I washed the towels... response: *"while he cleaned the kitchen."*

6. Encourage students to practice sentence expansion using conjunctive adverbs and subordinate conjunctions.

Lesson 246

Materials: articles about celebrities or sports figures

In this lesson, students will begin a series of oral presentations.

1. Demonstrate a three- to four-minute oral presentation on school manners and the creation of "Manners Banners."

2. Discuss which school problems might be alleviated if there were a code of manners among members of the school community (e.g., teachers, students, cafeteria workers, administrators, parents). Write the list of generated ideas in the front of the class.

3. Explain presentation requirements as follows:

   A. Students will work in small groups and select three areas of concern (e.g., trash in the courtyard, graffiti on desks, cars speeding through the school zone).

   B. One member of the group will present the areas of concern and the problems each creates (e.g., unkempt schoolyard, worn-looking desks, dangerous intersections where students must walk).

   C. Discuss ways the problems might be solved by implementing a "code of manners" for the school community to follow (e.g., if students and teachers put their trash in garbage cans, then everyone would be proud of this school because it is clean; if students took pride in school property and reminded others of their ownership in the school, then everyone would have clean desks; if parents stopped at crosswalks when they dropped off their children for school, then students and teachers would have a safe area in which to cross).

4. Divide students into groups of three or four. Give groups seven to ten minutes to prepare for their presentations. Students may use notes during their presentations. Each group should have a designated spokesperson to present ideas. The spokesperson will rotate with each assignment, providing each student several opportunities to speak in front of the class.

5. Have each group present its ideas to the class. Volunteers may go first. Pay careful attention to the oral output of each student, focusing on comprehension and grammar. Set a timer to limit each presentation to three to four minutes. After each speech, discuss any errors made and model correct sentence structure.

6. The topic for the next day will be "Sports Figures and Celebrities." Give each group a different article about a celebrity or sports figure. (All students should get a copy of their group's article.) Students may gather other sources of information if they choose. Encourage the class to watch a television show or clip an article from a newspaper or magazine about a sports figure or celebrity who interests them.

Lesson 247

Materials: clippings of weather forecasts

In this lesson, students will practice giving oral presentations.

1. Demonstrate a three- to four-minute oral presentation on "Sports Figures and Celebrities."
2. Have students break into the small groups formed in Lesson 246. Have the group members share information from the article they received or gathered on their own. Each group needs to decide on one celebrity or sports figure for its report.
3. Explain presentation requirements as follows:
   A. The group spokesperson will provide at least three facts about the sports figure or celebrity (e.g., name, occupation, age, sport, team).
   B. The students will give details of the story they are reporting (e.g., what happened, where, when, why).
   C. Reports should be given in a "live report" format. Have students pretend they are on television, covering a story for the news.
4. Give groups seven to ten minutes to prepare for their presentations. Students may use notes during their presentations. Each group should have a designated spokesperson to present ideas. The spokesperson will rotate with each assignment, providing each student several opportunities to speak in front of the class.
5. Have each group present its topic to the class. Volunteers may go first. Pay careful attention to the oral output of each student, focusing on comprehension and grammar. Set a timer to limit each presentation to three to four minutes. After each speech, discuss any errors made and model correct sentence structure.
6. The topic for the next day will be "Local/Regional Weather Forecasts." Give each group a newspaper or Internet clipping of a weather forecast for a different region of the country. (All students should get a copy of their group's clipping.) Students may use other sources of information if they choose. Encourage students to watch a weather forecast on television and take notes about the weather predictions.

Lesson 248

Materials: newspaper or magazine articles about national current events

In this lesson, students will practice giving oral presentations.

1. Demonstrate a three- to four-minute oral presentation on "Local/Regional Weather Forecast."

2. Have students break into the small groups formed in Lesson 246. Have the group members share information from the article they received or gathered on their own. Each group needs to decide on one specific region for its report.

3. Explain presentation requirements as follows:

   A. The spokesperson will discuss the unique area of the country the group will be speaking about and give its geographical characteristics (have a map available for students to refer to and point out different regional features).

   B. The students will give the current and short-term weather forecasts, including factors that are influencing the weather (e.g., cold front, warm front, hurricane, storms in surrounding states).

   C. Reports should be given in a "live report" format.

4. Give groups seven to ten minutes to prepare for their presentation. Students may use notes during their presentations. Each group should have a designated spokesperson to present ideas. The spokesperson will rotate with each assignment, providing each student several opportunities to speak in front of the class.

5. Have each group present its topic to the class. Volunteers may go first. Pay careful attention to the oral output of each student, focusing on comprehension and grammar. Set a timer to limit each presentation to three to four minutes. After each speech, discuss any errors made and model correct sentence structure.

6. The topic for the next day will be "National News." Give each group a different article about a newsworthy event. (All students should get a copy of their group's clipping.) Students may use other sources of information if they choose. Encourage students to watch the news or clip an article from a newspaper or magazine.

Lesson 249

Materials: newspaper or magazine articles about international news

In this lesson, students will practice giving oral presentations.

1. Demonstrate a three- to four-minute oral presentation on "National News."

2. Have students break into the small groups and share national news from the article they received or the information they gathered on their own. Each group needs to decide on one news item for its report.

3. Explain presentation requirements as follows:

   A. The spokesperson will provide several facts about the news item the group has chosen (e.g., who, what, where, when, why).

   B. The students will explain why this story is important to people in the United States (e.g., if the president is asking Congress to allocate more money for schools, all students, parents, and teachers may want to find out what this means to them. Will they get new books, buildings, or buses? Will there be more teachers next year? Will the classes be smaller?).

   C. Reports should be given in a "live report" format.

4. Give groups seven to ten minutes to prepare for their presentations. Students may use notes during their presentations. Each group should have a designated spokesperson to present ideas. The spokesperson will rotate with each assignment.

5. Have each group present its topic to the class. Volunteers may go first. Pay careful attention to the oral output of each student, focusing on comprehension and grammar. Set a timer to limit each presentation to three to four minutes. After each speech, discuss any errors made and model correct sentence structure.

6. The topic for the next day will be "International News." Give each group a different article about an international event. (All students should get a copy of their group's clipping.) Students may use other sources of information if they choose. Encourage the class to watch the news or clip an article from a newspaper or magazine covering an international story.

Lesson 250

In this lesson, students will practice giving oral presentations.

1. Demonstrate a three- to four-minute oral presentation on "International News."

2. Have students break into their small groups and share international news from the article they received or the information they gathered on their own. Each group needs to decide on one news item for its report.

3. Explain presentation requirements as follows:

   A. The spokesperson will provide several facts about the news item the group has chosen (e.g., who, what, where, when, why).

   B. The students will explain why this story is important to people in the United States (e.g., if the price of crude oil from Saudi Arabia is increasing, people in the United States may have to pay a higher price for gasoline).

   C. Reports should be given in a "live report" format.

4. Give groups seven to ten minutes to prepare for their presentations. Students may use notes during their presentations. Each group should have a designated spokesperson to present ideas. The spokesperson will rotate with each assignment. Make sure each student has spoken in front of the class once before other students go a second time.

5. Have each group present its topic to the class. Volunteers may go first. Pay careful attention to the oral output of each student, focusing on comprehension and grammar. Set a timer to limit each presentation to three to four minutes. After each speech, discuss any errors made and model correct sentence structure.

6. The topic for the next day will be "Selling a Product." Encourage students to think of a product; they will need to use persuasion to **sell** whatever product they choose. Briefly discuss commercials and what makes them effective.

Lesson 251

In this lesson, students will practice giving oral presentations.

1. Demonstrate a two- to three-minute oral presentation on "Selling a Product."

2. Have students break into their small groups and choose a product to present. Suggest different products to get them started (e.g., cereal, soft drink, sneakers, backpack, car, shampoo, board game). *(Note: Students are **not** to choose brand-name products. They may make up a brand name or talk about a product without using its brand name.)* Each group needs to decide on one product to "sell."

3. Explain presentation requirements as follows:

   A. Each spokesperson will present a two- to three-minute commercial about the chosen product, explaining what the product is and does.

   B. The students must explain why this product is the best on the market, using at least three examples (e.g., ballpoint pens are the best because they write smoothly, they come in a variety of colors, the ink can be washed out of clothes, they aren't expensive, they are comfortable to hold, they can be purchased at a variety of stores).

   C. The students will explain why everyone should use the product and why it is better than any other of its kind.

4. Give groups seven to ten minutes to prepare for their presentations. Students may use notes during their presentations. Each group should have a designated spokesperson to present ideas. The spokesperson will rotate with each assignment, providing each student several opportunities to speak in front of the class.

5. Have each group present its topic to the class. Volunteers may go first. Pay careful attention to the oral output of each student, focusing on comprehension and grammar. Set a timer to limit each presentation to two to three minutes. After each speech, discuss any errors made and model correct sentence structure.

6. Provide students with the topic for the next oral presentation, "Career Goals: What I Plan To Do With My Life." Encourage students to think about the topic and write some ideas on paper.

Lesson 252

In this lesson, students will practice giving oral presentations.

1. Demonstrate a two- to three-minute oral presentation on "Career Goals: What I Plan To Do With My Life."

2. Discuss different kinds of professions. Suggest specific ones to get students started (e.g., accountant, astronaut, barber, carpenter, dentist, doctor, electrician, engineer, firefighter, interior designer, lawyer, mechanic, plumber, telephone repair technician, teacher, zookeeper). Have students decide on one profession for their presentations.

3. Explain presentation requirements as follows:

    A. Each student will present a two- to three-minute speech on career goals. Have each begin with explaining goals and specifying the chosen profession. The student will list responsibilities (e.g., carpenter: build new houses, make repairs to older houses, build additions to houses, add porches, install appliances, install floors).

    B. The student must identify the educational/training requirements for their profession (e.g., carpenter: finish high school, go to technical college, get a job with a contracting firm, be an apprentice, study books on carpentry).

    C. The student will briefly share reasons for choosing this career. Will it be rewarding? Will this career choice be good for the community? For example: a student might say: *"If I am a carpenter, I would be building homes for families or office buildings for workers. I could build a playhouse for my children. I could volunteer to make home repairs for people with no money for repairs."*

4. Give students five minutes to prepare for their presentations. Students will speak about their chosen professions; however, they may work in small groups to share ideas, give feedback, and prepare. Encourage students to write notes to use during their presentations.

5. Have all students present their speeches to the class. Volunteers may go first. Pay careful attention to the oral output of each student, focusing on comprehension and grammar. Set a timer to limit each presentation to two to three minutes. After each speech, discuss any errors made and model correct sentence structure.

6. If there is not enough time for each student to present, have students continue the following day. Provide students with the topic for the next oral presentation, "Television Favorites."

Lesson 253

In this lesson, students will practice giving oral presentations.

1. Demonstrate a two- to three-minute oral presentation on "Television Favorites."

2. Have students make a short list of their favorite television programs. Students need to decide on one program for their presentations.

3. Explain presentation requirements as follows:

   A. Each student will present a two- to three-minute speech on their favorite television program. Have each begin by explaining the setting of the television show (e.g., Where does the story take place? Are the characters in a school, an apartment building, a hospital, on an island?).

   B. Students will introduce their favorite characters and give three facts about that character (e.g., a student might say: *"My favorite character is Jennifer. She is 22 years old, a college student at Glendale Community College, and her best friend is Maria"*).

   C. Students will explain why these are their favorite programs, sharing recent story lines that they particularly enjoyed.

4. Give students five minutes to prepare for their presentations. Students will speak about their favorite program; however, they may work in small groups to share ideas, give feedback, and prepare. Encourage students to write notes to use during their presentations.

5. Have all students present their speeches to the class. Volunteers may go first. Pay careful attention to the oral output of each student, focusing on comprehension and grammar. Set a timer to limit each presentation to two to three minutes. After each speech, discuss any errors made and model correct sentence structure.

6. If there is not enough time for each student to present, have students continue the following day. Provide students with the topic for the next oral presentation, "Getting To Know You."

Lesson 254

In this lesson, students will practice giving oral presentations.

1. Demonstrate a two- to three-minute oral presentation on "Getting To Know You."

2. Have students work in assigned pairs "interviewing" each other. Discuss questions that would allow them to get to know each other (e.g., What are your hobbies? How long have you lived here? Do you play sports? How many brothers and sisters do you have? What kind of music do you like? Where do you think you will live when you graduate from high school? Where would you go if you could go anywhere in the world?).

3. Explain presentation requirements as follows:

   A. All students will present a two- to three-minute speech about their partners. Have them begin by introducing their partners to the class with a brief biographical overview (e.g., how many brothers and sisters they have, where they live).

   B. Students will discuss their partners' interests and hobbies.

   C. Students should conclude by sharing something they learned about their partners that they did not know before the interview.

4. Give students seven to ten minutes to interview each other. Students will need to take notes and use them during their presentations.

5. Have all students present their speeches to the class. Volunteers may go first. Pay careful attention to the oral output of each student, focusing on comprehension and grammar. Set a timer to limit each presentation to two to three minutes. After each speech, discuss any errors made and model correct sentence structure.

6. If there is not enough time for each student to present, have students continue the following day. Provide students with the topic for the next oral presentation, "Explain Yourself: Knowing Right From Wrong."

Lesson 255

In this lesson, students will practice giving oral presentations.

1. Demonstrate a two- to three-minute oral presentation on "Explain Yourself: Knowing Right From Wrong."

2. Have students recall a time when they made a bad decision or choice. Prompt students to generate examples of bad judgment (e.g., telling a secret that hurt a friend, lying to a parent, spending hard-earned money on something foolish, taking a book from the library without asking). Emphasize that everyone makes poor choices at one time or another, and it is important to learn from our mistakes.

3. Explain presentation requirements as follows:

   A. All students will present a two- to three-minute speech describing a time they used poor judgment. More important than the incident is why their behavioral decision turned out to be a bad choice. Have students discuss the negative repercussions of their choices.

   B. Students will share what they would change if they could revisit the situation (e.g., have students finish the following statement: *"If I could do it over again, I would…"*).

   C. Students will conclude by explaining the lessons learned from their poor judgment.

4. Give students five minutes to prepare for their presentations. All students will discuss a personal incident; however, they may work in small groups to prepare. Remind students to focus on lessons learned. Encourage students to write notes to use during their presentations.

5. Have all students present their speeches to the class. Volunteers may go first. Pay careful attention to the oral output of each student, focusing on comprehension and grammar. Set a timer to limit each presentation to two to three minutes. After each speech, discuss any errors made and model correct sentence structure.

6. If there is not enough time for each student to present, have students continue the following day. Provide students with the topic for the next oral presentation, "Rewriting the Law."

Lesson 256

In this lesson, students will practice giving oral presentations.

1. Demonstrate a two- to three-minute oral presentation on "Rewriting the Law."

2. Have students name different types of laws, either here or in another country. Post the list in the front of the class. If necessary, offer some examples of laws in this country (e.g., say: It is against the law to drive without a license, assault another person, steal, fail to pay your taxes). Have students select a law they would like to see changed.

3. Explain presentation requirements as follows:

   A. All students will present a two- to three-minute speech on the law they have chosen. Have students identify the law, present the reasons this law is in place, and who benefits from the law. For example, a student might discuss the minimum driving age. The student could say: *"This law was made because driving a car is a big responsibility. People who drive need to be big enough to see out the windshield and reach the pedals and be coordinated enough to react quickly to their circumstances; otherwise, people could get hurt."*

   B. Students will explain why they want to change this particular law. For example, a student might say: *"I would like to be able to drive now and not have to wait until I'm older. If I could drive, I could drive myself to school and not have to wait for the bus. I would have more job opportunities because I could get a job at one of the businesses that is hard to get to by bus or bike. I could go places on my schedule and not just when someone else is available to drive me."*

   C. The students must also predict what would happen if the law were changed. For example, a student might say: *"If there weren't a minimum driving age, kids who aren't ready to drive might be on the roads and cause accidents. There might also be more traffic and pollution because more people would be driving."*

4. Give students five minutes to prepare for their presentations. All students will discuss a law they want changed; however, students may work in small groups to prepare. Encourage students to write notes to use during their presentations.

5. Have all students present their speeches to the class. Volunteers may go first. Pay careful attention to the oral output of each student, focusing on comprehension and grammar. Set a timer to limit each presentation to two to three minutes. After each speech, discuss any errors made and model correct sentence structure.

6. If there is not enough time for each student to present, have students continue the following day. Provide students with the topic for the next oral presentation, "If I Could Have Anything I Wanted, I Would Wish For..."

Lesson 257

In this lesson, students will practice giving oral presentations.

1. Demonstrate a two- to three-minute oral presentation on "If I Could Have Anything I Wanted, I Would Wish For..."

2. Have students share some of their wishes. If necessary, offer some examples of wishes (e.g., say: I wish I could spend more time with my children, I wish my house was bigger, I wish I could travel to Japan). Have students select three wishes for their presentations.

3. Explain presentation requirements as follows:

   A. Students will speak for two to three minutes about their top three wishes. Have students rank their wishes in order of importance.

   B. Students will explain how their lives would be enriched if these wishes came true. For example, a student might say: *"My first wish would be to learn to play a trumpet. If I could play a trumpet, I could be in the school band and go to all the sports events with the rest of the band members. I would make new friends. I would sometimes get out of classes to practice. I would be able to entertain my family and friends with the trumpet. When I go to college, I could play a trumpet in the band at the college and make new friends quickly. My second wish would be...."*

   C. Students will evaluate the possibility of any of their wishes coming true. Have students identify the steps they could take to make one of their dreams come true. For example, a student might say: *"I want to learn to play the trumpet. To make that happen, I could set up a meeting with the band director to see how long it takes to learn to play. I could go to a music store and ask how much it costs to buy or rent a trumpet. I could begin to listen to trumpet players to familiarize myself with trumpet playing. I could look in the phone book under "Music Lessons" and find a trumpet teacher. I could make money by doing odd jobs and put the money I earn toward lessons."*

4. Give students five minutes to prepare for their presentations. Each student will discuss their three wishes. Encourage students to write notes to use during their presentations.

5. Have all students present their top three wishes to the class. Volunteers may go first. Pay careful attention to the oral output of each student, focusing on comprehension and grammar. Set a timer to limit each presentation to two to three minutes. After each speech, discuss any errors made and model correct sentence structure.

6. If there is not enough time for each student to present, have students continue the following day. Provide students with the topic for the next oral presentation, "My Family: Only The Best."

Lesson 258

In this lesson, students will practice giving oral presentations.

1. Demonstrate a two- to three-minute oral presentation on "My Family: Only The Best."

2. Have students make a list of their family members (parents, brothers, sisters, grandparents, aunts, uncles, cousins, stepfamilies) and write down the things they like most about their family members. Students may use these notes in their presentations.

3. Explain presentation requirements as follows:

   A. Students will speak for two to three minutes about the things they most admire about the people in their family. The students may speak about individual members' attributes, or may speak about the family as a whole. For example, a student might say: *"My Uncle Mario is a good cook and always has a funny joke to tell me. My Aunt Jenny always plays ball with me when I visit. My family is very warm and loving."*

   B. Students will choose one family member and explain how the two of them are alike. For example, a student might say: *"My cousin Frank is a good mechanic; I like to take things apart and put them back together, too."*

   C. Finally, students will share what makes their family strong. Students may discuss how family relationships are different from friendships. For example, a student might say: *"Our family eats dinner together every night and we talk about the day's events."*

4. Give students five minutes to prepare for their presentations. Each student will discuss this topic. Encourage students to write notes to use during their presentations.

5. Have all students present their speeches to the class. Volunteers may go first. Pay careful attention to the oral output of each student, focusing on comprehension and grammar. Set a timer to limit each presentation to two to three minutes. After each speech, discuss any errors made and model correct sentence structure.

6. If there is not enough time for each student to present, have students continue the following day. Provide students with the topic for the next oral presentation, "My Fabulous, Funny, Fantastic, Foolish, Friend."

Lesson 259

In this lesson, students will practice giving oral presentations.

1. Demonstrate a two- to three-minute oral presentation on "My Fabulous, Funny, Fantastic, Foolish Friend."

2. Have students write down the name of a very good friend, followed by the words: **fabulous**, **funny**, **fantastic**, and **foolish**.

3. Explain presentation requirements as follows:

   A. Students will speak for two to three minutes about the friend they have chosen. They may use one or more of the adjectives from step 2 to describe that friend. Have all students tell a story to explain why their friends are fabulous, funny, fantastic, and/or foolish.

   B. Students need to give a specific example of their friend acting in one or more of the ways listed in step 2. For example, a student might say: *"My friend, Mark, is both funny and foolish. He was singing a song off-key, and we were laughing. He did it in class and got into trouble with our teacher. My fabulous friend Rita let me borrow her favorite sweater for the dance."*

   C. Students need to share why they like this friend. Have them use adjectives other than the ones listed in step 2 to describe their friends. Each presentation must include one sentence to describe what they think builds a good friendship. For example, a student might say: *"Tran is my friend because she is honest and kind. Carlos is my friend because he is funny and smart."*

4. Give students five minutes to prepare for their presentations. Each student will discuss this topic. Encourage students to write notes to use during their presentations.

5. Have all students present their speeches to the class. Volunteers may go first. Pay careful attention to the oral output of each student, focusing on comprehension and grammar. Set a timer to limit each presentation to two to three minutes. After each speech, discuss any errors made and model correct sentence structure.

6. If there is not enough time for each student to present, have students continue the following day. Provide students with the topic for the next oral presentation, "If I Were You."

Lesson 260

In this lesson, students will practice giving oral presentations.

1. Demonstrate a two- to three-minute oral presentation on "If I Were You."

2. Pair students and have them discuss problems they are having, big or small. Students should make a list of ideas that might help their partners deal with their problems. All students will address their partners directly during their presentations. Give students an example of possible ideas to suggest. For example, say: Since you are having trouble with geometry, I think you should speak with Mr. Soto about getting a tutor after school, talk with your parents about helping you with your homework, and ask Tina to help you because geometry is her favorite subject.

3. Explain presentation requirements as follows:

   A. Students will speak directly to their partners for two to three minutes. All students will share their advice in a positive and constructive way. The speaker will identify the problem their partner is having, then offer suggestions that might help the most. For example, a student will address the class and say: *"Donna needs extra money for a trip to Florida this summer."* The speaker will then talk directly to Donna, and say: *"I think what would help you most would be to talk with our school counselor about getting a part-time job after school. The counselor could show you how to locate jobs that would not interfere with your school work."*

   B. The student receiving the advice is to ask the presenting student two to three questions (e.g., *"Have you ever had a job after school? What kind of job did you have? When could I set up an appointment with the counselor?"*).

   C. The presenting student must answer the questions with complete sentences, providing as much information as possible. Emphasize that the content of their questions and answers is important, but the manner in which they speak is the focus of this exercise.

4. Give students five minutes to prepare for their presentations. Working in pairs, students will need to take notes as they listen to their partner. Students may use these notes during their presentations.

5. Have all students present their speeches to the class. Volunteers may go first. Pay careful attention to the oral output of each student, focusing on comprehension and grammar. Set a timer to limit each presentation to two to three minutes. After each speech, discuss any errors made and model correct sentence structure.

6. If there is not enough time for each student to present, have students continue the following day. Provide students with the topic for the next oral presentation, "Crazy English."

Lesson 261

In this lesson, students will practice giving oral presentations.

1. Demonstrate a two- to three-minute oral presentation on "Crazy English."

2. Ask students to think back on all their English lessons thus far. Have students brainstorm some of the most confusing parts of learning to speak English (e.g., pronunciation [read, read], word meanings [to, two, too], the difference between adjectives and adverbs). Put the list in the front of the class.

3. Explain presentation requirements as follows:

   A. Students will present a two- to three-minute speech on what makes English hard to learn. Students will discuss the most difficult aspects (for them) to master. Have students give a few examples.

   B. Students will identify the parts of learning to speak English that were the easiest for them and explain why.

   C. Students will decide if they think they could teach someone else to speak English. What would they change to make the difficult parts easier to learn?

4. Give students five minutes to prepare for their presentations. Encourage students to take notes to use during their presentations.

5. Have all students present their speeches to the class. Volunteers may go first. Pay careful attention to the oral output of each student, focusing on comprehension and grammar. Set a timer to limit each presentation to two to three minutes. After each speech, discuss any errors made and model correct sentence structure.

6. If there is not enough time for each student to present, have students continue the following day. Provide students with the topic for the next oral presentation, "Me, The Teacher."

Lesson 262

In this lesson, students will practice giving oral presentations.

1. Demonstrate a two- to three-minute oral presentation on "Me, The Teacher."

2. Ask students to think back on all their English lessons thus far. Have students make a list of the most important concepts to master when learning to speak English. All students will pick one important concept of spoken English and make notes on how they would teach this concept if they were teachers.

3. Explain presentation requirements as follows:

   A. Students will present a two- to three-minute speech about teaching others to speak English. The students should explain the meaning of their chosen concept to the class. For example, a student might choose plurals and say: *"One **bike**, two or more **bikes**. **Bikes** is the plural of **bike**. In English, regular plurals are made by adding* **–s**, *or* **–es**. *English is hard because so many words have irregular plurals, like one **mouse**, two **mice**."*

   B. Students will demonstrate the meaning of the concept using objects or drawings, or writing on the board (e.g., for plurals, the student could hold up one pencil, then two pencils).

   C. Students are to "teach" this concept to English learners in a clear and concise manner. Students need to decide if their methods differ from the ways in which the concepts were taught by the teacher and decide if they are more or less effective.

4. Give students five minutes to prepare for their presentations. Encourage students to take notes to use during their presentations.

5. Have all students present their speeches to the class. Volunteers may go first. Pay careful attention to the oral output of each student, focusing on comprehension and grammar. Set a timer to limit each presentation to two to three minutes. After each speech, discuss any errors made and model correct sentence structure.

6. If there is not enough time for each student to present, have students continue the following day. Provide students with the topic for the next oral presentation, "Way To Go."

Lesson 263

In this lesson, students will practice giving oral presentations.

1. Demonstrate a two- to three-minute oral presentation on "Way To Go."

2. Have students brainstorm different means of transportation and the various tasks related to these means. Put the list in the front of the class (e.g., dump truck: hauls dirt, sand, gravel; airplane: carries people, mail, and supplies a long distance in a short period of time; ship: transports people or things across water; wheelchair: provides a way to move around for people who cannot walk.

3. Explain presentation requirements as follows:

   A. Students will present a two- to three-minute speech about different modes of transportation and the tasks accomplished by each. Have students discuss a specific task to be completed, and then state the many different means of transportation that could be used to accomplish this task (e.g., if the task is hauling corn from Iowa to Mexico, a student may say: *"This can be done by car, plane, train, shipping service, and U.S. Mail"*).

   B. Students will then identify the best mode of transportation for their task (e.g., *"If a car, shipping service, or U.S. Mail is used, only a small amount of corn can be delivered. If a plane is used, a large amount could be shipped, but many places in Iowa and Mexico do not have convenient airports. If a train is used, the containers can carry many tons of corn at a time, and almost every town in Mexico and Iowa has train tracks. Therefore, the train would be the best way to go"*).

   C. Students will conclude by "inventing" a means of transportation that would complete the job more easily, faster, or cheaper than the means of transportation available at this time (e.g., *"A plane that could fly into Mexico and land on a road instead of a runway could get the corn there faster. The plane would not have to stop at train stations along the way between Iowa and Mexico"*).

4. Give students five minutes to prepare for their presentations. Encourage students to take notes to use during their presentations.

5. Have all students present their speeches to the class. Volunteers may go first. Pay careful attention to the oral output of each student, focusing on comprehension and grammar. Set a timer to limit each presentation to two to three minutes. After each speech, discuss any errors made and model correct sentence structure.

6. If there is not enough time for each student to present, have students continue the following day. Provide students with the topic for the next oral presentation, "The Best Place To Live."

Lesson 264

In this lesson, students will practice giving oral presentations.

1. Demonstrate a two- to three-minute oral presentation on "The Best Place To Live."

2. Have students brainstorm different types of places in which people live (e.g., house, apartment, condo, trailer, boat, hotel). Ask students to complete this sentence: *"I would prefer to live in a/an ________________ because...."*

3. Explain presentation requirements as follows:

   A. Students will present a two- to three-minute speech about the type of place in which they would like to live and, given the choice, why they would pick that place (e.g., a student might say: *"I would prefer to live in an apartment because there are always other people around, and I sometimes have to stay home alone. At my apartment building, someone else cuts the grass, which I do not like to do"*).

   B. Students will explain why they would not want to live in certain types of places (e.g., a student might say: *"I would not like to live in a boat because boats are not big enough for me to have my own room. The boat would rock back and forth during a storm, and I might be afraid"*).

   C. Finally, students are to finish this statement: *"The best place I've lived in so far was a/an __________. I liked it best because...."*

4. Give students five minutes to prepare for their presentations. Encourage students to take notes to use during their presentations.

5. Have all students present their speeches to the class. Volunteers may go first. Pay careful attention to the oral output of each student, focusing on comprehension and grammar. Set a timer to limit each presentation to two to three minutes. After each speech, discuss any errors made and model correct sentence structure.

6. If there is not enough time for each student to present, have students continue the following day. Provide students with the topic for the next oral presentation, "Taking Advantage."

Lesson 265

In this lesson, students will practice giving oral presentations.

1. Demonstrate a two- to three-minute oral presentation on "Taking Advantage."

2. Explain what it means to "take advantage" of a situation or a thing in a positive way. Have students list opportunities available to them that they could take advantage of (e.g., school, extracurricular activities, free time each week, the public library). Have students complete the following sentence: *"I am going to take advantage of ________________ because...."*

3. Explain presentation requirements as follows:

   A. Students will present a two- to three-minute speech about resources available to them and the ways to use those resources to get ahead. For example, a student might say: *"I am going to take advantage of the public library because I can read about anything or anyplace without spending money. If I take advantage and study the books available in the library, I can get an 'A' on my next science paper."*

   B. Students will explain what resources they have used in the past. For example, a student might say: *"I am good at basketball because there is a neighborhood court close to my home, and I practice there frequently."*

   C. Students will describe the ways in which their lives would be different if the resources presently available were no longer there. For example, a student might say: *"If I could not participate in extracurricular activities, I would not get to meet people with interests like mine. I might get bored with school if I didn't have activities other than studying to occupy my time."*

4. Give students five minutes to prepare for their presentations. Encourage students to take notes to use during their presentations.

5. Have all students present their speeches to the class. Volunteers may go first. Pay careful attention to the oral output of each student, focusing on comprehension and grammar. Set a timer to limit each presentation to two to three minutes. After each speech, discuss any errors made and model correct sentence structure.

6. If there is not enough time for each student to present, have students continue the following day. Provide students with the topic for the next oral presentation, "Happy Holidays."

Lesson 266

In this lesson, students will practice giving oral presentations.

1. Demonstrate a two- to three-minute oral presentation on "Happy Holidays."

2. Have each student choose their favorite holiday, either one celebrated here or in another country. Ask them to make a list of the ways this holiday is celebrated.

3. Explain presentation requirements as follows:

   A. Students will give a two- to three-minute presentation on their favorite holiday. The students should begin by discussing when the holiday is celebrated, what the reasons are for celebrating, who celebrates the holiday, and where it is celebrated.

   B. Students will share with the class how their individual family prepares for and celebrates the holiday.

   C. Students are to discuss how they will celebrate the selected holiday when they have families of their own. Will they celebrate it in the same way they do today? Will they begin their own traditions? If so, what will the new traditions be?

4. Give students five minutes to prepare for their presentations. Encourage students to take notes to use during their presentations.

5. Have all students present their speeches to the class. Volunteers may go first. Pay careful attention to the oral output of each student, focusing on comprehension and grammar. Set a timer to limit each presentation to two to three minutes. After each speech, discuss any errors made and model correct sentence structure.

6. If there is not enough time for each student to present, have students continue the following day. Provide students with the topic for the next oral presentation, "Fix It."

Lesson 267

In this lesson, students will practice giving oral presentations.

1. Demonstrate a two- to three-minute oral presentation on "Fix It."

2. Ask students if they have ever repaired an item of any kind (e.g., bicycle, toaster, flat tire). Have students list the item they repaired, what was wrong with it, and how they fixed it. If students have never repaired anything, have them imagine trying to fix something.

3. Explain presentation requirements as follows:

    A. Students will present a two- to three-minute speech on how to repair an item of their choice. The student must provide information on the item, including what is wrong with it. For example, a student might say: *"Let me teach you how to repair a broken plate. The plate has broken into three pieces. I will show you how to put the plate back together again."*

    B. Students will explain the tools needed to repair the item. For example, a student might say: *"In order to fix the plate, I will need some ceramic glue, a flat surface on which to work, and a bright light to help me see how the broken pieces fit together."*

    C. Students will present this information as if on a television show. They must explain the steps involved in the repair and demonstrate (when possible) to illustrate their points.

4. Give students five minutes to prepare for their presentations. Encourage students to take notes to use during their presentations.

5. Have all students present their speeches to the class. Volunteers may go first. Pay careful attention to the oral output of each student, focusing on comprehension and grammar. Set a timer to limit each presentation to two to three minutes. After each speech, discuss any errors made and model correct sentence structure.

6. If there is not enough time for each student to present, have students continue the following day. Provide students with the topic for the next oral presentation, "Can't Live Without It."

Lesson 268

In this lesson, students will practice giving oral presentations.

1. Demonstrate a two- to three-minute oral presentation on "Can't Live Without It."

2. Ask students to complete the following sentence: *"If I had to choose two items I could not live without, I would choose ______ and ________."* Give students a brief period of time to think about this before answering. Provide some examples if necessary (e.g., brush, computer, fan, flashlight, fork, glasses, knife, ladder, oven, pen, pencil, phone, refrigerator, saw, scissors, shovel, spoon, stapler, tape).

3. Explain presentation requirements as follows:

    A. Students will present a two- to three-minute speech on two implements they could not live without. Students must name the two chosen items and explain why they are so important for everyday survival. For example, a student might say: *"If I had to choose two items I could not live without, I would choose my refrigerator and my phone. If I did not have a refrigerator, my food would spoil, and I would starve. If I did not have a phone, I could not talk with my friends or call for help in an emergency."*

    B. Students will describe how their lives would be different without these implements. For example, a student might say: *"If I did not have a refrigerator, the only foods I could eat would be canned or fresh fruits and vegetables. I would not be able to keep food for a long period of time because it would rot. I would have to find another way to keep my drinks cold; I could use a cooler, but I would have to buy ice every day for the cooler."*

    C. Students are to choose a friend or family member and state one item that person could not live without and why. For example, a student might say: *"My sister could not live without her computer because she goes to college and must have it to study."*

4. Give students five minutes to prepare for their presentations. Encourage students to take notes to use during their presentations.

5. Have all students present their speeches to the class. Volunteers may go first. Pay careful attention to the oral output of each student, focusing on comprehension and grammar. Set a timer to limit each presentation to two to three minutes. After each speech, discuss any errors made and model correct sentence structure.

6. If there is not enough time for each student to present, have students continue the following day. Provide students with the topic for the next oral presentation, "Advice To Monolingual Friends."

Lesson 269

In this lesson, students will practice giving oral presentations.

1. Demonstrate a two- to three-minute oral presentation on "Advice To Monolingual Friends."

2. Ask students to think about reasons why everyone should be able to speak more than one language (e.g., to understand other cultures, to understand television programs or song lyrics in another language, to be able to make friends from different countries).

3. Explain presentation requirements as follows:

   A. Students will give two- to three-minute presentations on what it means to speak more than one language. Students will tell the class which languages they are able to speak fluently. Have them discuss the advantages of speaking more than one language.

   B. Students will identify friends or family members who have not learned to speak English. Have students describe the difficulties these friends or family members experience.

   C. Students must choose another language they would like to learn and tell why. For example, a student might say: *"I would like to learn to speak Mandarin so that I could one day visit China and not experience difficulties with the language."*

4. Give students five minutes to prepare for their presentations. Encourage students to take notes to use during their presentations.

5. Have all students present their speeches to the class. Volunteers may go first. Pay careful attention to the oral output of each student, focusing on comprehension and grammar. Set a timer to limit each presentation to two to three minutes. After each speech, discuss any errors made and model correct sentence structure.

6. If there is not enough time for each student to present, have students continue the following day. Provide students with the topic for the next oral presentation, "How I'll Benefit From Becoming Proficient In English."

Lesson 270

In this lesson, students will practice giving oral presentations.

1. Demonstrate a two- to three-minute oral presentation on "How I'll Benefit From Becoming Proficient In English."

2. Have students think of reasons why they are glad they learned to speak English.

3. Explain presentation requirements as follows:

   A. Students will present a one- to two-minute speech on what it means to speak English proficiently. Have students expand on the difficulties they faced before they were able to speak English and ways their lives have improved since learning English.

   B. Students will tell why it is important to speak English when living in the United States **and** in another country.

   C. Students will predict how knowing English will affect their future (e.g., Will it be easier to get a good education or a good job? How would their future have been affected if they had not learned to speak English?).

4. Give students five minutes to prepare for their presentations. Encourage students to take notes to use during their presentations.

5. Have all students present their speeches to the class. Volunteers may go first. Pay careful attention to the oral output of each student, focusing on comprehension and grammar. Set a timer to limit each presentation to two to three minutes. After each speech, discuss any errors made and model correct sentence structure.

6. Watch presentation times closely to ensure that each student has had an opportunity to speak.

Glossary & Appendices

Glossary of Terms

Adjectives: Adjectives comprise a word class used to describe nouns and pronouns. They include words like *acceptable, blue, last, lovely, silly, tall.* Adjectives can also occur after linking verbs (verbs like *are, seem, sound, taste*).

Adverbs: Adverbs comprise a word class used to describe verbs, adjectives, and other adverbs. They include words that tell *how*, like *comfortably, gratefully, fast*; words that tell *where*, like *up, in, away*; and words that tell *when*, like *never, sometimes, recently*. Adverbs that belong to the conjunctive adverb subclassification function both as adverbs and as conjunctions: *after, as, before, since, until, when, where, while* (see **conjunction**).

Basic sentence: An English basic (base) sentence is a statement in active voice without much modification. (*Mary sings. The man left. I saw the game. A day passed.*) A basic sentence is not derived from some other fundamental sentence.

Conjunction: Conjunctions join words, phrases, or clauses in a sentence. They are used to expand sentences. The most common, coordinate conjunctions *and, but,* and *or* connect words that have the same function (e.g., subjects, predicates, objects, modifiers). The subclassifications of conjunctions are not mutually exclusive. For example, conjunctive adverbs function both as adverbs and as conjunctions: *after, as, before, since, until, when, where, while*. Subordinate conjunctions are used to introduce clauses: *as, because, for, if, provided, since, so, than, that, then, until, where, while.*

Demonstratives: Demonstratives constitute a subclass of pronouns: *this, that, these, those.*

Determiners: Determiners are words that tell *which*, like *the, his,* and *that*, in structures like: *the* in *the old captain*; *his* in *his book*; *that* in *that ship*. Determiners usually occur with nouns. Some of them may occur with other word classes, as in *the young*, or *the poor*.

Form vs. Function: In English, *form* refers to the word itself. *Function* refers to the "job" the word does in a sentence or a context. Because English words may have several functions, it is important not to try to analyze words' functions out of context. For example, it would not be appropriate to use a list of words and assign them to a "part of speech." This is because many English words function differently in different contexts. For example, in *She will run, run* is an action verb, a part of the verb phrase, *will run*. In *She has a run, run* is a noun that functions as the direct object of the sentence.

Grapheme: A grapheme is the orthographic symbol used to represent a phoneme (speech sound) such as */t/* at the beginning of top; */sh/* at the end of wish, or */ck/* at the end of luck.

-ed form: The **-ed** form is the same as the **past tense verb form**.

-en form: The **-en** form is the same as the **past participle verb form**.

Indefinite pronouns: Indefinite pronouns are a subclass of pronouns that have nonspecific referents. They include *somebody, anybody, nobody, someone, anyone, no one, something, anything, nothing, either, neither, each, both, all, some, many, few, several, one, none, lots.*

Indirect object: An indirect object is a noun or pronoun that comes between the main predicate verb and the direct object, as in *John showed me the field*, or *She gave Maria a book.*

Infinitive: An infinitive is a simple, non-inflected verb form (*listen, calculate, walk, vote, read, cook, give*), sometimes indicated by a preceding *to*, as in *to listen, to calculate, to walk, to vote, to read, to cook, to give.*

Inflection: An inflection is a subclass of morpheme (*meaningful unit of a word*) that adds to a word's meaning. In English, all inflections are suffixes. The eight inflectional functions of English are: *plural, possessive, present participle, third person singular, past, past participle, comparative, superlative.* These functions may have more than one form. For example, *plural* can be represented by **-s** (*cat, cats*); **-es**, (*watch, watches*); internal change (*goose, geese*); or no change (*deer, deer*).

-ing verb form: **-ing** is the **present participle verb form**, which has an **-ing** inflectional ending. **-ing** verb forms may function as present progressive tense, as in *We are trying; She is sleeping; I am leaving.*

Intransitive verbs: Intransitive verbs are a subclass of verbs that do not pass action to an object: *Bears growl loudly; She arrived at three; We looked for her; Sr. Fernandez goes with his wife.*

Irregular Verbs: Irregular verbs are those English verbs whose forms differ from the regular forms. Regular English verbs follow this pattern for present, past, and past participle: *work, worked, worked; walk, walked, walked; bake, baked, baked.* Forms of the most common irregular verbs in English are listed in Appendix E.

L¹ : L¹ is the symbol commonly used to refer to a speaker's first language.

L² : L² is the symbol commonly used to refer to a speaker's second or target language.

Linking verbs: Linking verbs are a subclass of the verb word class. A verb that functions as a linking verb in a sentence takes no object. Some verbs, such as *be* and *go*, do not take objects. Other verbs may function as linking verbs or action verbs, depending upon context. For example, *grow* may function as a linking verb: The children *grow* much taller every year! *Grow* may also take an object: I like to *grow* tomatoes. As in all aspects of language, it is important to separate the concepts of form (*grow*) and function (*linking verb* or *action verb*).

Morpheme: A morpheme is a single unit of meaning in a word, such as these: *pre*; *scrip*; and *tion*—the three meaningful units of the word *prescription*. Morphemes include prefixes, suffixes, and whole words. Words like *in* or *go* are free morphemes; their meanings can stand alone. Bound morphemes, like **-ed** or **-ing**, are meaningful units that must be attached to other words. Morphemes are not to be confused with syllables, which are based on sound, rather than on meaning.

Nouns: Nouns constitute a major English word class. Nouns name a person, place, or thing—like *Maria, telephone, Grand Canyon, car, teacher, work*. Some of these words occur in other word classes, too. In English it is common for words (forms) to function in more than one class or subclass.

Direct object: A direct object is a noun or pronoun that receives the action of the main predicate verb, as in *John threw the ball*, or *She saw a movie*.

Object complement: The object complement follows the main predicate verb. The object complement may be a noun, as in *Elizabeth is queen*; or it may be an adjective, as in *Elizabeth is lovely*.

Past participle verb form: The past participle verb form is the same as the **-en form** and is used with the auxiliary, *had*. It includes verb forms such as *given, taken, eaten*. (In most English verbs, the forms for past tense and past participle are identical.) Not all past participle forms end with the **-en** spelling; **-en** is simply a referent for past participle forms. Other past participle forms include *come, done, driven, forgotten, heard, calculated, disintegrated*.

Past tense verb form: The past tense verb form is the same as the **-ed form**. (In English, the **-ed** inflection may be pronounced three ways: (1) /d/, as in *smiled, toiled, combed*; (2) /t/, as in *walked, hoped, dropped*; (3) /ǝd/, as in *waited, voted, repeated*). Not all past tense forms end with the **-ed** spelling; **-ed** is simply a referent for past tense forms. Other past tense forms include *blew, chose, did, drove, fell, gave, grew, rode, was, wrote.*

Personal pronouns: Personal pronouns include subject, object, and possessive pronouns. They include: *I, me, mine; you, yours; he, him, his; she, her, hers; it, its; we, us, ours; they, them, theirs.*

Phoneme: A phoneme is a single unit of sound in a spoken word, such as /t/ at the beginning of *top*; /m/ at the end of *column*, or /u/ in the middle of *cut*.

Phrasal verb: A phrasal verb is comprised of a verb and an adverb functioning together as an action verb. Examples of these structures that are frequent occurrences in English include: *sit in* on the lecture, *hang up* the phone, *look up* the answer, *drop in* on friends, *pick up* the check. See Appendix G, Phrasal Verbs, for a list to use in teaching.

Predicate: The predicate is the second of the two main parts of English sentences; *John went away; John intended to be here*.

Predicate nominative, or predicate noun: The noun or pronoun occurring after the form of *be* or other inactive verb in sentences like: *Elizabeth was queen; The Nigerian athlete was the winner; Nutrition is an important subject; Her major was engineering; Tran remained my friend; He became a teacher*.

Preposition: A preposition is an English function word that is used to introduce a prepositional phrase. When they stand alone, without objects, prepositions usually function as adverbs. The prepositions of English include words like *about, above, along, around, before, beside, between, during, for, from, inside, on, over, under*. A prepositional phrase may function either as an adjective or an adverb. Prepositional phrases are phrases like *above the trees, before six, during the concert, for all, under pressure*. See Appendix F for a list of English prepositions.

Present participle: Such verb forms as *seeing, thinking, relieving, industrializing.*

Present participle verb form: The present participle verb form is the same as the **-ing verb form**. It includes verb forms such as *giving, taking, eating*. Other present participle verb forms include *calculating, coming, disintegrating, doing, driving, forgetting, hearing, waiting*.

Present progressive tense: The present progressive tense indicates ongoing action in current time. The present progressive tense uses an **-ing** inflectional ending, as in *I am going; We are trying; She is seeing; They are telling*.

Pronouns: Pronouns are function words that are used in place of nouns. The several subclassifications of pronouns are not mutually exclusive. For example, personal pronouns include subject, object, and possessive pronouns. English pronouns include, but are not limited to, the following: (1) personal pronouns (*I, me, mine; you, yours; he, him, his; she, her, hers; it, its; we, us, ours; they, them, their, theirs;* (2) nominative (subject) pronouns (*I, you, he, she, it, we, you, they*); (3) objective pronouns (*me, you, him, her, it, us, you, them*); (4) possessive pronouns (*my, mine, your, yours, his, her, hers, its, our, ours, their, theirs*); (5) indefinite pronouns (*somebody, anybody, nobody, someone, anyone, no one, something, anything, nothing, either, neither, each, both, all, some, many, few, several, one, lots, a lot*); (6) reflexive and intensive pronouns (*myself, yourself, himself, herself, itself, ourselves, yourselves, themselves*); and (7) relative pronouns (*who, which, what, that*). Some pronoun words also function as determiners. Some grammars classify possessive pronouns as possessive adjectives.

-'s form: The **-'s** form is the same as the singular possessive form: an inflectional ending that shows singular ownership.

-s' form: The **-s'** form is the same as the plural possessive form: an inflectional ending that shows plural ownership.

-s form: The **-s** form is the same as the third person singular; an inflectional ending used with *he, she,* or *it* in the singular.

Sentence patterns: English has several basic sentence patterns and transformations of those patterns. See Appendix B, Basic English Sentence Patterns.

Simple verb form: The simple verb form is the same as the infinitive form. It includes simple, noninflected verb forms such as *listen, calculate, walk, vote, read, cook, give*.

Standard English: Standard English comprises the dialects of English normally used by educated native speakers.

Subject: The subject is the first of the two main parts of English sentences: *My mother arrived today; Nguyen arrived today.*

Third person singular verb form: The third person singular verb form is the same as the **-s form**. The predicate verb form agrees with a third person singular subject: *he, she, it, Mr. Soto, Tran, the principal.* Third person singular forms include *calculates, comes, disintegrates, does, drives, eats, finishes, forgets, hears, is, tries, washes, waits.*

Transitive verb: Transitive verbs comprise a subclass of verbs that can pass action to an object: *John hit the ball; She saw me; We gave a donation; Sr. Fernandez built it.*

Verb-adverb team: A verb and an adverb team (also called a phrasal verb) constitute a form functioning together as an action verb. These structures, frequent occurrences in English, are found in phrases such as *sit in on* the lecture, *hang up* the phone, *look up* the answer, *drop in* on friends, *pick up* the check. See Appendix G, Phrasal Verbs.

Verbs: Verbs are the English word class that represent action or state of being. English verbs have five possible forms:

1. simple, or infinitive form: *calculate, go, scrub, see, sit, walk, be*
2. third person singular form: *calculates, goes, scrubs, sees, sits, walks, is*
3. present participle form: *calculating, going, scrubbing, seeing, sitting, walking, being*
4. past tense form: *calculated, went, scrubbed, saw, sat, walked, was*
5. past participle form: *calculated, gone, scrubbed, seen, sat, walked, been*

Appendix A: Scope and Sequence

Lessons	Nouns	Pronouns	Verbs	Adjectives	Adverbs	Prepositions/ Conjunctions	Syntactic and Morphologic Constructs
1–5	people's names objects	possessive pronouns: **your, my, his, her**	third person singular of **be**: **is**	demonstratives: **this, that** (see possessive pronouns)			My name is Mr. Soto. Your name is Carlos. Her name is Karen. His name is Ngoc. This is a book. That is your book. This is her chair. This is his pencil. That is a chair. That is a desk.
6–10	animals common objects		third person singular of **be**: **is** action verbs animal sounds as verbs	color descriptors demonstratives: **this, that**			This is a dog. That is a cat. Dogs jump. Rabbits hop. This is a white rabbit. That is a yellow pencil.
11–15	animals familiar objects (initial graphemes: consonants only) <u>-s</u>; common plural marker for English nouns		third person singular of **be**: **is** present plural of **be**: **are** **take**	determiners: articles: **a, the** demonstratives: **this, these**			This is a zebra. That is a bear. These are markers. Those are pens. This is a book. These are books. Take a pencil. Take the pencil. (no vowels at this stage)
16–20	vocabulary development (initial graphemes: consonants and vowels)		third person singular of **be**: **is**	determiners: articles: **a, an** demonstrative: **this**			This is a (initial consonant grapheme). This is an (initial vowel grapheme).
21–25	vocabulary development (initial graphemes: consonants and vowels)	objective pronoun: **me**	third person singular of **be**: **is** **show**	determiners: articles: **a, an, the** demonstratives: **this, that**			This is a plate. This is an airplane. This is the airplane. That is a knife. That is an oven. That is the teacher's chair. Show me a globe. Show me an ant. Show me the red jacket.
26–30	familiar objects vocabulary development (initial graphemes: consonants and vowels)		first person plural of **be**: **are**	numbers (1-10)	adverbs of place: **here, there**		Here are three pencils. There are four windows.
31–35	people's names	subject: **I**	first and third person present tense of **be**: **am, is**	abstract: emotions abstract: identifiable characteristics			Ana is sad. I am sad. Isaac is tall. Norma is blonde.

Lessons	Nouns	Pronouns	Verbs	Adjectives	Adverbs	Prepositions/ Conjunctions	Syntactic and Morphologic Constructs
36–40	people's names	subject: **I, he, she**	semantically related words: touch, speech, movement present and past tense opposite concepts	determiner: **the**	**today, yesterday**		Touch the door. Tap on the door. **-ed**; past tense: Mrs. Tucker walks; Mrs. Tucker walked. Today I skip; yesterday I skipped. opposite concepts: I can push. I can pull.
41–45	predicate nouns	subject: **I, you, he, she**	question transformations of action verbs first, second, third person singular			preposition: **to**	statements to questions: You go to school. Do I go to school? Do you go to school? Yes, I go to school. Does he go to school? Yes, he goes to school. negative statements; contracted verb phrases: Do you drive to school? No, I don't drive to school.
46–50	people's names familiar objects as predicate nouns and indirect objects	pronoun referents	first, second, and third person singular	**good** pictures, **other** students determiners: **a, the**		preposition: **to**	statements to questions: Anita likes to sing. Does Anita like to sing? statements to questions using pronoun referents: Tran puts the books away. Does he put the books away? statements to negative questions: LaTanya dances. Doesn't LaTanya dance? statements to negative questions using pronoun referents: Kim plays ball. Doesn't he play ball?
51–55		first, second, third person personal pronouns (as subject): **I, you, he, she, it, we, they**	forms of **be** as auxiliary verbs: **is, are, am** forms of **be** (past tense): **was, were** action verbs		**here, there**		present progressive verb/personal pronoun: I am standing. You are standing. I was leaving. You were leaving.
56–60		first, second, third person personal pronouns (as subject): **I, you, he, she, it, we, they**	forms of **be** as auxiliary verbs: **is, am** past tense forms of **be** as auxiliary verb: **was, were** action verbs	emotions	**yesterday, today** **here, there**		I was leaving. You were leaving. Today, I am talking. Yesterday, I was talking.
61–65	food clothing school things tools toys vehicles		third person singular form of **be**: **is** third person plural of **be**: **are**	deletion of **a/an** before plurals and some English nouns demonstratives: **that, those**			That is an orange. Those are Ø oranges. That is Ø lettuce.

Lessons	Nouns	Pronouns	Verbs	Adjectives	Adverbs	Prepositions/ Conjunctions	Syntactic and Morphologic Constructs
66–70		personal pronouns as objects: **I, you, she, he**	action verbs: present, present progressive, past, future tenses high-frequency irregular verbs, past and present tense: **be, go**	determiner: **the**	**yesterday, today, tomorrow, now**		I walk. You are walking. She walked. He will walk. I empty the trash. Now, you are emptying the trash. Yesterday, she emptied the trash. Tomorrow, he will empty the trash.
71–75	students' names: direct/indirect usage familiar words as direct objects	objective case pronouns: **me, you, him, her, it, us, them** personal pronouns as subjects: **I, you, he, she, it, we, they**	past singular of **be**: **was** past plural of **be**: **were** action verbs	determiners (articles): **a, an, the**		prepositional phrases after verbs: **beside, by, for, near, to, with**	passive/active voice: I was found by Ana. Ana found me. They lived in a house near Mona. Mona lived in a house near them.
76–80		personal pronoun as subject: **I**	regular and irregular action verbs, present, present progressive, past, and future tenses		**now, yesterday, tomorrow**		I bend. Now, I am bending. Yesterday, I bent. Tomorrow, I will bend.
81–85		personal and object pronoun usage	action verbs			preposition: **with**	I can run. You run with me. We can run. You run with us.
86–90	review: familiar objects	personal, possessive, and object pronoun usage	review: verb tense review: forms of **be**	**this** (see possessive pronouns)	**yesterday, tomorrow**	prepositions: **to, with**	subject/verb agreement I smile. I am smiling. Yesterday, I smiled. Tomorrow, I will smile. I run. Run with me. This is their seat. This seat is theirs.
91–95	familiar objects animals	subject pronouns: **I, you, he, she, it, we, they**	action verb vocabulary development				student production of sentences with action verbs
96–100	familiar objects animals	subject pronouns: **I, you, he, she, it, we, they**	helping verb: **be** inflectional endings: **-ing** (present progressive) **-ed** (past tense)				We cough. Today, we are coughing. Yesterday, we coughed. Mr. Soto hums. Today, he is humming. Yesterday, he hummed.
101–105		subject pronouns: **I, you, he, she, it, we, they**	helping verbs: **be, have** inflectional endings: **-ing** (present progressive) **-ed** (past tense)				I am going. We were singing. I have worked. He has hoped. Have you heard? I have heard. Has she begun? She has begun.

Lessons	Nouns	Pronouns	Verbs	Adjectives	Adverbs	Prepositions/ Conjunctions	Syntactic and Morphologic Constructs
106–110		subject pronouns: **I, you, he, she, it, we, they**	helping verbs: **be, have, do** inflectional endings: **-ing** (present progressive) **-ed** (past tense)				I do sleep. He does try. I am going. I have climbed. Is he standing? He is standing. Was she walking? She was walking.
111–115		subject pronouns: **I, you, he, she, it, we, they**	modals: **can, could, shall, should, will, would, may, might, must** practice forms of **be, have, do** (with negative contractions: **do not** and **don't**)				I can finish it. We could hear you. Am I speaking? I am speaking. Have I spoken? I have spoken. Does he sit here? He does not (doesn't) sit here. Can you help? You can't help. Will they pitch? They won't pitch.
116–120		subject pronouns: **I, you, he, she, it, we, they**	review helping verbs: **be, have, do,** and **modals**				I am calling. We were gasping. I have chuckled. We have giggled. I do sleep. You do sing. I can finish it. She may stay.
121–125		indefinite pronouns as subject: **anybody, anyone, anything, nobody, nothing, somebody, something**	present/past participle forms of common verbs				Is somebody knocking? Yes, somebody's knocking. Did anyone knock? No, nobody knocked. No, no one knocked. Is something burning? Yes, something's burning. Is anything missing? No, nothing's missing.
126–130	food people places			demonstratives: **this, these**			student production of sentences with vocabulary words: This is an apple. This is a cook. This is a bridge.
131–135	school things tools vehicles			demonstratives: **this, these**			student production of sentences with vocabulary words: This is an eraser. This is a van. This is a broom.
136–140	body parts clothing		action verbs	demonstratives: **this, these**			student production of sentences with vocabulary words: This is an arm. These are toes. This is a jacket. These are shoes. This shows driving. This shows sleeping.

	Nouns	Pronouns	Verbs	Adjectives	Adverbs	Prepositions/ Conjunctions	Syntactic and Morphologic Constructs
141–145	appliances buildings containers furniture machines musical instruments			demonstratives: **this, these**			student production of sentences with vocabulary words: This is a barn. This is an oven. This is a bed. This is a plate. This is a computer. This is a banjo.
146–150	animals insects money plants shapes			demonstratives: **this, these**			student production of sentences with vocabulary words: This is grass. This is a spider. This is a circle. This is a quarter. This is a bat. This is a lion.
151–155	direct and indirect (familiar) objects	object pronouns: **her, us** possessive pronouns: **her, his, my, their**	familiar action verbs contracted and non-contracted forms of **be, do, have,** and **familiar modals**	(see possessive pronouns)	adverbs of place: **here**		Are the students in their seats? No, the students are not (aren't) in their seats. Are they bringing the ball? Yes, they are (they're) bringing the ball. Would they like to sit here? Yes, they would (they'd) like to sit here.
156–160	direct and indirect (familiar) objects	indefinite pronouns: **anybody** object pronouns: **it, me, us** possessive pronouns: **her, his, my, our, their**	familiar action verbs contracted and non-contracted forms of **be, do, have,** and **familiar modals**	demonstratives: **the, these, this, those** (see possessive pronouns) **broken, new, right**		prepositions: **in, on, to**	converting grammatically incorrect sentences to Standard English
161–165	direct and indirect (familiar) objects	indefinite pronouns: **anybody, anything** object pronouns: **me, us, you** possessive pronouns: **her, his**	familiar action verbs contracted and non-contracted forms of **be, have, do,** and **familiar modals**	demonstratives: **the, these, this** (see possessive pronouns) **both, pretty**	adverbs of place: **here**	prepositions: **in, on, with**	converting grammatically incorrect sentences to Standard English
166–170	direct and indirect (familiar) objects	indefinite pronoun: **something** object pronouns: **me, us, you** possessive pronouns: **her, our**	familiar action verbs contracted and non-contracted forms of **be, do, have,** and **familiar modals**	demonstratives: **a, that, the, these, this, those** (see possessive pronouns) **funny, good, wonderful**	adverbs of place: **here, in, there, out**	prepositions: **at, in, on, to, with**	slight sentence variations change sentence meaning: They walk home. They can walk home. They will walk home. He had a dog. He has a dog. He wants a dog. This is a banana. These are bananas. Those are bananas. We saw our friends. You saw our friends. She saw our friends.

Lessons	Nouns	Pronouns	Verbs	Adjectives	Adverbs	Prepositions/ Conjunctions	Syntactic and Morphologic Constructs
171–175	familiar objects	indefinite pronouns: **anybody, anyone, anything, nothing, something, someone** possessive pronouns: **her, my, your**	familiar action verbs contracted and non-contracted forms of **be, have, do,** and **familiar modals**	demonstratives: **a, that, the, this** (see possessive pronouns)	adverbs of place: **here, this**		
176–180	familiar objects	possessive pronouns: **my, your**	past, present, future tenses	(see possessive pronouns)	**alone, most**	prepositions: **about, at, on, to, with**	expository speaking
181–185		indefinite pronouns as objects: **a lot, all, anybody, anyone, anything, both, each, either, few, lots, many, neither, no one, nobody, nothing, one, several, some, somebody, someone, something**	action verbs				Either of us will stand. Neither of us will stand. Each of us will stand. Both of us will stand. Each of us must stand. Each of us should turn. Neither of us should turn. Each of us should turn. Both of us should turn.
186–190				positive, comparative (**-er, more**), and superlative (**-est, most**) inflections irregular adjectives: **bad, worse, worst; good, better, best; little, less, least; many, more, most**			Maria is short. Maria is shorter than Dominic. Maria is the shortest girl in her family. Lee is a courteous student. Lee is more courteous than Paul. Lee is the most courteous person I know.
191–195	familiar objects sports equipment tools vehicles	objective pronouns: **her, him, it, me, them, us, you**		prepositional phrases as adjectives	prepositional phrases as adverbs	prepositional phrases demonstrating: **how, how many, what kind of, when, where, which, why**	She raked with you. I read with help. Dad sat between us.

Lessons	Nouns	Pronouns	Verbs	Adjectives	Adverbs	Prepositions/ Conjunctions	Syntactic and Morphologic Constructs
196–200		reflexive pronouns: **herself, himself, itself, myself, ourselves, themselves, yourself, yourselves** intensive pronouns: **herself, himself, itself, myself, ourselves, themselves, yourself, yourselves**				review prepositional phrases	I blamed myself for the trouble. You helped yourself to water. I myself wrote this. She herself grew these. I myself wrote this for class. She herself grew these at home.
201–205					adverbs of time adverbs of place adverbs of manner adverbs of degree	review adverbs as prepositions	When do you like to wake up? I like to wake up late. How do you study? I study quietly. How much does she swim? She hardly swims.
206–210		review indefinite, intensive, objective, and reflexive pronouns		review prepositional phrases as adjectives	review adverbs of time, place, manner, and degree	review adverbs as prepositions	students generate sentences using objective, indefinite, intensive, reflexive pronouns; adverbs; and prepositional phrases: I like both subjects. We washed ourselves. We ourselves baked the pie. She drew a picture for me. I finished it around nine.
211–215			phrasal verbs				students discuss meanings of the separate words, then meanings of the phrases: "act" + "up" versus "act up" Students create and deliver short dialogues using phrasal verbs
216–220			phrasal verbs				students create and deliver short dialogues using phrasal verbs
221–225			present, past, and past participle forms of irregular verbs				students generate sentences using three tenses of irregular verbs: I hide. She hid. It is hidden.
226–230			present, past and past participle forms of irregular verbs				students generate sentences using three tenses of irregular verbs: You shouldn't steal. He stole an apple. My bike was stolen.

Lessons	Nouns	Pronouns	Verbs	Adjectives	Adverbs	Prepositions/ Conjunctions	Syntactic and Morphologic Constructs
231–235	familiar objects					conjunctions: **and, or, but, either…or**	Rashad and Ennis took the test. Apples or bananas make a good snack. We'll bake chicken or fry fish for dinner. My cat sat and purred in the sunshine. Ed or Sam drank milk and ate crackers. Mia and I rented an apartment, but they found a house and bought it.
236–240		relative pronouns: **that, what, which, who**					students identify the base sentence, relative pronoun, and relative clause of given sentences: He is the player who won the game. He is the player. He won the game.
241–245					conjunctive adverbs: **after, as, before, since, until, when, where, while**	subordinate conjunctions: **as, as if, because, for, if, provided, since, so that, than, until, where, while**	I want to see you after they go. The band played as she entered. The books arrived before he did. I waited in the gym because she was late. I can't imagine it, so I won't do it. The silence ended when the bell rang. When the bell rang, the silence ended. We stood when she entered. She entered when we stood.
246–250							oral presentations (topics provided)
251–255							oral presentations (topics provided)
256–260							oral presentations (topics provided)
261–265							oral presentations (topics provided)
266–270							oral presentations (topics provided)

Appendix B: Basic English Sentence Patterns

Basic English Sentence Patterns

N/V	noun/verb	The class sang.
N/V/N	noun/verb/noun	The class sang a song.
N/V/ADV	noun/verb/adverb	The class sang a song happily.
N/LV/N	noun/linking verb/noun	The teacher is Mr. Soto.
N/LV/ADJ	noun/linking verb/adjective	The teacher is tall.
N/V/N/N	noun/verb/noun/noun	The teacher gave the class a test.

Some Transformations of Basic English Sentence Patterns

Negative transformation	*The class did not sing.*
Question transformation	*Did the class sing? Didn't the class sing?*
There statement insertion	*There was a song.*
Request transformation (**you** implicit)	*Sing a song.*
Passive transformation	*A song was sung by the class.*
Prepositional phrase insertion	*The class sang before school. Before school, the class sang.*
Adverbial clause insertion	*When we arrived, the class sang. The class sang when we arrived.*

Appendix C: Pronouns by Category

Pronouns are function words that are used in place of nouns. The several subclassifications of pronouns are not mutually exclusive. For example, personal pronouns include subject, object, and possessive pronouns. English pronouns include, but are not limited to, the following:

Personal Pronouns

I	you	he	she	it	we	they
me	your	him	her	its	us	them
mine	yours	his	hers		our	their
					ours	theirs

Subject (Nominative) Pronouns

I	you	he	she	it	we	they

Object (Objective) Pronouns

me	you	him	her	it	us	them

Possessive Pronouns (also called possessive adjectives)

my	you	his	our	their
mine	yours	her	ours	theirs
		hers		
		its		

Indefinite Pronouns

all	anything	either	many	nobody	one	somebody
anybody	both	few	neither	none	several	someone
anyone	each	lots	no one	nothing	some	something

Reflexive and Intensive Pronouns

myself	himself	itself	ourselves	themselves
yourself	herself		yourselves	

Relative Pronouns

who	which	what	that

Appendix D: Positive, Comparative, and Superlative Adjective Forms

This is an incomplete list. English has hundreds of regularly and irregularly inflected adjectives.

REGULAR

POSITIVE	COMPARATIVE *(comparing two)*	SUPERLATIVE *(comparing more than two)*
big	bigger	biggest
brave	braver	bravest
bright	brighter	brightest
clear	clearer	clearest
dark	darker	darkest
easy	easier	easiest
happy	happier	happiest
hot	hotter	hottest
jolly	jollier	jolliest
lazy	lazier	laziest
large	larger	largest
narrow	narrower	narrowest
noisy	noisier	noisiest
pretty	prettier	prettiest
pure	purer	purest
quick	quicker	quickest
rich	richer	richest
ripe	riper	ripest
rosy	rosier	rosiest
sad	sadder	saddest
safe	safer	safest
slim	slimmer	slimmest
small	smaller	smallest
soft	softer	softest
sunny	sunnier	sunniest
tall	taller	tallest
tame	tamer	tamest
warm	warmer	warmest
wealthy	wealthier	wealthiest
wide	wider	widest
wise	wiser	wisest

IRREGULAR

POSITIVE	COMPARATIVE *(comparing two)*	SUPERLATIVE *(comparing more than two)*
little	less	least
bad	worse	worst
good	better	best
many	more	most
much	more	most
late	later	latest
far	farther	farthest
old	elder	eldest

REGULAR (with more/most)

POSITIVE	COMPARATIVE *(comparing two)*	SUPERLATIVE *(comparing more than two)*
courteous	more courteous	most courteous
difficult	more difficult	most difficult
famous	more famous	most famous
generous	more generous	most generous
glorious	more glorious	most glorious
natural	more natural	most natural
numerous	more numerous	most numerous
obedient	more obedient	most obedient
radiant	more radiant	most radiant
reliable	more reliable	most reliable
special	more special	most special
tender	more tender	most tender
unusual	more unusual	most unusual
valuable	more valuable	most valuable

Appendix E: Irregular Verb Forms

This list represents only the most commonly used irregular verb forms of English.

PRESENT	PAST (stand alone)	PAST PARTICIPLE (need helping verbs)
am	was	been
awake	awoke	awaken
beat	beat	beaten
bend	bent	bent
bet	bet	bet
bind	bound	bound
bite	bit	bitten
blow	blew	blown
break	broke	broken
bring	brought	brought
build	built	built
burn	burned	burned
burst	burst	burst
catch	caught	caught
choose	chose	chosen
come	came	come
do	did	done
draw	drew	drawn
dream	dreamed, dreamt	dreamed, dreamt
drink	drank	drunk
drive	drove	driven
eat	ate	eaten
fall	fell	fallen
find	found	found
fly	flew	flown
forget	forgot	forgotten
freeze	froze	frozen
give	gave	given
go	went	gone
grow	grew	grown
hang	hung	hung
have	had	had
hear	heard	heard
hide	hid	hid, hidden
hold	held	held
hurt	hurt	hurt

PRESENT	PAST (stand alone)	PAST PARTICIPLE (need helping verbs)
keep	kept	kept
kneel	kneeled, knelt	kneeled, knelt
know	knew	known
lay	laid	laid
leave	left	left
lend	lent	lent
let	let	let
lie (recline)	lay	lain
lose	lost	lost
make	made	made
mean	meant	meant
meet	met	met
read	read	read
ride	rode	ridden
ring	rang	rung
rise	rose	risen
run	ran	run
say	said	said
see	saw	seen
shake	shook	shaken
sing	sang	sung
sink	sank	sunk
sit	sat	sat
speak	spoke	spoken
spin	spun	spun
stand	stood	stood
steal	stole	stolen
stick	stuck	stuck
swim	swam	swum
swing	swung	swung
teach	taught	taught
tear	tore	torn
throw	threw	thrown
wear	wore	worn
write	wrote	written

Appendix F: Prepositions

about	among	beside	except	of	to
above	around	between	for	off	toward
across	at	by	from	on	under
after	before	down	in	over	up
against	behind	during	near	through	with

Appendix G: Phrasal Verbs

act like
act up
add up
add up to
ask out

back down
back off
back up
beg off
blow up
bone up on
break down
break in
break into
break up
bring back
bring off
bring up
brush up on
build up
burn down
burn up
butt in
butter up

call off
call on
calm down
care for
catch on
catch up (with)
check in
check into
check off
check out
check out of
cheer up
chew out
chicken out
chip in

clam up
come across
come down with
come to
count on
crack down
crack down on
cross out
cut back
cut back on

do in
do over
drag on
draw out
draw up
drop by
drop in
drop in on
drop off
drop out
drop out of

eat out
egg on
end up

face up to
fall through
feel up to
figure out
fill in
fill in for
fill out
find out
find out about

get across
get along with
get around
get around to

get by
get in
get off
get on
get out of
get over
get rid of
get up
give up
go out with
go with
goof off
grow up

hand in
hand out
hang up
have to do with
hold up

iron out

jack up
jump all over

keep at
keep on
kick out
knock out

lay off
leave out
let down
let up
look back on
look down on
look forward to
look in on
look into
look like
look over

look up
look up to
luck out

make for
make fun of
make up
make up (with)
mark down
mark up
mix up

nod off

pan out
pass away
pass out
pick on
pick out
pick up (for)
pitch in
pull off
pull over
put away
put back
put off
put on
put out
put up
put up with

rip off
round off
run into
run out of

set back
set up
show up
slip up
stand for

stand out
stand up

take after
take back
take care of
take off
take up
tell off
throw away
throw out
throw up
tick off
try on
try out
try out for
turn around
turn down
turn in
turn off
turn on
turn up

wait on
wake up
watch out for
wear out
work out
wrap up
write down
write up

zonk out

Appendix H: Helping (Auxiliary) Verbs Used to Build Verb Phrases

Forms of Be

am	was	be
are	were	been
is		being

Forms of Have

have	has	had

Forms of Do

do	does	did	done

Modals

can, could	shall, should	will, would	may, might	must

Appendix I: Conjunctions

Coordinate Conjunctions

and	but	or	nor

Conjunctive Adverbs

after	before	until	where
as	since	when	while

Subordinate Conjunctions

as	for	since	until
as if	if	so that	where
because	provided	than	while

Appendix J: Picture Cards by Category

(All categories of picture cards depict nouns, except for the "action" category, which depicts action verbs.)

Category	Word	Card Number
action	bathing	75
action	biking	86
action	climbing	138
action	closing	140
action	coloring	144
action	combing	146
action	cooking	152
action	cutting	163
action	dancing	166
action	dressing	185
action	driving	186
action	eating	190
action	emptying	195
action	exercising	198
action	fishing	214
action	gluing	237
action	helping	263
action	hoeing	269
action	hopping	270
action	hugging	277
action	jogging	288
action	juggling	289
action	jumping	292
action	keyboarding	294
action	kicking	295
action	kissing	297
action	locking	317
action	looking	319
action	marching	327
action	mixing	338
action	opening	362
action	painting	372
action	petting	393
action	planting	402
action	punching	412
action	pushing	416
action	raking	426
action	reading	428
action	riding	433
action	running	441
action	sharing	456
action	sick	468
action	singing	470
action	sipping	472
action	sitting	473
action	skating	475
action	skipping	476
action	sleeping	481
action	sliding	482
action	standing	501
action	sweeping	515
action	swimming	516
action	talking	523
action	telephoning	529
action	wagging	562
action	walking	564
action	winning	572
action	writing	575
animal	alligator	46
animal	animals	49
animal	ape	53
animal	bat	74
animal	bear	78
animal	beaver	79
animal	bird	87
animal	camel	116
animal	cat	125
animal	chick	131
animal	chipmunk	133
animal	cow	155
animal	cub	159
animal	deer	167
animal	dog	176
animal	donkey	180
animal	duck	188
animal	elephant	193
animal	fish	213
animal	fox	222
animal	frog	223
animal	giraffe	229
animal	goat	238
animal	goose	239
animal	gorilla	240
animal	guinea pig	247
animal	hamster	255
animal	hen	264
animal	hippopotamus	268
animal	horse	272
animal	kangaroo	293
animal	lamb	302
animal	lion	312
animal	lizard	314
animal	monkey	340
animal	mouse	347

Category	Word	Card Number
animal	owl	368
animal	ox	369
animal	parrot	380
animal	peacock	383
animal	penguin	390
animal	pig	397
animal	pup	413
animal	puppy	415
animal	rabbit	421
animal	rat	427
animal	rooster	437
animal	seal	453
animal	sheep	457
animal	skunk	478
animal	snake	485
animal	tiger	535
animal	turkey	552
animal	turtle	553
animal	whale	569
animal	wing	571
animal	yak	577
animal	zebra	580
appliance	coffee pot	142
appliance	oven	366
appliance	refrigerator	430
appliance	stove	509
appliance	television	530
appliance	vacuum cleaner	555
body part	ankle	50
body part	arm	57
body part	back	63
body part	calf	115
body part	chin	132
body part	eye	199
body part	eyebrow	200
body part	eyelid	201
body part	face	202
body part	finger	209
body part	foot	218
body part	hair	250
body part	hand	256
body part	lap	304
body part	leg	305
body part	lip	313
body part	mouth	348
body part	neck	352
body part	nose	358
body part	shin	459
body part	shoulder	465
body part	stomach	506
body part	thigh	533
body part	toe	536
body part	waist	563
building	apartment building	52
building	barn	69
building	hospital	274
building	house	276
building	school	451
building	shop	463
building	silo	469
clothing	baseball cap	71
clothing	bib	84
clothing	blouse	90
clothing	boots	97
clothing	cap	120
clothing	coat	141
clothing	collar	143
clothing	dress	184
clothing	gloves	235
clothing	gown	241
clothing	hat	258
clothing	hats	259
clothing	jacket	282
clothing	jeans	285
clothing	mittens	337
clothing	overalls	367
clothing	pajamas	374
clothing	pants	376
clothing	raincoat	423
clothing	shirt	461
clothing	shoes	462
clothing	shorts	464
clothing	skirt	477
clothing	slacks	479
clothing	slippers	483
clothing	sneakers	486
clothing	sock	489
clothing	suit	512
clothing	sweater	514
clothing	swimsuit	518
clothing	tie	534
clothing	vest	558
color	black	22
color	blue	23
color	brown	24
color	gray	25
color	green	26
color	orange	27

Category	Word	Card Number
color	pink	28
color	purple	29
color	red	30
color	white	31
color	yellow	32
container	bag	64
container	box	98
container	can	117
container	cup	160
container	dish	172
container	dishes	173
container	envelope	196
container	garbage can	225
container	net	355
container	pan	375
container	plate	403
container	pot	409
container	sack	442
container	vase	557
food	apple	54
food	apples	55
food	banana	66
food	biscuits	88
food	burrito	107
food	cake	113
food	carrots	123
food	cherries	129
food	chips	134
food	cookies	151
food	corn	153
food	egg	191
food	eggs	192
food	fajita	204
food	grapefruit	242
food	grapes	243
food	green beans	246
food	gum	249
food	ham	251
food	hamburger	252
food	hot dogs	275
food	ice cream cone	278
food	jam	284
food	jelly	286
food	juice	290
food	lemon	306
food	lettuce	307
food	lime	311
food	milk	335
food	nut	360
food	onion	361
food	orange	363
food	oranges	364
food	pasta	381
food	peach	382
food	peanut butter	384
food	pear	385
food	pie	396
food	pineapple	399
food	pizza	400
food	potato	410
food	rice	432
food	salad	445
food	salt	446
food	sandwich	447
food	soda	490
food	soup	492
food	spaghetti	495
food	squash	499
food	steak	505
food	strawberries	510
food	taco	521
food	tomato	538
food	watermelon	566
furniture	bed	80
furniture	bookcase	96
furniture	chair	127
furniture	chest	130
furniture	couch	154
furniture	crib	157
furniture	desk	169
furniture	easel	189
furniture	sofa	491
furniture	table	520
insect	ant	51
insect	bee	81
insect	beetle	82
insect	bug	105
insect	butterfly	111
insect	caterpillar	126
insect	dragonfly	183
insect	grasshopper	245
insect	ladybug	301
insect	mosquito	344
insect	moth	345
insect	spider	496
insect	wasp	565
machine	computer	148
machine	fan	205

Category	Word	Card Number
machine	fax machine	207
machine	sewing machine	455
money	dime	171
money	dollar	178
money	nickel	357
money	pennies	391
money	penny	392
money	quarter	418
musical instrument	banjo	67
musical instrument	bell	83
musical instrument	clarinet	136
musical instrument	drum	187
musical instrument	guitar	248
musical instrument	piano	394
musical instrument	sax	449
musical instrument	tambourine	524
musical instrument	trombone	548
musical instrument	trumpet	551
musical instrument	violin	561
musical instrument	xylophone	576
number	0	1
number	1	2
number	2	3
number	3	4
number	4	5
number	5	6
number	6	7
number	7	8
number	8	9
number	9	10
number	10	11
number	11	12
number	12	13
number	13	14
number	14	15
number	15	16
number	16	17
number	17	18
number	18	19
number	19	20
number	20	21
object	balloon	65
object	bathtub	76
object	battery	77
object	bracelet	100
object	calendar	114
object	candle	118
object	clock	139
object	comb	145
object	curtains	161
object	door	181
object	flag	215
object	floor	217
object	fork	221
object	gas	227
object	gate	228
object	glass	231
object	hanger	257
object	hopscotch	271
object	knife	299
object	lamp	303
object	license plate	309
object	lid	310
object	lock	315
object	magazine	320
object	mailbox	322
object	mat	330
object	match	331
object	mirror	336
object	napkin	351
object	necklace	353
object	nest	354
object	newspaper	356
object	pad	370
object	paper towel	378
object	quilt	420
object	ring	434
object	rock	436
object	saddle	443
object	shell	458
object	sink	471
object	smoke	484
object	soap	487
object	spoon	497
object	stamps	500
object	stop sign	507
object	stoplight	508
object	swing	519
object	tag	522
object	teapot	527
object	tent	531
object	toilet	537
object	toothbrush	539
object	toothpaste	540
object	towel	542
object	umbrella	554
object	wave	567
object	web	568

Category	Word	Card Number
object	window	570
people	alien	45
people	angel	48
people	astronaut	61
people	boy	99
people	carpenter	122
people	cook	150
people	crossing guard	158
people	custodian	162
people	dad	164
people	dentist	168
people	doctor	175
people	elf	194
people	fairy	203
people	firefighter	212
people	girl	230
people	infant	279
people	king	296
people	librarian	308
people	mail carrier	321
people	man	324
people	mechanic	332
people	men	333
people	mom	339
people	monster	341
people	musician	350
people	nurse	359
people	painter	371
people	police officer	406
people	principal	411
people	queen	419
people	secretary	454
people	teacher	526
people	vet	559
people	woman	573
people	women	574
place	aquarium	56
place	barber shop	68
place	bridge	101
place	bus stop	109
place	classroom	137
place	dock	174
place	farm	206
place	forest	220
place	highway	266
place	hill	267
place	island	281
place	mall	323
place	moon	342
place	park	379
place	playground	404
place	police station	407
place	post office	408
place	restaurant	431
place	road	435
place	space station	493
place	stars	504
place	sun	513
place	swimming pool	517
place	train station	544
plant	acorn	43
plant	bush	110
plant	daisy	165
plant	grass	244
plant	log	318
plant	mum	349
plant	pine	398
plant	plant	401
plant	rose	438
plant	tree	545
plant	vine	560
school things	board	91
school things	book	94
school things	book bag	95
school things	bulletin board	106
school things	chalk	128
school things	construction paper	149
school things	crayons	156
school things	eraser	197
school things	globe	233
school things	glue	236
school things	ink	280
school things	locker	316
school things	map	325
school things	marker	328
school things	paints	373
school things	paper	377
school things	pen	386
school things	pencil	387
school things	pencil sharpener	388
school things	pencils	389
school things	ruler	440
school things	scissors	452
school things	tape dispenser	525
shape (outline)	arrow	33
shape (outline)	circle	34
shape (outline)	diamond	35
shape (outline)	heart	36

CATEGORY	WORD	CARD NUMBER
shape (outline)	hexagon	37
shape (outline)	oval	38
shape (outline)	rectangle	39
shape (outline)	square	40
shape (outline)	star	41
shape (outline)	triangle	42
shape (color)	arrow	58
shape (color)	circle	135
shape (color)	diamond	170
shape	dot	182
shape (color)	heart	260
shape (color)	hexagon	265
shape (color)	oval	365
shape (color)	rectangle	429
shape (color)	square	498
shape (color)	star	503
shape (color)	triangle	546
shape	zigzag	581
sports equipment	arrow	59
sports equipment	arrows	60
sports equipment	baseball	70
sports equipment	basketball	72
sports equipment	bat	73
sports equipment	fin	208
sports equipment	football	219
sports equipment	glove, baseball	234
sports equipment	helmet	262
sports equipment	skateboard	474
sports equipment	soccer ball	488
tool	ax	62
tool	broom	102
tool	brush	103
tool	bucket	104
tool	compass	147
tool	fire extinguisher	211
tool	flashlight	216
tool	glasses	232
tool	hammer	253
tool	hammers	254
tool	hose	273
tool	ladder	300
tool	microscope	334
tool	mop	343
tool	pick	395
tool	rake	424
tool	rakes	425
tool	saw	448
tool	scale	450
tool	shovel	466
tool	shovels	467
tool	stapler	502
tool	telephone	528
tool	thermometer	532
tool	yardstick	578
toy	blocks	89
toy	doll	177
toy	dollhouse	179
toy	game board	224
toy	jacks	283
toy	jump rope	291
toy	kite	298
toy	marbles	326
toy	mask	329
toy	puppets	414
toy	puzzle	417
toy	sled	480
toy	top	541
toy	tricycle	547
toy	yo-yo	579
vehicle	airplane	44
vehicle	ambulance	47
vehicle	bicycle	85
vehicle	boat	92
vehicle	boats	93
vehicle	bus	108
vehicle	cab	112
vehicle	canoe	119
vehicle	car	121
vehicle	cars	124
vehicle	fire engine	210
vehicle	garbage truck	226
vehicle	helicopter	261
vehicle	jet	287
vehicle	motorcycle	346
vehicle	police car	405
vehicle	race car	422
vehicle	rowboat	439
vehicle	sailboat	444
vehicle	ship	460
vehicle	spaceship	494
vehicle	submarine	511
vehicle	train	543
vehicle	truck	549
vehicle	trucks	550
vehicle	van	556

Appendix K: Manner and Place of Articulation of Phonemes

Different shapes of the vocal tract cause different sounds to be produced; the sounds produced also depend on whether or not the larynx vibrates. The vocal tract consists of the mouth, nose, and pharynx (the very back wall of the mouth). The placement of the tongue and lips and the closure of the pharynx all affect the shape of this tract. The tongue may come into contact with the teeth, alveolar ridge, hard palate, soft palate, or pharynx (see diagram), or may lie on the floor of the mouth, which is known as the "neutral" position. The lips may be open or closed, rounded or spread during sound production. The valve between the nose and the throat may also be open or closed. (Unless otherwise stated, it is assumed in the following descriptions of sounds that this valve is open.)

The larynx is commonly known as the voice box. The larynx is located at about the level of the Adam's apple; its vibrations can be felt by touching the Adam's apple and saying "ah." The larynx generates sound (voice), and many phonemes differ from one another only in terms of whether or not they are voiced.

1. Lips
2. Teeth
3. Alveolar ridge (behind teeth)
4. Hard palate (roof of mouth)
5. Soft palate-velum (back of mouth)
6. Throat-glottis
7. Tip of tongue
8. Blade (middle) of tongue
9. Back of tongue
10. Pharynx
11. Larynx

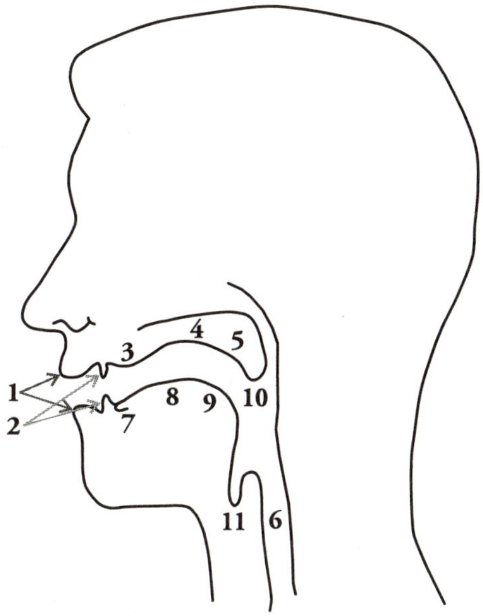

Consonant Sounds

/b/ is produced by closing the lips with the tongue in a neutral position. Air is allowed to build up behind the lips and is released by pushing the air through the lips as they open. The larynx vibrates to produce sound.

/c/ is produced as the */k/* phoneme (see following).

/ch/ is produced with the first third of the tongue pressed up against the alveolar ridge. The lips are slightly rounded. The tongue drops to release the pressure built up behind it. No sound is generated at the larynx.

/d/ is produced with the tip of the tongue pressed behind the top teeth on the alveolar ridge. The tongue drops to release the pressure built up behind it. The lips are slightly open. The larynx vibrates to produce sound.

/f/ is produced with the top teeth resting on the lower lip. The tongue is in a neutral position and air is allowed to slowly escape between the teeth and lip. No sound is produced at the larynx.

/g/ is produced with the mouth slightly open and tongue and lips in a neutral position. The part of the tongue that is furthest back pushes up against the pharynx (far back in the lower portion of the throat), producing a valve. Air builds up behind this valve and pushes it open. The larynx vibrates to produce sound.

/h/ is produced in the back of the throat with a completely open vocal tract. The air flows out of the tract in a similar fashion to a sigh. No sound is produced at the larynx.

/j/ is produced with the lips slightly rounded and the middle of the tongue raised toward the highest point of the palate, without touching it. The tongue tip is pressed against the alveolar ridge. The tongue drops to release the pressure that is built up behind it. Sound is produced at the larynx.

/k/ is produced with the mouth slightly open, the lips in a relaxed position, and the tongue in a neutral position. The part of the tongue that is furthest back pushes up against the pharynx (far back in the lower portion of the throat), producing a valve. Air builds up behind this valve and pushes it open. No sound is produced at the larynx.

/l/ is produced with the tongue tip against the alveolar ridge. Air flows over both edges of the tongue and sound is produced at the larynx. The lips are in a wide but relaxed position.

/m/ is produced with the lips pressed together and the valve between the throat and the nose open so that air can flow through it. Sound is generated at the larynx and a buzzing sound is produced. No air escapes through the mouth.

/n/ is produced with the tongue pressed against the alveolar ridge and the edges of the tongue against the other teeth to create a seal. The valve between the nose and throat is open to allow air to flow through it. Sound is generated at the larynx but escapes through the nose, not the mouth.

/ng/ is produced with an open mouth and the back of the tongue pushed up against the pharynx. The valve between the pharynx and nose is open so that air escapes through the nose, not the mouth. Sound is generated at the larynx.

/p/ is produced by closing the lips with the tongue in a neutral position. No sound is produced at the larynx. Air is allowed to build up behind the lips and is released by pushing the air through the lips as they open.

/q/ is produced using a */k/* phoneme followed by a */w/* phoneme. The */kw/* sound is considered voiced because of the production of */w/*, which is voiced.

/r/ is produced with the tongue tip curled slightly back and toward the alveolar ridge. The edges of the tongue are curled up gently against the rest of the teeth and air flows over the edges of the tongue. Sound is produced at the larynx.

/s/ is produced with the teeth together and the lips spread apart. The tongue tip may be behind either the top or bottom teeth. Sound flows smoothly through the space between the tongue and teeth, creating a hissing sound. No sound is generated at the larynx.

/sh/ is produced with rounded lips and the front of the tongue lightly touching the alveolar ridge. Air flows smoothly over the tongue. No sound is generated at the larynx.

/t/ is produced with the tip of the tongue pressed against the top teeth. The tongue drops to release the pressure built up behind it. The lips are slightly open. No sound is produced at the larynx.

/th/ There are two phonemes that are represented by **th**; they differ in terms of voicing. Both are produced with the tongue tip between the upper and lower teeth. The air flows over the tip of the tongue and between the teeth. The larynx produces voice in **this** and **that**, but not in words like **thick** and **thin**.

/v/ is produced with the top teeth resting on the lower lip. The tongue is in a neutral position and air is allowed to slowly escape between the teeth and lip. Sound is produced at the larynx.

/w/ is produced with the lips rounded. The soft palate is slightly raised so that the back of the mouth has a bigger cavern. The air flows through the mouth and out through the lips smoothly. Sound is generated at the larynx.

/x/ is produced by making a quick transition from the */k/* sound to the */s/* sound.

/y/ is produced with the middle of the tongue slightly raised toward the highest point of the palate. Air flows over the tongue smoothly. Sound is generated at the larynx.

/z/ is produced with the teeth together and the lips spread apart. The tongue tip may be behind either the top or bottom teeth. Sound flows smoothly through the space in the teeth, creating a hissing sound. Sound is generated at the larynx.

/zh/ This is the sound in **beige** and **measure**. It is produced with rounded lips and the front of the tongue lightly touching the alveolar ridge. Air flows smoothly over the tongue. Sound is generated at the larynx.

Vowel Sounds

Vowel sounds have minimal constriction (valving) through the oral mechanism. Some tension of the tongue does occur, which results in the perception of the production of some vowels as further forward in the mouth than others. All vowels are voiced.

/a/ (as in **apple**): This vowel is formed with an open mouth position and the tongue a little lower than neutral position. The air flows straight out of the mouth.

/a/ (as in **make**): This sound is produced with an open mouth position and the tongue fairly high and in the front of the mouth. The lips are slightly pulled back with some tension.

/ar/ (as in **cart**): This vowel is produced with an open, relaxed mouth and the tongue slightly retracted (pulled back).

/e/ (as in **pet**): This vowel is produced with a wide lip shape and the tongue in a neutral position.

/e/ (as in **me**): This sound is produced with a wide lip shape and a more relaxed mouth posture than the */i/* in **pin**. The front of the tongue (behind the tip) is raised, but less so than in **pin**.

/er/ (as in **earth**): This sound is produced with a relaxed rounded lip shape and the tongue in a neutral position.

/i/ (as in **pin**): This sound is produced with a wide lip shape. The front of the tongue (behind the tip) is slightly raised toward the palate.

/i/ (as in **my**): This sound is produced with a wide lip shape and an open mouth posture. The back of the tongue is slightly raised toward the palate.

/o/ (as in **pot**): This sound is produced with a slightly round lip shape. The back of the tongue is slightly raised. The tongue is relaxed.

/o/ (as in **vote**): This sound is produced with a round lip shape. The back of the tongue is slightly raised and the tongue is tense.

/o/ (as in **or**): This sound is produced with a very tense, rounded lip shape. The back of the tongue is raised toward the pharynx, but does not touch it.

/u/ (as in **up**): This sound is produced with an open mouth posture and slightly widened lips. The middle of the tongue raises slightly.

/u/ (as in **food**): This sound is produced with a very tense, rounded lip shape with the back of the tongue raised toward the pharynx so that it approaches it, but does not touch it.

/aw/ (as in **saw**): This sound is produced with an open mouth and the tongue relaxed and slightly raised in the back.

/oo/ (as in **good**): This sound is produced with an open mouth posture and slightly rounded lips. The back of the tongue raises slightly.

Diphthongs (*/oi/* as in **boy**; */ow/* as in **cow**): These are produced by moving from one vowel sound to another with a smooth motion.

Schwa (as in **about**): A schwa is a neutral vowel in which the mouth, tongue, lips, and pharynx are all in open, relaxed positions.

Appendix L: Research Institute Web Sites

http://www.cal.org/	Center for Applied Linguistics
http://www.cal.org/crede/	Center for Research on Education, Diversity & Excellence
http://www.cal.org/ncle/	National Center for ESL Literacy Education
http://www.ceousa.org/READ/	The Institute for Research in English Acquisition and Development (READ)
http://www.ed.gov/	United States Department of Education
http://www.sil.org/ethnologue/	SIL International: Ethnologue, Languages of the World

Appendix M: Contrastive Analysis of English Learners' First Languages

English contrasts with: **Chinese** (Cantonese, Mandarin, Wu and other dialects)		
Phonology	**Orthography**	**Morphology/Syntax**
With 1.25 billion speakers, more people speak Chinese than any other language. Phonologic and vocabulary differences make oral communication difficult for speakers of various Chinese dialects; nevertheless, the writing is always the same, so the written language is mutually intelligible. But even within the dialects, the phonology of subvarieties differs. Modern Standard Chinese (Mandarin) is based on the Beijing dialect. Mandarin, spoken in the North, has about 1300 different syllables. Northern dialects are more similar to each other than the Southern dialects are. Modern Standard Chinese has nine vowel phonemes, several of which can combine into clusters. There about 1300 different syllables and 22 initial consonants. In the final position, the only consonants that can occur are the nasals **n/ng** and **r**, and the semivowels **w** and **y**. English phonemes that do not exist in most Chinese dialects include: */b/, /ch/, /d/, /j/, /g/, /sh/, /th/, /v/*, and */z/*. The English phonemes projected to be most difficult for native speakers of Chinese include */b/, /ch/, /d/, /f/, /g/, /j/, /l/, /m/, /o/, /sh/, /th/, /v/, /z/*, l-clusters, and r-clusters. Feature variants can cause difficulty in production of English phonemes for native speakers of Chinese dialects. Several books and web sites, listed on page 318, provide additional information.	In different regions of China, different dialects of Chinese are spoken; however, the Chinese written word is universal, so written communication is possible between and among speakers of hundreds of Chinese dialects. The Chinese orthographic system is based on image (form), sound, and meaning. Its thousands of distinctive characters, called ideographs, have six symbol types, including pictographs, indicatives, ideatives, harmonics, transmissives, and borrowed words. The official Chinese transcription system today, the Pinyin System, was devised to translate Chinese orthographic characters to the Romanized alphabet, making Chinese words decodable and encodable for native speakers of English and other Roman alphabetic systems.	Modern Standard Chinese words have three possible syllabic/morphemic structures: they may consist of one syllable; of two or more syllables, both carrying an element of meaning; or of two or more syllables that carry no individual meanings. Each word in Chinese carries at least one meaning, but meaning can change based upon the four tones in which words are uttered. In some Chinese dialects, tones may also add grammatical meaning. Tonal units may be compared to the inflectional and derivational affixes of English (e.g., -**s**, -**tion**, -**ing**, -**ly**), which can add to or modify a word's meaning. Chinese has no inflectional suffixes (such as -**ed**, -**ing**, -**est**, -**'s** in English), which may cause native Chinese speakers to struggle with the concept of inflection when learning English. Chinese languages distinguish nouns and verbs, but the two overlap to some degree. Noun suffixes can form different kinds of nouns (e.g., concrete, abstract, diminutives). Adjectives are a category of verb. Chinese does not use articles, so the article use concept is difficult for native Chinese speakers. Syntactically, word order is critical, since Chinese uses no inflection or case to provide function information. SVO (subject-verb-object) is the most common word order.

English contrasts with: Hmong (Mon, Meo)

Phonology	Orthography	Morphology/Syntax
Hmong, a subgroup of Miao, has 8 million speakers, scattered by history through China, Southeast Asia, Australia, Europa, and America. The Hmong language has 13 vowels and 56 consonants. Like its cousin, Vietnamese, Hmong is a tonal language, one in which the same word can be produced with various tones that give the word several different meanings. Production of phonemes is complex, so a pronunciation Web site is provided in the resources section on page 318. This Web site features production of each of the Hmong phonemes. Feature variants can cause difficulty in production of English phonemes for native speakers of Hmong. Hmong consonants are difficult for English speakers because the consonant phonemes may be represented by up to four letters. The only consonant phoneme that can occur at the close of a syllable is */ng/*, which may cause native Hmong speakers to struggle with final consonant sounds. As in English, a Hmong symbol (grapheme) may represent more than one sound (phoneme).	Hmong's orthographic system, RPA (Romanized Popular Alphabet), is only 50 years old. In the sense that phoneme-grapheme associations determine production, Hmong's orthography is like that of English.	Because it has been so recently coded, and because of the difficult recent history of its speakers, relatively little has been written regarding the grammar, morphology, and syntax rules of Hmong. Hmong is an isolating language; that is, it has no inflection in its nouns or verbs, no endings such as -**ed** or -**ing** to indicate verb tense, and no endings such as -**s** or '**s** to extend meanings of nouns. In Hmong, each syllable carries a meaning of its own. In speech, however, some syllables are produced more closely than others. Each syllable has a tone that is represented by a consonant letter written at the close of the syllable. This causes no confusion to Hmong speakers, since the only consonant permitted at the end of a syllable is */ng/*. The ordinary syllable pattern is CV (one consonant, followed by one vowel). However, the consonant may be represented by two, three, or even four consonant letters, and the vowel by one or two letters. Hmong's basic sentence structure is SVO (subject-verb-object). Literate Hmong speakers attempting to learn English can be predicted to have difficulty, since the same letters can represent different sounds (phonemes) in the two languages.

English contrasts with: Khmer (Cambodian)

Phonology	Orthography	Morphology/Syntax
The Khmer language, official language of Cambodia, is spoken by about 7 million people. Linguistically, Khmer is related to Hmong and Vietnamese, although Khmer is nontonal. Khmer has 33 consonants, 24 dependent vowels, 12 independent vowels, and several diacritical markings to assist in pronunciation of its phonemes. Khmer permits numerous combinations of consonant clusters in the initial position of a word, which is very unlike English. Feature variants can cause difficulty in production of English phonemes for native speakers of Khmer. Khmer Web sites, listed on page 319, can provide native speakers of Khmer with help in production of English phonemes.	The orthographic system of Khmer had its origins in southern India. The letters, which originated in southern India and were derived from Pali, are unlike those of English's Roman alphabet. The Khmer alphabetic symbols represent the phonemes of the language's consonants and dependent and independent vowels. Native speakers of Khmer who are learning English must reconceptualize the alphabetic system. It will be important for these students to have much practice in the sound-to-symbol correspondences of English, with explicit, systematic, sequential and cumulative teaching and abundant practice.	Khmer uses roots from Sanskrit and Pali, much as English uses Latin and Greek roots, to derive new words. Khmer also has borrowed words from Chinese, French, and English, most recently to name items of modern Western technology. Khmer has a system of affixes, including infixes, for derivational morphology (word additions that give information about the word's grammatic function in the sentence). Khmer has nouns, verbs, adverbs, and particles. Usual sentence structure is SVO (subject-verb-object). Grammatic relations are signaled by word order and by particles. Modifiers usually follow nouns, but numbers precede nouns. Number is conveyed by modifiers and context. Khmer does not use articles, either definite or indefinite, so the article use concept is difficult for Khmer speakers who are learning English. The Khmer system of personal pronouns acknowledges speakers' perceived status, age, and level of intimacy. Khmer is an isolating language; that is, it has no inflectional morphology in its nouns or verbs. (In English, inflectional endings such as -**ed** or -**ing** indicate verb tense; inflectional endings such as -**s** or '**s** extend meanings of nouns; inflectional endings such as -**er** and -**est** extend meanings of adjectives.) Most native words are monosyllabic. Polysyllabic words, usually of literate nature, have been borrowed from Sanskrit and Pali. Khmer has also borrowed from Thai, Vietnamese, Chinese, and French.

English contrasts with: Korean (Kugo)		
Phonology	**Orthography**	**Morphology/Syntax**
Korean, which many speakers call Kugo, is about 2000 years old and is spoken by about 72 million people. It is linguistically similar to Japanese. Korean has ten simple vowels and three series of stops and affricates: plain, aspirated, and glottalized. This complicates the task of relating their alphabetic system to that of English, since more than one Roman letter may represent a single Korean phoneme. Feature variants can cause difficulty in production of English phonemes for native speakers of Korean. Korean Web sites, listed on page 319, provide native speakers of Korean with help in production of English phonemes.	Korea's orthographic system incorporates Chinese characters, On-Mun, and Romanization. The modern Korean orthographic system is alphabetic, but it is written top-to-bottom, with spaces between words. The alphabetic system illustrates the CVC (consonant-vowel-consant) syllabic grouping structure of Korean. Each of the alphabet's 24 letters represents a single consonant or vowel. Vowels are represented by 11 letters, of which there are three basic forms. Korean borrowed many Chinese characters over the centuries, but this practice has been gradually phased out since the end of World War II.	Korean words may consist of more than one morpheme. While Korean has borrowed many Chinese words, the language is unrelated to Chinese and the grammar and syntax of Korean are more similar to Japanese. Korean, an agglutinative language that makes much use of morphology, adds suffixes to nominal and verbal stems for purposes of derivation and inflection. (Derivational morphemes can change the grammatic function; inflectional morphemes add or modify meaning.) Changing vowels to make a morphologic distinction (such as present/past) in verbs does not exist in Korean. SOV (subject-object-verb) is the usual syntactic order, but while the verb is always the last constitutent of a sentence, other constituents can be placed anywhere in the sentence.

English contrasts with: Pilipino (Tagalog)

Phonology	Orthography	Morphology/Syntax
Pilipino, the modern, standardized version of Tagalog, belongs to the Austronesian language family, and is spoken by 25 million people. Pilipino is the official language of the Phillipines. (The other official language of the Phillipines is English.) Tagalog, the base for Pilipino, is spoken by 14 million people. Since 1973, it has been mandatory for schools to teach Pilipino. The language has fifteen consonants, five vowels, and five diphthongs (vowel glides). Syllable stress distinguishes sounds in words that are otherwise similar. A highly phonetic language, the only sound in Tagalog that is not written is the glottal stop. Feature variants can cause difficulty in production of English phonemes for native speakers of Tagalog and Pilipino. Pilipino/Tagalog Web sites, listed on page 319, may be helpful for native speakers of Tagalog who are learning to produce the phonemes of English.	Pilipino, the name given to standardized Tagalog when it was made the national language of the Philippines in 1962, has an alphabetic orthographic system based on the Roman alphabet. Pilipino has a regular sound-to-symbol correspondence orthographic system. It is punctuated much like English. Because of these regularities and similarities, readers and writers of Pilipino are not expected to have extraordinary difficulty in learning to read and write English.	Hundreds of Spanish words were incorporated into Tagalog during three centuries of Spanish rule. Tagalog grammar is known for its complex verbal system, which includes three different types of passive verb constructions. Many Tagalog words are multisyllable, and its morpheme structures work in much the same way as those of English.

English contrasts with: Russian

Phonology	Orthography	Morphology/Syntax
Russian consists of 21 consonant sounds and 5 vowel sounds. Most consonants have both a soft and hard pronunciation, which is determined by the vowel that follows it. Consonant blends and clusters occur frequently. Often one of the consonants is omitted in the pronunciation of clusters. When unstressed, vowel sounds are reduced to a sound similar to the English schwa.	The Russian language is encoded using an alphabetic system, Cyrillic. Many letters are similar to those used in the Greek alphabet. The written language is phonetically regular. There are no consonant or vowel digraphs. The Cyrillic alphabet has 33 letters: 21 represent consonant sounds; ten represent vowel sounds; and two letters (the hard sign and soft sign) have no sound themselves but affect the pronunciation of the preceding consonant. While there are five vowel sounds, there are ten letters representing the vowel sounds. The letter determines the pronunciation of the consonant preceding it (soft or hard).	This highly inflected language has six cases affecting the forms of nouns, adjectives and pronouns. Verbs also have specific endings dependent on person and number. Russian has no present tense form of the verb **to be**, so this concept may be difficult for native Russian speakers. Word order within a sentence is less strict than in English because case endings help determine the function of words within the sentence. Verb phrases are not used per se; rather, verbs occur in pairs with different aspects (perfective and imperfective) to convey subtleties in meaning. Russian does not use articles, either definite or indefinite, so the article use concept is difficult for Russian speakers who are learning English. One phenomenon related to Russian vocabulary is its families of words which are derived from a single root, by addition of prefixes and suffixes. Because of its conjugations and declensions, Russian word order is not as strict as that of English.

English contrasts with: Spanish

Phonology

Spanish, a Romance language derived from Latin, is the official language of Spain (40 million speakers) and 19 Latin American countries (1 million) and by 17 million people in the United States.

Spanish has five vowels that are consistently articulated. Stress is also consistent: it is placed on the next-to-final syllable in words ending in a vowel, **n**, or **s**; and it is placed on the final syllable in words ending in other consonants. The complex vowel system of English is difficult for native Spanish speakers. Until the English vowels are differentiated via phonemic awareness and phoneme-grapheme correspondence rules, speakers may experience difficulty learning to read and write English. Symbol-sound correspondences differ slightly with Spanish consonants as well. It is important to teach the English code to automaticity, if Spanish speakers are to become literate in English.

Basic accent rules of Spanish include: (1) For words ending in a vowel, or **n** or **s**, stress falls on the next-to-last syllable; (2) For words ending in a consonant other than **n** or **s**, stress falls on the last syllable; and (3) If the word has an accent mark, then that syllable is stressed, ignoring the rules above. Consequently, the complexities of stress in English may be difficult for native Spanish speakers.

Spanish has a one-to-one symbol-sound orthographic system. Its alphabet includes three letters not found in English (**ch**, **ll**, and **ñ**).

Orthography

Like English, Spanish has an alphabetic orthographic system.

Vowel letters represent these phonemes:

a—as in **water**
e—for a syllable ending in a vowel, as in **grey**; for a syllable ending in a consonant, as in **set**
i—as in **machine**
o—for a syllable ending in a vowel, as in **home**; for a syllable ending in a consonant, as in **hot**
u—as in **mule**; silent after **q** and in the groups **gue** and **gui**
y—when used as a vowel, as the Spanish **i**

Diphthongs (vowel glide) represent these phonemes:

ai, **ay**—as in **hide**
au—as in **bout**
ei, **ey**—as in **they**
eu—as in **you**
oi, **oy**—as in **toy**

Semiconsonants represent these phonemes:

i, **y**—as y in **yet**
u—as **w** in **wet**

Consonants represent these phonemes:

b—when found at the beginning of a word or following a consonant, like */b/*; otherwise, it falls between English's */b/* and */v/* phonemes
c—before a consonant or **a**, **o**, or **u**, as */k/*; before **e** or **i** as */s/*
ch—*/ch/*
d—as the English */d/*; when between vowels and following **l** or **n**, pronounced as in **this**
f—*/f/*

Morphology/Syntax

Spanish has a morphologic system that is typical of Romance languages, and not dissimilar to English.

One important syntactic difference in Spanish: modifiers follow the words they modify in Spanish. For example, adjectives follow nouns. A Spanish speaker would refer to the "house red" rather than to the "red house" as in English.

Spanish requires a double negative; this can cause syntactic confusion for English learners, since English does not permit a double negative.

Conjugation of verbs in Spanish is dependent upon the verb's form/spelling, a phenomenon which does not translate to English and may cause confusion.

Spanish has two distinct forms of the verb **to be** (**estar**, which denotes a temporary state, and **ser**, which denotes a stable condition and is used before a predicate noun).

Reflexive verbs in Spanish often function as do passive verbs in English.

Because the Spanish verbal conjugations' inflectional process (different endings required for each form) indicates person (first, second, third) and number clearly, subject pronouns aren't necessary as they are in English.

Spanish has several dialects. Although the language is basically from Latin, its vocabulary has been expanded by many loan words from Arabic, French, Italian, and various central and South American languages.

English contrasts with: Spanish		
Phonology	**Orthography**	**Morphology/Syntax**
English phonemes not used in Spanish include */j/*, */sh/*, */th/*, and */z/*. Problem English phonemes for Spanish speakers can be predicted to include */b/*, */d/*, */dg/*, */h/*, */j/*, */m/*, */n/*, */ng/*, */r/*, */sh/*, */t/*, */th/*, */v/*, */w/*, */y/*, */z/*, and */s/*. Feature variants can cause difficulty in production of English phonemes for native speakers of Spanish. Spanish Web sites, listed on page 319, may be helpful in dealing with the differences between and among phonemes for native speakers of Spanish.	**g**—before **e** or **i**, like the Spanish **j**; otherwise as in **get** **h**—silent **j**—as an **h** but stronger; silent when at the end of a word **k**—*/k/* **l**—*/l/* **ll**—as in **you** **m**—*/m/* **n**—*/n/*; except where it appears before a **v**, as */m/* **ñ**—as in the final **n** in **onion** **p**—*/p/* **q**—*/k/* **r**—pronounced with a strong trill at beginning of a word and following an **l**, **n**, or **s**; little trill when at the end of a word; and medium trill in other positions **rr**—strongly trilled **s**—before **b**, **d**, **g**, **l**, **m**, **n**, as */z/*; otherwise, as */s/* **t**—*/t/* **v**—when found at the beginning of a word or following a consonant, like */b/*; otherwise, it falls between English's */b/* and */v/* phonemes **w**—*/v/* **x**—when between vowels, as */ks/*; before a consonant, as */s/* **y**—as in **yes** **z**—*/s/*	

English contrasts with: Vietnamese (Annamese)

Phonology	Orthography	Morphology/Syntax
Vietnamese is spoken by about 59 million people. Vietnamese phonology is complicated by its series of six tones, which affect not only production but also meaning. Vietnamese uses a large number of vowels and groups of vowels to create different phonemes. While the system is complex, context helps to simplify them. In modern Vietnamese, there is a trend to pronounce consonant blends and clusters as single phonemes. Consonants located at ends of words are not pronounced at all, which may cause native Vietnamese speakers to struggle with final consonant sounds. A Vietnamese/English dictionary Web site is provided on page 319 to help clarify and simplify these issues.	Since 1945, Vietnamese has had an alphabetic orthographic system that serves as the conventional orthography throughout the country. Diacritical marks indicate tone and some vowel sounds; a letter may have two different diacritical marks. The system creates a nearly one-to-one symbol-sound correspondence code.	Vietnamese words are monosyllabic. Ten centuries of Chinese rule in Vietnam resulted in a vocabulary in which nearly half its words are borrowed from Chinese; however, while the Vietnamese language is related to Hmong and Khmer, it is linguistically unrelated to Chinese. Each Vietnamese word carries at least one meaning, but meaning can change based upon the tone (pitch) in which the word is uttered. Vietnamese has no inflectional suffixes that can add to or modify a word's meaning. Nouns and verbs are not marked for subject agreement, tense, number, gender, or case. Instead, nouns are marked by classifiers that identify categories such as inanimate or animate objects, vehicles, books, or people. Common linguistic phenomena include compounding and reduplication, which may be repetition of the entire word or of a portion of the word. This linguistic process can be used to indicate plural, intensification, extension, or repetition of a situation. Syntactic word order in Vietnamese is SVO (subject-verb-object). Because the language is noninflected, it is highly dependent upon syntax (order of words in sentences) to convey meaning.

Definition of Terms

Language/Dialect

Nearly 7500 distinct languages are known to be spoken in the 191 countries of the world. Fewer than 2000 of those language have invented orthographic (writing) systems. Linguists have identified distinct families of languages from which modern languages have emerged. For example, English is a member of the Indo-European family of languages. From the original Indo-European language are other major branches, such as the Germanic language (of which English is a member) and the Romance languages, which derived from Latin. Some languages are technically not distinct languages since they are mutually intelligible. They are categorized as different languages based on their countries' geographic boundaries. Linguists would say that such languages are really dialects of the same language. Other languages have dialects that are so distinct that they are not mutually intelligible; for example, many of the dialects of Chinese are actually different languages. However, many categorize them as one language because of China's borders. Every speaker speaks a dialect, or a particular version of a language. Dialects may be ethnic or regional. In the United States, speakers of English are almost always able to code-switch; that is, they are able to change from one dialect to another. The English dialect that is most widely used by educated speakers and writers is called Standard English.

Phonology

Phonology is the study of sounds produced in spoken language. In each language, each isolated speech sound is called a phoneme. Phonology examines how phonemes interact with each other. Phonology explains the phonological processes in a language as they are related to the rules of production.

Orthography

Orthography is the study of writing systems. The English writing system is alphabetic, so its orthographic system is spelling, a sound-to-symbol code. Speakers of various languages have invented various orthographic systems to map speech to print. Most of the world's spoken language have no orthographic systems; that is, they have no written forms.

Morphology

Morphology is the study of word formation and structure. In each language, the smallest units of meaning are called morphemes. Morphology studies how words are put together from their smaller parts and the rules governing this process. The English word cats, for example, contains the free morpheme, **cat** and the bound morpheme for plural, **-s**. Students whose languages do not have these kinds of suffixes can be predicted to have difficulty conceptualizing them linguistically. They will need to understand the linguistic process of adding or altering meaning via morphology before they can be expected to understand and apply the meanings of English morphemes.

Syntax

Syntax is the study of sentence structure. All languages are rule-governed; sentence structure rules differ among languages. Syntax decribes how sentences may be grammatically structured in a particular language. In some languages, the rules of syntax are simple; only a few possibilities exist. In English, syntax is complex. For example, while English typically has a subject-verb-object sentence order (e.g., *Juan threw the ball*), the transformational process permits alteration of word order to produce sentences with similar meanings (e.g., *The ball was thrown by Juan*) or to ask questions (e.g., *Did Juan throw the ball?*). In each transformation, the word order is altered.

Resources

Books and Articles

Campbell, G.L. (1991). *Compendium of the World's Languages, Vols. 1–2*. London and New York: Routledge Press.

Celce-Murcia, M., Brinton, D.M., & Goodwin, J.M. (2000). *Teaching Pronunciation: A Reference for Teachers of English to Speakers of Other Languages*. Cambridge: University Press.

Cressey, W.W. (1978). *Spanish Phonology and Morphology: A Generative View*. Georgetown University Press.

Crystal, D. (1987). *The Cambridge Encyclopaedia of Language*. Cambridge, UK: Cambridge University Press.

Diffloth, G. (1992). "*Khmer*" in W. Bridge, Ed. International Encyclopedia of Linguistics, Vol 2:271-275. New York and Oxford; Oxford University Press.

Greene, P.J.F. (1981). *The Morpheme Conceptualization Barrier: Non-inflected Asian speakers' acquisition of English morpheme structures*. University of New Orleans: Doctoral dissertation.

Grimes, B.F., ed. (2000). *Ethnologue: Languages of the World*. Dallas: Summer Institute of Linguistics, Inc.

Hashimoto, A. Oi-Kan Yue (1972). *Phonology of Cantonese*. Cambridge: Cambridge University Press.

Harris, J.W. (1969). *Spanish Phonology: MIT Press research monograph* # 54. Cambridge: M.I.T. Press

Huffman, F.E. & Proum, I. (1987). Cambodian System of Writing and Beginning Reader.

Huffman, F.E. & Proum, I. (1987). Modern Spoken Cambodian.

Johnson, K. (1987). *Intonation in Cantonese*. OSU Working Papers in Linguistics 36:1-15. Columbus: Ohio State University.

Kao, D. L. (1971). *Structure of the Syllable in Cantonese*. The Hague: Mouton.

Karlgren, B. (1934). *Word families in Chinese*. Bulletin of the Museum of Far Eastern Antiquities 5.9-120.

Katzner, K. (1975). *The Languages of the World*. New York: Funk and Wagnalls.

Kwok, H. (1984). Sentence Particles in Cantonese. Hong Kong: Centre of Asian Studies.

Liem, N.D. (1970). *Vietnamese Pronunciation*. Honolulu: University of Hawaii Press.

Law, Sam-po. (1990). *The Syntax and Phonology of Cantonese Sentence-Final Particles*. Boston University: Doctoral dissertation.

Los Angeles County Office of Education. (1984). *Materials for Indochinese students: an annotated bibliography*. Los Angeles.

Matthews, S. & Yip, V. (1994). *Cantonese: A Comprehensive Grammar*. London and New York: Routledge.

Ouk, M., Huffman, F.E., & Lewis, J. (1988). *Handbook for teaching Khmer-speaking students*. Folsom, CA: Folsom Cordova Unified School District.

Ruhlen, M. (1987). *A Guide to the World's Languages*, Vol. 1: Classification. London: Edward Arnold.

Resources

Te, H.D. & Ouk, M. (1996). *Helping your child achieve in school. A handbook for Southeast Asian parents*. English-Cambodian bilingual edition. Southeast Asian Culture and Education Foundation.

Vance, T. and Walker, C.A. (1976). *Tone and intonation in Cantonese*. Papers from the Regional Meeting of Chicago Linguistic Society (CLS) 12:640-655.

Multi-Language Web Sites for Teachers and English Learners

Interactive Dictionary 240 Languages
http://www.yourdictionary.com/

- 240 language dictionaries
- over 30 multilingual dictionaries
- grammar rules of languages
- language identifiers
- research
- thesaurus
- rhyming
- phrases
- pronunciation
- acronyms
- synonyms
- homophones
- antonyms
- language games to help with complexities and nuances
- translations among European languages
- endangered languages information

READ Institute of the Center for Equal Opportunity
http://www.ceousa.org/READ

Dave's ESL Café
http://www.eslcafe.com/

Center for Applied Linguistics
http://www.cal.org/

TESL/TEFL/TESOL/ESL/EFL/ESOL Links

Registered Links of Interest to Students & Teachers of English as a Second Language
http://www.aitech.ac.jp/~iteslj/links/

CHINESE (CANTONESE, MANDARIN, and other dialects)

Marjorie Chan's China Links
http://www.cohums.ohio-state.edu/deall/chan.9/c-links.htm

Cantonese, Mandarin: It's all Chinese to me
http://www.unique.net/allenwu/

Mandarin Pronunciation Guide and Dictionary
http://www.1jn.com/1/chinese.html

HMONG (MON)

Pronunciation
http://ww2.saturn.stpaul.k12.mn.us/hmong/pronunciation/pronunciation1.html

English/Hmong Dictionary
http://ww2.saturn.stpaul.k12.mn.us/hmong/dictionary/enghmong/newmenu.html

Hmong/English lesson plans
http://ww2.saturn.stpaul.k12.mn.us/hmong/lessonplans/lessonplans.html

Resources

KHMER

Khmer Language and Literacy Project
http://psrtec.clmer.csulb.edu/Khmer_site/index.html

Cambodia Web: Khmer Language
http://camweb.org/khmer/

KOREAN (KUGO)

Survival Hangul: The Korean Language
http://soback.kornet.nm.kr./~pixeline/heeyun/hangul.html

Education Planet: Linguistics and Language Arts; Korean Language
http://www.educationplanet.com/search./Linguistics_and_Language_Arts/Software/Korean_Language

PILIPINO (TAGALOG)

Interactive Language and Filipino Culture Resources
http://www.seasite.niu.edu/tagalog/

English/Tagalog Online Dictionary
http://www2.seasite.niu.edu/tagalogdict/reverse_lookup.asp

RUSSIAN

Russian Grammar, Pronunciation, and Online Dictionary
http://www.departments.bucknell.edu/russian/ruslang.html

SPANISH

English/Spanish Online Dictionary
http://dictionaries.travlang.com/EnglishSpanish/

The Spanish Language
http://www.eden.infohwy.com/~tomzap/spanish.html

VIETNAMESE

English/Vietnamese Dictionary
http://www.ksvn.com/